# MIND, CAUSATION AND ACTION

# MIND, CAUSATION & ACTION

*Edited by*

LESLIE STEVENSON

ROGER SQUIRES

JOHN HALDANE

BASIL BLACKWELL

First published 1986

Basil Blackwell Ltd
108 Cowley Road, Oxford OX4 1JF, UK

Basil Blackwell Inc.
432 Park Avenue South, Suite 1505,
New York, NY 10016, USA

*British Library Cataloguing in Publication Data*
Mind, causation and action.
1. Causation
I. Stevenson, Leslie II. Squires, Roger
III. Haldane, John
122        BD591

ISBN 0–631–15045–5

*Library of Congress Cataloging-in-Publication Data*
Mind, causation, and action.
1. Causation.  2. Intellect.  I. Stevenson,
Leslie Forster.  II. Squires, Roger, 1940–.
III. Haldane, John.
BD541.M46 1986      128′.2      86–6080
ISBN 0–631–15045–5 (pbk.)

Typeset by Katerprint Co. Ltd, Oxford
Printed in Great Britain by Page Brothers (Norwich) Limited

# CONTENTS

# EDITORIAL FOREWORD

The essays printed here may look at first sight to be a somewhat heterogeneous collection in the broad area of philosophy of mind, but a more distinct common theme can be discerned running through them, namely the exact elucidation of the role of causation in our concept of mind.

The pendulum of philosophical thought has swung to and fro, and around and around, on this issue. Cartesian dualism offered an ontology of distinct but interacting substances as a metaphysical interpretation of what appear to be common sense truisms – that physical inputs to our sense-organs cause mental states (notably our perceptual judgments), and that mental states (notably our intentions) cause bodily events and actions. Materialism offered ontological economy by cutting out the mental states (in so far as dualism conceived them to be immaterial in nature), replacing them by physiological states inside the body, particularly the brain, thus trying to eliminate any mystery about causal interaction between the mental and the physical.

This however still seemed to leave out of the picture much that is very important, notably our assessment of reasons for actions, and our everyday explanation of each others' actions in terms of such reasons. So there arose a tendency to emphasize very strongly a distinction between reasons and causes – exemplified in the work of Ryle, Melden, Peters and others. As the slogan of the day had it, reasons could not be causes; and thus a dualism of concepts replaced the ontological dualism of substances or events. It was left to the sciences to investigate the bodily causes and effects of our mental states, but our everyday talk of actions, beliefs and desires was thought to be entirely within the non-causal language of reasons.

Then it came to be generally recognized – a change notably pioneered by the work of Davidson – that reasons and causes could not be kept so separate, since our talk of reasons is in an important sense also causal. Perhaps the pendulum of opinion has come, if not to rest, at least to swing within a smaller area roughly indicated by the previous sentence. (Though it must be admitted that old-style ontological dualism still finds its forthright spokesmen like Popper and Eccles; and various forms of reductive or eliminative materialism also attract the tough-minded like Armstrong or Rorty.)

The articles in this collection can all be seen as contributing to the study of the subtle relationship between the rational and the causal. The grand battles between rival 'isms' in the philosophy of mind have left their memories (and scars!), but they are here largely succeeded by detailed, sometimes very technical, analyses of how causation enters into our various mental concepts. To help orientate the reader for these intricate discussions, we have invited Simon Blackburn, newly-appointed Editor of *Mind*, to contribute a guest introduction to the present state of the art in the philosophical discussion of how propositional attitudes enter into the causal explanation of action. We think readers will find that he has provided them with a very helpful overview of recent work, making interesting connections between the philosophies of mind and language.

In the first main article, Morris distinguishes subtly different senses (which he thinks philosophers have hitherto conflated) in which mental states such as believings may be said to cause behaviour. The Macdonalds defend Davidson's views on the causal role of the mental (and therewith his non-reductive version of materialism) against recent criticisms. Owens criticizes David Lewis's various "functionalist" accounts of mental states in terms of their typical causes and effects, and concludes that we should abandon "the last lingering legacy of positivism", namely the search for reductive analyses of the mental.

Budd's sensitive elucidation of Wittgenstein's negative and positive views on the self-ascription of sensation, and their connections with the much-disputed topics of rule-following and private language, may seem foreign to the main theme of this volume, but the connection appears in his last section, where he finds that Wittgenstein fails to take into account the causal role of sensation in producing behaviour. Charlton is also concerned with the self-ascription of mental states, but he suggests making the connection with action very directly, by defining belief and desire in terms of reasons for action.

The next two papers, by Mele and Graham, are concerned with the causation of belief, and in particular with the non-rational, or at least imperfectly rational, situations in which desire unduly influences what is believed – cases which are often labelled 'self-deception' or 'wishful thinking'.

The two papers by Kapitan and Fischer take up points in the long-standing set of conundrums about the freedom of the will. The issues are now seen to involve very subtle questions about the exact sense of 'can' and 'could have' claims, which depend in turn on views about the role of causality in the mental. Our collection closes with critical studies of two important recent books by Stephen Stich and Christopher Peacocke: both of which are concerned in their different ways with the themes discussed in Blackburn's introduction.

This volume is undoubtedly philosophers' philosophy – written by professionals for professionals. We think it represents some of the cutting edge of current research in the philosophy of mind.

# INVITED INTRODUCTION: FINDING PSYCHOLOGY

BY SIMON BLACKBURN

The philosophy of mind is largely a chase after fugitive facts; facts about meaning, thought, agency, consciousness, whose nature escapes our understanding. They escape it for two reasons. Firstly, what we would allow as success in understanding them is constrained by various principles, and the constraints are very tight. Misinterpreted even a little, they become impossible to satisfy. They include:

(1) That we should not deny first/third person asymmetries – yet we should not make knowledge of other minds impossible.
(2) That we should not abandon a physicalist ontology – yet we should not make intentionality (agency, etc.) impossible.
(3) That we should not ignore "the holism of the mental" – yet we should not deny that beliefs (etc.) have their own content and identities.
(4) That we should respect the apparent identity of belief over identically appearing ("doppelganger") possible worlds – yet we should make proper place for genuine reference and intentionality in describing psychologies.

Each member of these four pairs stands in some tension with the other; perhaps more philosophers are keen to stress allegiance to one than have succeeded in exorcizing the pull to the other.

These tensions are familiar. But the second main obstacle, I believe, to progress is more abstract. It is that we come to these issues with a set of doubtful categories. These include certain distinctions (causal vs. non-causal explanations; realist vs. instrumentalist construal of theories) and technical terms (notably, I suggest, 'truth-condition', 'representation', and most treacherously, 'state').

In this brief introductory article I shall say little about the particular constraints on a proper psychology, but more about the importance of understanding the categories we bring to it. If I have a theme, it is this: in today's climate, philosophical psychology has ousted philosophy of language as the Queen of the philosophical sciences – yet what it needs is a better philosophy of truth and of fact. My theme is intended to impinge on assumptions which seem to be present in many writers in the "cognitive psychology" tradition, regardless of differences amongst them. Indeed, those differences (for example between representative and syntactic theories of mind, or instrumental and realist theories of intentional ascription) seem to me a response to pressures which can actually be released by better understanding of truth and fact.


I


In recent years the best hope for forging an understanding of mind has been functionalism. This starts with the observation that we use psychological attributions to explain and predict the things each other does. So common-sense psychology is a "folk-theory", or attempt at explanation. If not itself a theory, at least it is a kind of proto-theory, or framework for fuller theory. It specifies links internally amongst psychological "states", and between them and inputs ("stimuli") and outputs ("behaviour"). Furthermore (goes the dominant story) these explanations are causal: it must be *because* I believe that the cat is under the bed that I am inclined to say that it is there, or feel uneasy about its being there.

A complete psychological model of a subject would provide the entire dynamics of this system; the suggestion is not that folk psychology ever enables us to do this for an actual subject, but that it contains enough principles and concepts for us to be able to frame the outline of such a theory. Its rough generalizations can be related both to an evolutionary understanding of ourselves, and to norms such as those of decision theory or logic. For instance, common sense might suppose that the belief that there is a cat in front of me is typically caused (using normal vision and hearing in normal circumstances) when and only when there is indeed a cat in front of me; or that a tendency to believe that $p$ normally follows upon a tendency to believe that $p$ & $q$: a teleological/evolutionary story is in the wings waiting to say why such things should be true. Creatures set to act on cats under the bed when there are none, or not set so to act when there *is* one, do worse. But there will also be occasions where (for natural reasons) our systems are set to form inappropriate beliefs and desires, and these too can be identified.

The liberating effect of this conception of psychology is well known: it gives psychological terms the freedom from strict particular behavioural connections that logical behaviourism wrongly required, and since it can be quite silent about the precise "realization" of the causal pathways, it can be charitable to machines and Martians, giving psychology the right degree of autonomy from neurophysiology.

Or, it may seem to do so. But now, it may be suggested, on this causal version of functionalism, we only believe, desire, etc. if there exist states with very particular places in our causal organization. For instance, as Stich points out, in common sense theory my believing that the cat is under the bed explains both why I say that it is, and why I reach down to pull it out.[1] So it will be a promise of causal functionalism that there exists one state causally responsible for both the saying and the doing. But then (the argument continues) physicalism ensures that the only kind of state able to explain *both* those things would be at a neurological node somewhere in the head, and there may be no such node. It might turn out, for example, (Stich and Churchland cite empirical work pointing tentatively in this direction) that notwithstanding what it feels like from the inside, behaviour control and verbal control could be under the command of quite different systems, with yet another part of the brain ensuring some kind of co-ordination.[2] The physical investigation of the brain would reveal no such thing as "the state causally responsible for both the saying and the doing", and in that case the folk-theory implies a falsehood.

I think this is a good specimen of the kind of argument that leads theorists to see folk psychology as "scientifically doubtful". Does it work? Perhaps it seems plain that if folk psychology says that there is something that causes both A and B, yet science shows that A has a different cause from B, then either folk psychology is wrong, or it needs to abandon any pretence of descriptive accuracy. Yet consider this analogy. Folk meteorology tells us that crops fail to grow, and people feel miserable, because of the bad weather. And this 'because' is causal. So, it is a promise of folk meteorology that there is one state causing each of these effects. But good empirical work could well show that in fact one state (persistent cold, say) causes the crops not to grow, whereas another state (persistent wet, say) causes people to be miserable. The best full physical story of the atmosphere and its effects may acknowledge no one state with both consequences. Similarly perhaps folk geology talks of earthquakes causing buildings to fall. Perhaps physical geologists separate different things (transverse from vertical wave movements in rock, say) each with different effects (shaking and rolling, say). Do these discoveries undermine folk meteorology or geology? Didn't folk-theory say that one *thing* or *state* caused the shaking and the rolling?

Here is the natural solution to this strained problem. So long as the two wave movements, or the wet and the cold, or the tendency to say and the tendency to do, *typically* occur together, the folk-terms have a role. They tell of a *syndrome*, and their utility depends on the general co-ordination of its different aspects. The concepts would lose their propriety (and utility) if, typically, the unity of the phenomena broke up. (Would harmless shaking without rolling be an earthquake?) But the realization that the phenomenon is complex does not break up this unity. If earthquakes (bad weather, beliefs)

[1] Stephen Stich, *From Folk Psychology to Cognitive Science* (London, 1983), p. 231.
[2] Stich, *op. cit.*, p. 231 ff. Paul M. Churchland, *Matter and Consciousness* (London, 1984), p.79.

typically involve different aspects which science can separate, we learn that the folk-story can be filled out further, but in no case are we apt to abandon it. A chair causes me to maintain my present posture regardless of whether some of its properties are irrelevant to that power.[3]

There are pressures which cause thinkers to resist this simple reconciliation. It is as if we think: well, if the vertical movements brought down the buildings and the transverse movements are harmless then it *wasn't really* the earthquake (not that overall *state*, or *event*) that caused the damage. The villain of this piece is the notion of a state, and a change of state. We too easily slide into a billiard-ball model of the notion: a proper state should be physically identifiable and located, causing things by the exertion of scientifically respectable forces. How else are we to accommodate the physicalist pressure? Agglomerated states like bad weather, earthquakes, the presence of a chair or of a belief, become simple obstacles to clear identification of the causal lines.

If it seems unlikely that so innocent-sounding a term as 'state' should play us false, consider how the flight into the head started. Belief states explain both acting and saying, so they must "consist in" states far back along the causal chains science finds. This is what leads to difficulty if a causal isomorphism with neurological states fails. But is common sense embroiled in any such theory? Certainly it allows that I am often in a psychological state – but it does not insist or even allow that psychological states are often in me. In folk-theory, being in a state is like being in a tizzy or a bother. I believe that the cat is under the bed; very well, I am in a state of believing that the cat is under the bed. But is this state a locatable part of me, causally influential through emitting gravitons and electrons? Is it amenable to tweezers and microscopes? Obviously not. It is right to say that I am in such a state, because I am set to control myself appropriately in response to information as from the cat. States involved in that control, either in the acceptance of the information or in the subsequent modifications of my actions, gain their title – their right to be thought of as "representing" the presence of the cat, in virtue of their role in this agency. It is the whole person which has a psychology, not internal bits of him.

The trick is to realize that although the neurophysiological truth shows us how internal states cause and explain behaviour, the direction which illuminates the philosophical and psychological problems of intentionality – and which is fully consistent with functionalism – is the reverse. It is only in virtue of its being a part of the signals in neural pathways in the whole active person that an electrical or chemical modification can be said to represent

---

[3] The concept 'chair' need not be any part of the final scientific Book for it to be true that the presence of chairs explains things. Chairs *are* physical, even if to physics they form a class with which it has no truck.

the impending tiger or the death of Hastings. The grounds for saying that the signals encode information about the tiger or the death of Hastings is that they play some role in the dynamic organization of the whole person. One could not detect what is encoded from any investigation of the internal, intrinsic properties of the configurations of *any* particular part of the animal.[4]

## II

Consider another philosophical argument for internal "representations". The propositional attitude idioms are on the face of it relational, so that if we suppose that they identify literal truths we ought to find a real object to which the subject is being related.[5] If a subject is related to some*thing* when he believes that *p*, then since relating us to abstract propositions offends against metaphysical constraints, the best bet becomes an inner "represen- tation", a "sentence in the head" – the internal representative thing which, somehow, stands for the cat being under the bed. This would be something there in the brains, with representative properties. It is true that its capacity for these properties is a little puzzling ("Of the semanticity of mental representations we have, as things now stand, no adequate account" – Fodor[6]), but theorists bent on rescuing the propositional attitudes have struggled to assure themselves that this "semanticity" is going to be there. The scene is set for people to recognize that the properties of things in the head (cells and pathways) are the first instance connected with other things in the head, and only mediately and accidentally with parts of the outside world – there is no real (spatially) inner state which is essentially connected with the cat, in that had the cat not been there, or had there been no cathood in the world, *it* could not have existed. But a belief-state involving a cat must, *essentially*, involve it. But since spatially configured states are all that there are (physicalism), there is no such thing as belief.

My alternative is simple: if belief-states both "have semanticity" and cause behaviour, then they must be thought of as states of an animal in an environment – something which includes as well the feedback from action. Like Evans, I think we can have the scientific and psychological insights of the computational theory of mind, and also keep a firm grip on the need to explain intentionality from outside in – to form a naturalistic psychology which cites the typical causes and functions of the agent.[7] I think that it is literally true that we believe and desire, and represent the world to ourselves:

[4] Here I have been especially helped by conversations with Derek Bolton.
[5] Stich, *op. cit.*, pp. 24, 78. J. A. Fodor, "Fodor's Guide to Mental Representation", *Mind* 94 (1985), p. 88.
[6] Fodor, *op. cit.*, p. 99.
[7] Gareth Evans, "Comment on Jerry A. Fodor's 'Methodological Solipsism Considered as a Research Strategy in Cognitive Psychology'", *Collected Papers* (Oxford, 1985), p. 400.

the relational expressions are entirely proper, yet they imply no "representations", no sentences in the head or inner bits advantageously thought of like sentences on a cathode-ray tube, whose presence somehow carries the semantic burden. It is no offence against physicalism to suppose that when we relate people to propositions, the only *relatum* is abstract (indeed, the offence would be if that were *not* so: physicalism only fails if there are real causally acting things which escape the physicist's ontology). The proposition is literally an abstraction from the psychological similarities of all those whose mental lives are organized with that proposition as a focus – doubters, believers, hopers alike. The content of a belief is not an item in space and time to which a subject is related. It is an abstraction from facts we want to know about the organization and awareness of the subject. This is what functionalism needs to say, and can say. Propositional description of people is precisely that which invents an object to stand at that point. Telling how someone is related to a particular proposition is telling something literal about him, but the proposition needs no spatial and temporal identity to function as it does in this story. Of course, in saying this I cheerfully stand opposed to the dreary tradition of finding sentences, utterances, representations – anything, so long as it be not abstract – to stand as the object of the demonstratives introducing 'that'-clauses.

But, comes the reply, this avoids the ontological problem only at the cost of abandoning "realism" about the intentional. Propositions become "abstracta" – "calculation-bound entities or logical constructs", like lines in a parallelogram of forces, or like directions on a Fregean construction.[8] And how can such things play any role in genuine causal explanation? The answer of course is that by themselves they don't: propositions do not bump into people or emanate light rays. What does play a role in explanation is possession of a propositional attitude – believing, hoping, etc. that *p*. Similarly "velocities" play no role in causal explanation – only the fact that particular things are travelling at particular velocities. Possession of a propositional attitude plays a role in causal explanation, because a subject can be so typed only if he is in a state – and his being in that state can be cited in explanation.

But, to repeat, his being in such a state makes no reference to any state which is in him. Perhaps another opposition to this may stem from allegiance to Quine's ontological attitudes. If propositions are values of variables in our best theories of people – if people believe, doubt, assert and deny these *things*, then we who hold these truths about them are "ontologically committed" to the propositions which we mention. Physicalism then forces us to bring them down to earth. But this is far too crude a picture of reference. It is just not the case that a belief has to be a physically identifiable thing for it

[8] Stich, op. cit. p. 243.

to be true that people have beliefs and act because of them – even in a purely physical universe. This is not so even if, having related people to propositions, we also find it convenient to quantify over the *abstracta*: say that there is one thing which two people each believe, and so on. All that has to be so is that the real, gross, physically identifiable things – the people – get into dispositional or other states, which play a part in explaining their actions, and which we recognize as such. Science may tell us that when such states change, so do the internal patterns of electrical and chemical impulses, but folk psychology is gloriously silent about that: there is simply no "substantive commitment about underlying internal mechanisms".[9]

III

We escape inner representations by reminding ourselves of the external, natural, relationship between the subject and how he is best to behave in his world. Now there is a dispute which, as far as I can see, cross-cuts this, but which tends to get involved with it, and I hope readers will forgive me if I digress to say why it should not. This is the issue of whether there is a distinct category of thoughts which are essentially individuated by reference: the "singular thoughts" or "Russellian thoughts" of current debate.[10] In my terminology, "universalists" are sufficiently impressed by "doppelganger" cases to suggest that no thoughts should be essentially classified by reference (ways of reporting thinkers however, using names, and indexicals, are of course bound to their actual referents).[11] My universalists defend themselves by pointing to functional equivalences between persons and their doppelgangers; Gareth Evans and John McDowell think that this idea is only tempting if we already sympathise too much with the flight inside the head, and this in turn will lead either to the "darkness within" following the collapse of representational theories, or to distressing Cartesianism.[12]

The hardest case is that of the perceptual demonstrative. It seems useful to distinguish at least three different aspects involved in an ordinary case of using such a demonstrative. There is the identity of the object; the identity of the features whereby it is perceived; and there is the initial way it is taken by the subject, or "what he makes (perceptually)" of the scene. It is possible to rotate these against each other: the same object may appear differently, or the appearance may be taken differently although it is the same, and

---

[9] Stich denies this, p. 244–5.

[10] Evans, *The Varieties of Reference* (Oxford, 1982), ch. 4.

[11] The universalist does not deny that singular terms used in 'that'-clauses have a distinct semantic role – he only queries whether this role is to introduce a *sui generis* singular thought. See my *Spreading the Word*, (Oxford, 1984), ch. 9.2.

[12] John McDowell, "Singular Thought and The Extent of Inner Space", forthcoming in *Subject, Thought, and Context*, ed. John McDowell & Philip Pettit (Oxford, 1986).

different objects can display identical features. We thus get thought-experiments of the kind I call "spinning the possible worlds", providing substitute and empty cases, and no doubt others, and we can ask what stays constant and what changes as we do so. It is clear that paying attention to these thought experiments in no way prevents us from accommodating the cognitive differences between, say, concentrating upon a perceptually presented object, and merely describing one. The mental state of a subject who takes himself to be in the presence of an object and who is, for instance, paying attention just to it, has to be distinguished sharply from that of someone thinking generally, e.g. by using definite descriptions à la Russell. It was, I think, absolutely right of Evans to hammer this point home in chapter 6 of his book.

Nothing seems to follow about the identity of these mental states, and in particular there is no reason yet to associate their identity with that of the object, forcing just one answer to the question: if it had not been *that* object, could the subject yet have been thinking the same, or would it follow that he would be thinking differently? It was too quick of Evans to associate the perfectly correct points about the quite different nature of the thinking involved in perceptual demonstrative use, with any doctrine of the individuation of what is going on psychologically – of thoughts.

It may be that we ought not to pursue the question of individuation – that it already concedes too much to the notion of a "mental state" attacked above, so that in thinking of such states as having definite, if controversial, identity conditions we are already in error. If we do pursue the question of individuation, it must depend upon what we want to individuate thoughts for – which aspects of sameness and difference across mental lives are to *matter*? One common aim is to satisfy the Fregean principle that it must not be possible without irrationality to hold rationally conflicting attitudes to one and the same thought. But this is hard to satisfy, and doubly hard if the identity of the object thought about is brought in. It is hard to satisfy if 'mode of presentation' is independently intelligible (it can of course be introduced simply as "whatever it is which enables thoughts to satisfy Frege's constraint"). In any ordinary sense we can have the same object presented in the same way to someone occupying the same perspective, and thought of in the perceptual demonstrative way – *that object* – whilst contradictory ascriptions of predicates are rationally made. Someone might be in a position in which he rationally supposes that it is a different object, although in fact it is not: object *and* mode of presentation are the same, but contrary predicates get applied (e.g. I am told by a conjuror that I will be presented with a succession of boxes, one of which will have a £5 note in it. Whilst I look at the one visible box, I rationally come to believe that a different one has been substituted as I blink, and think that although *that* one did not have a note in it, *this* one does. One might try saying that this is a different perspective, because of the passage of time, but then the difficulty will be to connect senses cut *this* fine with the theory of communication. There is no independent motivation, that I am aware of, for denying that the phrase 'that box' introduces the same thought (certainly: the same modification of the subject's mental life) on each occasion.

In this case, it is true, the passage of time is connected with something which can be called *a* change in the subject's perspective, or the mode of presentation, because he remembers the earlier (stages of the) box, and perhaps his perspective on the box changes as time goes by. But the same case can arise without that. A man may be on a production line: thinking "this glass is perfect" . . . then (remembering the criteria better) . . . "*this* glass is flawed"; but unknownst to him the supervisor has sent round the same glass again. Here we have the same glass, same public appearance, same way of taking it, and no perspectival change brought about because of a memory of the first judgement – but rationally different propositional attitudes.

Frege's principle needs a colder look than it normally gets. But in any case, once the theoretical need is identified, the individuation of thoughts will follow on. It is hard to make more of this issue than that, and this does nothing to connect the recognition of singular thoughts with the attainment of a genuinely "anti-Cartesian" theory of mind.

In a fully Cartesian picture we have:

(i)   the autonomy of the mental realm;
(ii)  the transparency of the realm to the introspection of the subject (this means: infallibility);
(iii) the correspondingly problematic access of subjectivity to the rest of the world.

Is a universalist either committed to these three doctrines, or covertly motivated by them? The issue is whether there is a theoretically important truth, or way of characterizing the mental life of the subject, which has the thought the same in either substitute or empty cases. It is admitted on all sides that *something* is the same: how things seem to the subject. Even McDowell admits that "by itself there is nothing dangerous about the idea that how things seem to one is a fact, knowable in a way that is immune to the sources of error attending one's capacity to find out about the world about one". One might have expected, then, that by itself there is nothing dangerous about the idea that how one is thinking is a fact knowable in ways which are immune to the sources of error attending one's capacity to find out about the identity of objects in the world about one. In other words, the issue about thinking could be settled by association with the admittedly harmless concept of seeming (in other words *not* taken Cartesianly). The deluded subject, thinking "It's coming to get me" when in the grip of a hallucination, would indeed be thinking in the characteristic, attention-focussing way, and so describing him would be *like* describing how things seem to him – and this is admitted to be legitimate. McDowell seeks to make the legitimate notion of seeming the same somehow disjunctive (so that entirely different facts make things seem the same on different occasions). But even if this move had anything to commend it, which I rather doubt, it could be made about thoughts as much as about experience.

In an hallucination case the functioning, as normally specified (propositionally), needs a thought slot, whereas on the Evans and McDowell conception, no singular thought is entertained. And it may need the same slot where on that conception, a different thought is being entertained (the unnoticed substitution of an identically appearing object, for instance). Still, there is a difference between substitute possibilities and empty ones: the doppelganger faced with a substitute but identically appearing object is possibly functionally identical with the original subject; one who hallucinates so that things seem to him exactly as they do to the original subject, is surely not. One aspect of his functioning may be the same, but another is different – the one causing the hallucination. Once again, this reminds us that questions of identity of thought need a theoretical background to come alive. I do not doubt that theorists such as McDowell would accept this: it is not a conflict of mere intuition. But I do doubt whether the theoretical need which forces us to give prominent place to the singular thought has yet been identified. Evans and McDowell share the naturalistic aim of placing psychology in the life of the agent in the world. But if we can have a position which is as genuinely opposed to methodological solipsism, as genuinely naturalistic about psychology, but does not incur the counter-intuitive costs of singular thoughts, it is obviously important to separate it from its vulnerable associates.

Is the debate important to epistemology? McDowell has again claimed, doubtfully: "allowing intrinsic object-dependence, we have to set whatever literally spatial boundaries are in question outside the subject's skin or skull. Cognitive space incorporates the relevant portions of the 'external' world. So its relations to that world should not pose philosophical difficulties in the Cartesian Style". It is essential, on my view to deny that *any* literal spatial (or temporal) boundaries are in question.[13] The right response to those setting the boundaries of the mind inside the head is not to set them instead some civilized distance outside it. And as far as epistemology goes, the only result

[13] Literal spatial boundaries would be in question only if the concept of a state attacked above were in order. Considered as a metaphor, however, the spatial vocabulary needs very careful interpretation – much better go for the literal truth, expressed in terms of possibilities and chances.

of identifying thought by a criterion which includes the identity of external objects, is to make one's own cognitive space an object of possible doubt: if substitutes and empty possibilities were more common, one would literally not know what one was thinking.

## IV

Let us return to the suggestion that we identify belief, desire, thought, in the life the subject lives in his world. I have tried to diagnose some reasons why this kind of naturalism is so easy to overlook. The final, perhaps the basic reason lies in the theory of truth. If the ontology is one of physical atoms in their places, exerting their forces, then it must be some distribution of these that gives the "truth condition" for someone's believing that $p$. It takes a spatial configuration to represent spatial configurations. This is the Tractarian conception of the relation of language and the world, and notwithstanding Wittgenstein's recantation, it still dominates our thinking. One can imagine the thoughts I have sketched about the way to relate psychology and the science of configurations in the neural pathways as "later Wittgensteinian", and hence unscientific; or one can imagine them being taken to licence an instrumentalist view of psychological description, in the manner of Dennett.[14] But I deny that at this point we have a good distinction between "taking up an intentional stance" towards a person, and "describing a set of truths about him". Sometimes, surely, there is such a distinction which does real work (in the theory of morals, and modals, for instance). But folk psychology is genuinely explanatory, and where we accept explanations, it seems to me, we are not at liberty to turn around and say that we do so but only in an "anti-realist" spirit.

Seeing the psychological as essentially large-scale, dealing with facts about the organization of the whole subject, is not, of course, denying any of the scientific interest of discovering how information is encoded, channelled, and dealt with in the head. Nor is it taking an *a priori* stance on the likely success of computational research programmes in empirical psychology (although it is, perhaps, offering a way to wean ourselves away from the model of the digital processing of something thought of as formulae). Certainly there is no *a priori* reason to expect this level of science to be conducted in linguistic categories. Electrical impulses are not sentences – even if we can regard them as representative in the same way that we can regard impulses in a telephone-line as representative of a conversation. Believing, as I do, that semantics rules syntax (the syntactical organization of a sentence or indeed the identity of anything as a sentence, is a reflection of

---

[14] D. Dennett, "Intentional Systems" in *Brainstorms* (London, 1978).

the *kinds* of semantic power of its various components) I think it is equally artificial to talk of the encodings possessing a "syntax".

Traps still wait. One development of a "macro" approach to psychology is to think exclusively in terms of our attribution of psychologies to others. The interpreter and his principles (charity, humanity, etc.) is certainly an alternative to the telephone engineer. Concentrating on the interpreter tells us a good deal about the epistemology of psychological attribution. But it must be doubted whether it brings similar success in thinking about its metaphysics or ontology. For once more it proves difficult to keep hold of the idea that the interpreter is *discovering* genuine truths, and not just *imposing* a scheme of description. And in any case, from the standpoint of the metaphysics of the mental, there is always the background residue – the unspoken reliance on the interpreter's own powers (the "frog in the mug" problem). The closer one studies those writings which concentrate upon interpretation, the more the matter turns out to hinge on preconceptions about the powers the interpreter brings to his task. Unless we have a regress, a "disappearance" theory of mind, in which the only way to think of those powers is to postulate another interpreter, there must be a point of escape, in which we consider just the thinker, his organization, and his world. So why start on the regress at all?

*Pembroke College, Oxford*

# CAUSES OF BEHAVIOUR

## By Michael Morris

A huge variety of kinds of human behaviour can be explained by revealing a subject's beliefs and desires. What kind of explanation is this? It seems both plausible and suggestive to say that it is causal explanation, that beliefs and desires are causes of behaviour. Indeed this seems so natural that Davidson can regard the onus of proof as resting on someone who denies that the connexion is causal:

> One way we can explain an event is by placing it in the context of its cause; cause and effect form the sort of pattern that explains the effect, in a sense of 'explain' that we understand as well as any. If reason and action illustrate a different pattern of explanation, that pattern must be identified.[1]

I shall argue that the causal pattern of explanation is not well enough understood for us to be content with this. In particular, the causalist hypothesis is ambiguous, in advance of linguistic stipulation, between several different claims. The hypothesis remains plausible and suggestive, but the interpretation on which it is most suggestive is not that on which it is most plausible. The issue is of some importance, for the significant division between philosophies of mind on this point appears to lie not between causalist and non-causalist views, but between two views which, in advance of linguistic reform, it is natural to count as causalist.

## I

What is special about causal explanation? I propose that we take an explanation as causal if it satisfies two conditions, which I shall call the "Non-*a priori* requirement" (NAP) and the "Independent existence requirement" (IE).

Consider an explanation of the form: *p* because *q*. We can restrict our attention to claims of that form which are in fact explanatory. Then, I suggest, such an explanation is causally explanatory if the replacements for '*p*' and '*q*' meet these conditions:

[1] D. Davidson, "Actions, Reasons, and Causes", in his *Essays on Actions and Events* (Oxford, 1980), p. 10.

(NAP) It is not possible to know *a priori* that *p* on the basis of knowing that *q*, or *vice versa*;

(IE)    the replacements for '*p*' and '*q*' are true in virtue of facts about states or events *e* and *c*, respectively, such that:

c does not depend for its existence upon the existence of *e*.[2]

This requires some comment. First, it should be emphasised that no attempt is being made to analyse the *explanatoriness* of causal explanation: I am taking it for granted that we have an explanatory connexion, and am simply pointing to what marks out such a connexion as a *causal* one. This means that remarks about support by significant generalisations, or counterfactual analyses, are out of place here, for they are equally required, if they are required, for the understanding of all explanatory connexions.

Secondly, (NAP) concerns only particular explanations, not general laws which support them, and takes these explanations in the form in which they are offered. It is thus silent about explanatory claims in which the replacements for '*p*' and '*q*' are in turn replaced by deep-level analyses of the concepts employed in those replacements. If we are concerned with the psychological aspect of an explanation, we need an argument to show that we should really be concerned with the laws (if any) which cover that explanation, or with some other form of words than that originally offered.

Thirdly, (IE) follows Davidson in taking causal statements to express relations between individuals, although it widens the class of possible *relata* to include states as well as events. I choose this reified form because it is the one most congenial to the position I want to question. Although it leads at times to rather baroque forms of expression, it is not obvious that there is anything to object to in this, as far as present purposes are concerned, provided that reification is not taken to imply ontological basicness. (In particular, we should not be distracted by considerations in favour of formulations of the form 'The fact that ... caused it to be the case that –' which do not undermine reification. For these are either concerned with psychological aspects of explanation, which are irrelevant to this point, or can be reconstrued, in reifying style, as alternative proposals about the individuation of states and events.) The class of possible *relata* is widened simply in order to count connexions which we naturally take to be causal as causal.

Fourthly, although I shall be concerned to distinguish between different kinds of independent existence, I shall not attempt to analyse the considerations relevant to the modality of 'depend for its existence upon ... '.

---

[2] The two conditions are obviously inspired by Hume: see, e.g., *A Treatise on Human Nature*, P. Nidditch, ed. (Oxford, 1978), p. 405.

Nevertheless, I should make my commitments clear. (IE) must be understandable in such a way that the relevant modal considerations are different from those relevant to causal determinism. This is not because I see any need to believe in causal determinism. But the considerations relevant to determinism, vaguely alluded to by the phrase 'causal necessity', may on occasion make an effect a necessary consequence of a cause, with respect to those considerations, when we still want to hold that the cause and the effect satisfy (IE). The considerations relevant to (IE) are rather those alluded to by the phrase 'metaphysical necessity'.

This is most easily understood within a framework according to which all modal claims are to be taken as relativised or indexed to certain kinds of consideration (often made clear by context). These considerations then provide the constraints needed for the construction of possible worlds relevant to the modal claim in question. Metaphysical considerations can then be characterised as those which, if they make something impossible, make it *absolutely* impossible, i.e. there are no considerations at all with respect to which it is possible. In adopting (IE) I take myself to be committed to these two theses:

(i)   There are considerations which are metaphysical by this test;
(ii)  causal laws do not provide considerations which are metaphysical by this test.

(i) and (ii) taken together can be taken to express the belief that there is a *philosophical* task, not merely a scientific one, of explaining the nature of reality. I know no independent argument for (i).[3] I see no reason for denying (ii): remarks about the success of physics are obviously beside the point. And there is at least a *prima facie* reason for affirming (ii), namely our strong intuitions about freedom of action. In addition, we have a pragmatic reason for accepting (IE), so understood: it provides a characterization of causality.

It is a slightly surprising consequence of accepting (IE) that, although some theses of essentiality of origin might be tenable, any claim of essentiality of causal consequence would be incoherent: if we want essentiality of consequence, the consequence in question cannot be a causal consequence. I think this could only seem unacceptable if we assumed that the considerations relevant to essence were just those relevant to causal determinism; which, of course, is what I am denying.

Why think that (NAP) and (IE) capture what is distinctive about causal explanation? I do not claim that every reasonable use of the English word

---

[3] I assume that so-called "epistemic possibility" is *not* to be treated in a way parallel to metaphysical necessity or causal necessity. Rather 'It is epistemically possible that $p$' is to be read as "It seems (to someone, under certain conditions) to be possible that $p$" or as "It is possible (for someone, under certain conditions) to believe that $p$".

'cause' conforms to these requirements. What is important is that, with two provisos to be mentioned below, they seem to isolate just that class of explanations which, if we are making distinctions, it is natural to isolate as causal. (NAP) rules out those explanations which can be called semantical, conceptual, logical, or mathematical. And (IE) rules out explanations which connect something *c* with something *e*, in such a way that the connexion is not *a priori* knowable, but in which *c* is held to constitute, or partially constitute, or constitute part of, *e*. In addition, (IE) provides a characterisation of causal priority; it thus supplies a want which should seem pressing if we are sceptical about the possibility of using temporal relations to do the job.

The two provisos are these. First, nothing has been said about teleological explanation. It is possible that some teleological explanations are best seen as meeting these two requirements. If we believe that, and also think it best to keep causal explanation separate from teleological explanation, we should hope to be able to make further refinements to deal with this. Secondly, if the distinctions made below are adopted, it may seem best to reserve the title 'cause' for a special class of those explanations counted as causal by (NAP) and (IE). I shall not attempt to decide these points. The proposal to take (NAP) and (IE) as distinctive of causal explanation is provisional only. The claim I want to make out is just that the significant division between philosophies of mind on this point falls within the class of views which accept that psychological explanations meet (NAP) and (IE).


II

The ambiguity in causalist hypotheses about a given form of explanation lies in the account of the *way* in which the items specified as cause and effect by such a hypothesis satisfy (IE). (IE) simply says that for each effect of a given cause, the cause must exist independently of it. It says nothing about the independence of a cause of that kind with respect to the whole class of its effects. To get clear on this point we can lay out a series of increasingly strong independence claims. They can be represented semi-formally, with the modality understood as indexed to the relevant kinds of consideration, by means of the following schemata:

$$(1) \quad \forall e \ [c \text{ causes } e \rightarrow \Diamond[\exists x(x=c) \ \& \ \sim\exists y(y=e)]]$$
$$(2) \quad \Diamond \ \exists x \ [x=c \ \& \ \sim\exists e \ [\text{Actually } (x \text{ causes } e)]]$$
$$(3) \quad \Diamond \ \exists x \ [x=c \ \& \ \sim\exists e \ [e \text{ is of kind } K \ \& \ x \text{ causes } e]]$$
$$(4) \quad \exists x \ [x=c \ \& \ \sim\exists e \ [x \text{ causes } e]]$$

At this point (4) is simply a special case of (3), with kind *K* suitably specified to include all of *c*'s effects in the relevant world. The point of keeping (4) separate appears when we formulate causal claims which set limits to the kind of independence ascribed to a cause of the kind in question. If we do that, we get four alternatives:

(RI)  = (1) & ~ (2)   $c$ could have existed without having any *particular* one of its actual effects, but not without having at least one of them.

(IK)  = (2) & ~ (3)   $c$ could have existed without having any of its actual effects, but not without having some effect of kind $K$.

(TK) = (3) & ~ (4)   $c$ could have existed without having any effect of kind $K$, but not without having some effect.

(RT)  = (4)            $c$ could have existed without having any effect.

These schemata can be used to make different claims about the independence of a given cause from its effects. It will be convenient to have a label for them. Let us say that (RI) takes $c$ to be a Radically Immanent cause; (IK) regards $c$ as an Immanent cause with respect to kind $K$; (TK) makes $c$ a Transcendent cause with respect to kind $K$: and (RT) makes $c$ a Radically Transcendent cause.

(TK) and (RT) are perhaps the schemata most naturally associated with causation. Part of the point of holding a causal theory of perception is to affirm a realism about the external world, which needs something at least as strong as (TK), with the kind $K$ taken to include all of a particular subject's experiences, or all of human experience generally. (RT) is naturally associated with the causal relations discovered by physics and kindred sciences. Interestingly, (RT) commits us to the possibility of causal cul-de-sacs, states or events which are caused but which themselves cause nothing. This can seem surprising if we think of nature as tidy-mindedly purposive, but is not obviously incoherent.

The fact that (TK) and (RT) are the schemata most naturally associated with causation does not, however, rule out (IK), at least, as capturing a causal kind of independent existence. For the possibility of independence of the kind offered by (IK) is likely simply to be overlooked by philosophers whose logic contains treatment of singular but not plural reference, and no consideration of 'Actually'. (RI) is slightly different: the problem here is whether, in fact, we ever have any motivation for thinking that a cause satisfies (1) but fails to satisfy (2), with kind $K$ taken to include any effect that such a cause might be expected to produce. In a spirit of linguistic liberalism, I shall continue to count all four lettered schemata as characterising kinds of cause: if (RI) is never satisfied, that can do no harm.

### III

The questions we need to ask a causalist about psychological explanation should now be obvious. Is he claiming that beliefs and desires are Immanent or Transcendent causes, and, if he holds some relativised thesis, how does he specify the kind $K$ with respect to which he makes his claim? I think it is also clear that if he is to be able to answer these questions, the causalist must have some more precise motivation than the failure of some alternatives. This does not require of him that he produce a conclusive argument for his view: I doubt if such an argument is available. Nevertheless, he must produce enough detailed argument to make clear what steps he is taking, and at which points he is making crucial choices.

I shall observe, to begin with at least, two restrictions upon the choice of thing offered as a candidate for the role of cause in psychological explanation. The first is terminological; there is a familiar ambiguity in the terms 'belief' and 'desire': they can refer either to what is believed or desired, or to the believing or desiring of it. The causalist is only concerned with the latter, so I shall speak only of believings and desirings. The second point is more substantive: to begin with, I shall confine my attention only to believings. The reason for thus excluding desirings from initial consideration will appear later.

How should we specify the kind $K$ with respect to which a causalist hypothesis about believings should be assessed? It seems reasonable to begin by considering the widest interesting class of putative effects that it is natural to associate with believings. The kind $K$, accordingly, will include all of the kinds of events we normally explain by citing believings. I shall call these 'reactions'. Reactions include actions, but much more besides. For example, Tom overtakes on a dangerous bend, and winces as he presses his foot down: we can explain his wincing by saying that he believed he was going to crash. Nor are we restricted to reactions which are overt, in the sense that they involve obviously perceptible bodily movements. Suppose that at some time a little before the wincing Tom felt a sudden burst of panic. The burst of panic can also be explained by saying that Tom believed that he was going to crash.

Are these causal explanations? It is certainly intelligible that Tom should have had that belief, even if he had not winced and had felt no burst of panic. Similarly, it seems intelligible that Tom should have winced then, and panicked then, and not believed that he was going to crash: perhaps he was thinking of his overdraft. If these things are intelligible, it seems that we cannot know *a priori* that Tom had that belief, on the basis of knowing that he winced and panicked, or *vice versa*. (NAP) seems satisfied.

Our intuitions are less definite when it comes to (IE). The difficulty is that we have little grasp on the particularity of believings. What is essential to a believing? It seems at least that we would not have had the same believing unless the same person had had the same belief in relevantly similar circumstances. But it is not obvious how we should specify the relevant similarity. We are inclined to require that the time and place at which the person has the belief be the same, but there may be room for some vagueness even here. A requirement we might plausibly impose is to insist that the grounds for believing a belief are essential to a believing.

In the face of such vagueness, the causalist cannot do more than present a *prima facie* case. Consider again the case of Tom, the timid road-hog. Could that believing have obtained even if he had not winced? It seems easy: he could have controlled his facial muscles. Even if he did not think of doing so, he could have done. Could that believing have obtained even if there had been no burst of panic? Tom might have drunk a stiff brandy before setting out; in that case we can imagine him having the same belief, at the same time, as a result of the same awareness of his circumstances, without the burst of panic. Would this have been the same believing? The causalist must reply: why not?

This seems not unreasonable. The causalist is responding to more than is required for the existence of a believing of the same type, a believing of the same belief, even if we take it that identity of belief requires identity of what the belief is about. He can accordingly claim to have made sense of the thought that we have individuals here. He is also responding to conditions stronger than those imposed by (NAP). Given that, the onus of proof seems to be on an opponent to motivate a finer notion of particularity of believings.

In addition, it seems clear that if this is right the very same believing could have existed in this case, even if Tom had neither winced nor panicked. The same stiff brandy might have removed both effects, without making him insensible. This means that on two plausible assumptions, believings can be held to satisfy both (1) and (2). The two assumptions are these: first, that what holds for the wincing and the burst of panic holds also for all remoter effects of this believing; secondly, that what holds for this believing may be taken to hold for all believings and their effects. Granting the same assumptions, belief explanation in general satisfies (NAP). The result is that believings are plausibly held to be the causes of reactions, and in more than an extremely minimal sense; for in the satisfaction of schema (2), believings are shown not to be Radically Immanent causes.

It might be thought that this is a strange and inconclusive line of argument for what seems to be a natural intuitive thesis, and that this results from choosing to take the thesis in relation to every event explained by a given believing. There is something right about this thought. What it shows is that the natural intuitive thesis says nothing about the nature of believings. For that thesis is restricted in its application to those events which are caused by other events which themselves are explained by believings. In our case, suppose that Tom's wincing was caused by a sudden burst of panic; if the burst of panic is itself explained by the believing, there is no intuitive obstacle to regarding the believing as the cause of the wincing. But it is obvious that this says nothing about how the believing itself fits in. The same goes for the kind of case the intuitive thesis most directly concerns: the explanation of actions. Many actions can be taken to be caused by decisions. If a decision is itself explicable by reference to the believing which explains the action it causes, then we can regard the believing as a cause of the action. But again this tells us nothing about the nature of believings. I have preferred to take a causalist view as proposing a substantial thesis about believings. As a result, I have found only an inconclusive argument; nevertheless I see no reason to deny it.

## IV

The important question is whether believings satisfy schema (3), with kind $K$ taken to include all of the reactions of the subject in the relevant possible world. This is the question whether believings are only Immanent causes of reactions. At this level of abstraction, we can rely upon intuitions no longer. I shall consider an argument that believings are Immanent with respect to reactions. Although the motivation of the argument is epistemological, it will be clear that its consequences are directly metaphysical.

The danger of using such arguments is that any apparent success they may have may be due to illiberal epistemological views. Setting reasonable epistemological restrictions requires complications which may obscure the argument's structure. Since the basic structure is very simple, and it is important to keep assessment of its validity separate from assessment of the truth of its premisses, I shall lay out the argument in summary. I suggest this as an epistemological requirement:

(a) For any $y$, for any $d_1 \ldots d_n$
  *if* (i) $y$ is a $G$: and
  (ii) $d_1 \ldots d_n$ are of kind $K$: and
  (iii) $y$ causes $d_1 \ldots d_n$; and
  (iv) $y$ could have existed without having any effect of kind $K$; and
  (v) $y$ together with $d_1 \ldots d_n$ constitute a favoured case; and
  (vi) it is possible to verify the existence of some $G$s–
  *then it is possible to verify the existence of $y$*

>  *either*  (i) without verifying the existence of any $d_i$ from among $d_1 \ldots d_n$;
>  *or*  (ii) by verifying the existence of some $d_i$ from among $d_1 \ldots d_n$ such that $d_i$ is *insulated* from the rest of $d_1 \ldots d_n$

The aim of the argument is to use *modus tollens* on an appropriate interpretation of the conditional embedded in (a), together with the acceptance of all but clause (iv) of the antecedent, to show that believings cannot exist without causing some reaction.

That is, even when we hold

> (b) $b$ is a believing by $a$;
> (c) $r_1 \ldots r_n$ are reactions of $a$;
> (d) $b$ causes $r_1 \ldots r_n$;
> (e) $b$ together with $r_1 \ldots r_n$ constitute a favoured case;

and accept

> (f) it is possible to verify the existence of some believings;

– even then, we should also hold

> (g) it is not possible to verify the existence of $b$
> *either*  (i) without verifying the existence of any $r_i$ from among $r_1 \ldots r_n$;
> *or*  (ii) by verifying the existence of some $r_i$ from among $r_1 \ldots r_n$ such that $r_i$ is *insulated* from the rest of $r_1 \ldots r_n$.

Given (a)–(g) we can derive

> (h) $b$ could not have existed without causing some reaction of $a$.

Of these premises, (b), (c), (d), and (e) can be taken to be true by stipulation; we just restrict attention to cases for which they hold. Denying (f) would be desperate. The question turns, then, on whether (a) and (g) are more plausible than the denial of (h).

Despite its superficial complexity, the motivating thought behind (a) is very simple. The leading idea is just that a metaphysical thesis about a given subject-matter must have epistemological consequences: it must make a difference to what it would be to know about that subject-matter. The superficial complexity of (a) arises just from attempting to make the epistemological consequences plausible.

(a) is an attempt to state the epistemological consequences of holding that a given kind of cause could have existed even if it had had no effects of kind K. It is intuitive to think that if it is possible to verify the existence of such a cause at all, it will always be possible (in principle) to do so without verifying the existence of any effects of kind $K$. The reason why this *seems* plausible is that it is hard to see what content the metaphysical thesis could have unless it had some such consequence; if metaphysical theses are not to be constrained in this kind of way, it is hard to see how they could be subject to any constraints at all.

Nevertheless, the intuitive thought is too strong in two respects. First, it is not clear that we can give a sense to 'in principle possibility' under which it is reasonable to expect that it is always in principle possible to verify the existence of the cause in the demanding way suggested. Cutting clear of this problem, I am taking it to be enough for verification of the existence of such a cause, if the methods of verification in fact available exhibit enough similarity between the evidence relied on in this case, and that available in a case where the demanding requirements can be met (what I call "a favoured case"). The idea is that we can accept slacker requirements for verification in some cases, if, but only if, the title to verification applies to those cases in a way that is parasitic upon the more rigorous verification available in a favoured case.

Secondly, only in very simple examples (like Hume's billiard balls) will it be possible to verify the existence of the cause without verifying the existence of any of the effects of the kind in question. Schema (3) is supposed to represent what can be satisfied in the case of the external world with respect to human experience, on natural realist assumptions. Insisting on verification without verifying the existence of any effects of kind $K$ would be too quick a route to anti-realism. The same applies to paradigm cases in physics. We therefore need some more liberal method. For this purpose I introduce the notion of an *insulated* indicator. The core idea here is that if you cannot get at the cause except by means of its effects, you have no right to a strong claim of independent existence unless some of those effects give evidence for the existence of the cause which is independent of that provided by the others. A first shot at spelling out what this amounts to in the theoretical case might run like this:

> (Ins)　$e_i$ is an indicator of the existence of a cause $c$ which is *insulated* from the rest of $e_1 \ldots e_n$ only if
>   (i)　The existence of $e_i$ can be verified without verifying the existence of any of the rest of $e_1 \ldots e_n$;
>   (ii)　we have a (successful) theory T which enables us to infer the existence of $c$ from the existence of $e_i$ on the basis of some law (or laws) $L$ with reasonable probability relative to conditions $O$, and

(a) $L$ is grounded on observation of circumstances which
are not of the same type as any of $e_1 \ldots e_n$ (apart from
$e_i$)

(b) the obtaining of $O$ can, in a favoured case, be verified
without verifying any of $e_1 \ldots e_n$;

(iii) It is essential to the role of objects like $c$ in T that they
satisfy schema (3), with kind $K$ specified as including
anything of the same kind as $e_1 \ldots e_n$.

This is likely to need some refinement. For a non-theoretical case we
should replace the notion of a theory, perhaps with that of an area of
discourse, and instead of laws it will be reasonable to advert to the kinds of
rules of thumb following which is constitutive of correct participation in that
area of discourse. 'Reasonable probability' in (ii) need not be thought of
quantitively: what is important is that belief that $c$ exists is reasonable. Also,
in a non-theoretical case, it may be inappropriate to talk of inference.

I take the need for clause (i) to be obvious. Clause (ii) is an attempt to spell
out the idea that the route from an insulated indicator to what it is an
indicator of must not be just another case of whatever route connects the
other effects with the cause. The intuitive thought supporting it is just that
there must be more than one way of getting at an object which is endowed
with independent existence.

Clause (iii) is needed to tie the notion of an insulated indicator to the
subject in hand. Satisfaction of (i) and (ii) by itself does not seem enough to
provide favoured case verification for an object which exists independently in
the way required by schema (3): indeed it seems appropriate for schema (2).
Clause (iii) is an attempt to block reconstructions of (e.g. physical) theories
which aim to defuse their causal claims. This should not be confused with an
attempt to block an instrumentalism about the subject-matter which takes
the truth of the relevant theory to be constituted by its predictive success. I
shall take instrumentalism to be a view which accepts that a theory is
committed in the way that clause (iii) requires, and, partly because of that,
takes an anti-realist attitude to the whole theory, perhaps denying that the
theory corresponds to the facts in some sense. Clause (iii) is trying to block a
different kind of view which may also be revisionist; this kind of revisionism
allows that the statements of the theory are as literally true as you please, but
holds that the theory should not be taken as committed to strong independent existence claims. The point of clause (iii) can now be seen clearly: it is
only if the theory is itself committed to the strong independent existence of
causes of a given kind that use of that theory could provide favoured case
verification of such independent existence.

It might be thought that the presence of clause (iii) undermines the point of taking an epistemological route to consideration of the Transcendent causal thesis. This is not so. For without the epistemological connexion, it might seem reasonable to take believings to be Transcendent with respect to reactions, even if it was not essential to do so. This position is put under pressure by the presence of clause (iii) in a condition for favoured case verification.

Let this, then, stand, as an outline of the motivation for premiss (a). It would be foolish to be completely confident about its formulation. It ought to take account of the kinds of verification we should expect in paradigm cases in physics and kindred sciences, on the assumption that such causes are held to satisfy schema (3) with kind $K$ widely specified; it must therefore be revisable in the light of further understanding of these sciences. As it stands it seems to me at least *prima facie* plausible.

## V

I shall now argue for the second main premiss, (g). The question is whether, even in the most favourable case imaginable, the verification conditions set by premiss (a) can be met. I shall consider two general methods of verification: one at the psychological level, employing the concepts and standard criteria central to the use of psychological discourse; the other at what I shall call the physical level.

At the psychological level, it seems clear, first of all, that in no case could the existence of a believing be verified without verifying at least some of the reactions caused by that believing. I doubt if this can be proved, but consideration of a few cases should make it plausible. Our most direct access to another's beliefs in many circumstances is by means of what he says. However, we can only tell what someone believes on the basis of what he says in this direct way if we take him to be being sincere. But then we can say that he said that *because* he believed it, and this is another instance of the same explanatory relation between a believing and a reaction. Alternatively, we might take $b$ to be a believing of a belief which it is reasonable to suppose a subject has in a given perceptual situation: say when he is standing in front of some obvious object with his eyes open. The difficulty is that we cannot know what the subject is believing in a favoured case without knowing what he is looking at or paying attention to, and we cannot know that without observing his reactions; and these reactions themselves will be liable to explanation by citing the very believing of which they are an indication. Again, although we should not ignore cases of introspection, there seem to be not even phenomenological grounds for thinking that we can verify the existence of our own believings without verifying at least some of the reactions they cause.

This means that if there can be favoured case verification at the psychological level, it must be by verifying the existence of an insulated indicator. There seems to be no difficulty about meeting the first two clauses of II. Suppose that $b$ is a believing acquired in circumstances of perceptual confrontation, which has considerable consequences throughout a large period of the subject's life; Freudian cases would provide examples. There are many effects of this believing, some widely separated in time from others. If we were present at the original perceptual confrontation, we would have no difficulty in verifying the existence of the believing. Suppose the subject is standing in front of a statue in a museum. The statue begins to fall towards him. We can easily supply an adaptation of a rule of thumb for the case: if a large object is falling towards someone, and he leaps back suddenly, then (probably) there is a believing by him of the belief that the object is falling towards him. When he does leap back, we could reasonably count as having verified the existence of the believing. The claim that this believing exists is, of course, revisable, but that does not make it unreasonable. This verification is surely sufficiently insulated from that of the other reactions caused by the believing; the rule of thumb is not supported by circumstances of the same type as the other reactions – for all we know, these reactions could be of any kind whatever; and we verify the falling of the statue quite independently of verifying any of the reactions caused by the believing.

The issue at the psychological level therefore depends upon whether it is essential to psychological discourse that believings be taken to satisfy schema (3) with respect to reactions. The final answer to this depends upon consideration of the physical level, but there are at least some intuitions which suggest that the satisfaction by believings of schema (3) with respect to reactions is not essential to psychological talk. First, there is nothing in talk of believings analogous to crude mechanistic hypotheses in other areas. Consider, for example, a primitive theology according to which God is thought to be the cause of thunder. If it is thought that God is a Transcendent cause of thunder, we expect there to be, essential to the primitive view, some conception of the mechanism whereby God causes thunder: perhaps some awesome striking. If scientific enquiry discerns no such striking, the primitive theology collapses. In the case of believings, there is no such conception of a mechanism linking believings and reactions. Secondly, there is nothing in talk of believings analogous to what is found in psychological cases where it is plausible to say that states of a certain kind do satisfy schema (3) with respect to the reactions they cause. It is plausible to say, for example, that it is essential to talk of pain that pains are conceived of as Transcendent with respect to the reactions they cause. But this is because pains are not *causes* of feelings of pain: there are *a priori* connexions between ascriptions of pain and ascriptions of feelings of pain. And this means that it is essential to third-person verification of the existence of a pain to think of pains as thus Transcendent, just because the subject can verify the existence of a pain of his own without verifying the existence of any of the reactions the pain causes. There is nothing analogous in the case of believings. And, thirdly, where there are no reactions for a believing to be cited to explain, we in fact feel no pressure at all to think that there really is such a believing there. If, for example, we only say that the agent *would*, in certain circumstances, react in a way explicable by that believing, we have no reason yet to say that he *actually* believes that. These intuitions combine to challenge someone who claims that the relevant Transcendence of believings is essential to psychological talk to provide some motivation for his view.

Such motivation might be found in the alternative method of verification, at the physical level. By 'the physical level' I do not mean to restrict consideration to verification provided by physics, or even to that provided by kindred sciences, following their present explanatory aims. The physical level is intended also to include any extension or development of such sciences which would occur if they were concerned specifically to connect higher with lower levels of discourse, and followed their present empirical methods. Presumably verification at such a level would not need to be verification by means of insulated indicators; it ought to be able to get behind the reactions caused by a particular believing. Indeed, this is just the point of appealing to the physical level.

What would it be to verify the existence of a particular believing at this level? It does not seem to be required that the believing be identified with some physical state. It would be sufficient if we could verify the existence of a state which stands in a constitutive relation to the believing.[4] For this to make sense, we need to be able to arrange psychological ascriptions in such a way that particular states and events at the psychological level can be paired off with particular states and events at the physical level. It is plausible to look for some form of functionalism to explain what sort of arrangement this might be.

This need not commit us to the standard functionalist claim that there is no more to psychological states than the causal role such an arrangement ascribed to them. But there is still a natural worry about functionalism which is allied to a point more directly relevant to our concerns. The natural worry

---

[4] I leave the notion of constitution appealed to here without substantial explanation. What is crucial for the argument is just that there should be a difference between what stands in a constitutive relation to a given state, and a cause or effect of what stands in a constitutive relation to that state. I assume that this would be acceptable to a physicalist who does not accept even a token identity thesis.

is this. In correlating a functional level arrangement of the psychological states ascribed to a subject with the physical states which realise them, the functionalist needs to begin from inputs and outputs. He seems to need to assume that it is unproblematic which physical states constitute the reactions caused by a given psychological state; whereas, in fact, this seems far from unproblematic. This is an expression of a general worry about whether the causal relations expressed at the two levels can be mapped on to one another.

This general worry can be given a sharper point, if we suppose that conditions are more favourable for physical level verification than most functionalists think that they in fact are. Let us suppose that there is no variable realisation, at least as far as human beings are concerned. This allows us to suppose that for an ideal ascriber of psychological states, there is just one physical property which is present in any subject whenever that ascriber ascribes the same type of psychological state to a subject. So we can take there to be, for every such psychological predicate in such an ascriber's use, a physical kind predicate which is co-extensive and co-projectible with it. I shall not be concerned with the question how this might be known: let us suppose there are adequate inductive grounds. The question is: under such favourable circumstances, would verifying the existence of the correlated physical state count as verifying the existence of the believing?

It might seem obvious that it would, but given the concerns of the argument we have reason to be fussy about this. For the presence of a correlation of the kind imagined does not itself guarantee that the physical state whose existence we have verified constitutes the believing: it might, for instance, be a cause of a state which constitutes the believing. This possibility in particular must be ruled out for the purposes of this argument: to pass over it would beg just the question at issue. And until the problem is settled, there can be no reason to expect the kind of isomorphism the functionalist requires. If it remains unresolved, there is simply no fact of the matter which physical state constitutes a given believing: nothing could count as verifying its existence at the physical level in the way required. And, presumably, if this were true even in the favourable circumstance imagined, it would be true as things actually are.

What would decide the point? It is at least a necessary condition for the claim that in these circumstances the identified physical state would constitute the believing, that in these circumstances it would be reasonable for an ascriber to defer to a scientist in possession of the physical facts, in much the way that on the Kripke-Putnam model of natural kinds it is reasonable for the layman to defer to the scientist about gold.[5] If the argument is to be

[5] See S. Kripke, "Naming and Necessity" in D. Davidson and G. Harman, eds., *The Semantics of Natural Language* (Dordrecht, 1972), pp.253–355, and H. Putnam, "The meaning of 'meaning'" in his *Mind, Language, and Reality* (Cambridge, 1975), pp. 215–271.

pushed through, and premiss (h) maintained, it is tempting to draw an analogy, and make plausible a claim about the points compared.

The analogy in question is between the ascription of beliefs and the ascription of value.[6] The favourable circumstances for verification imagined are precisely similar to what would hold if a form of ethical naturalism were true; we would then have a natural predicate co-extensive and co-projectible with the word 'good' as that word is used in moral judgments by an ideal ascriber. To push the argument through we would need to claim two things. First, that even if such a correlation obtained, it would be irrational, or bad, to defer to an expert about natural facts in the ascription of value. And, secondly, that the ascription of beliefs is analogous to the ascription of value in just the feature which, it is claimed, makes deference bad in the moral sense.

An argument for the first point might run like this. For deference of the right kind to the expert to be rational in the moral case, it would have to be rational for an *ordinary*, competent but not ideal, ascriber to count as authoritative over his ascriptions the satisfaction of any natural predicate which the expert about natural facts regarded as theoretically significant, and which was approximately co-extensive and co-projectible with the applications of 'good' he in fact tends to make. This would keep an ascriber in line, in a certain respect, with his already-formed habits. But there is no reason to think that he would thereby be kept in line in the right respects; and worse, by such deference he would rule out improvements in his own ascriptions of value which arose from his own increased moral sensitivity.

The analogy might be made out like this. What makes it bad to defer in the ethical case is that what counts as consistent or improved ascription is determined by features internal to morality, which no naturalised method can be guaranteed to capture. Just the same feature appears in the case of the ascription of beliefs. For in ascribing a belief to a subject, we commit ourselves to a view about the rationality of the reactions we thereby explain; precisely by attempting to verify the existence of a believing without verifying the existence of the reactions it causes, the physical level method of verification debars from consideration the very factors which determine what counts as consistency and improvement in the ascription of beliefs.

This argument should connect back with the psychological level method of verification. For, in need of a motivation for denying counter-intuitions, someone holding that it is essential to psychological discourse that believings be taken to be Transcendent causes of reactions is likely to hold that in the case imagined we should defer to the scientist. And once the connexion is made, it can be used to support the later argument. For it seems no accident

---

[6] This analogy is exploited by Davidson, but to different effect; see "The Material Mind", in his *Essays on Actions and Events* pp. 253 ff. I comment on the difference below.

that psychological discourse takes pains to be Transcendent with respect to the reactions they cause, and that at the same time an ascription of pain does not commit the ascriber to a view about the rationality of the subject.

A proponent of the argument is not, of course, committed to ruling out all kinds of deference to the scientist in these cases. In both areas, it would obviously be rational to take the scientist's observations into account; all that is denied is that authority should be handed over, as in the case of natural kinds on the Kripke-Putnam model. And it would be reasonable, I think, to defer to the scientist who had correlated a predicate with the actual use of an ideally sensitive or virtuous ascriber; but that is not really deference to the scientist, but to the ideal ascriber.

This argument is reminiscent of a point made by Davidson; but it is also, I think, significantly different from it. Davidson claims that the significant difference between psychological ascriptions and the applications of physical predicates is that the former are governed by "the constitutive ideal of rationality", while the latter are not.[7] He concludes from this that "there cannot be tight correlations between the realms if each is to retain allegiance to its proper source of evidence".[8] This conclusion does not obviously follow from the initial claim, and I see no reason for believing it. The argument here works differently. I assume that there could have been tight correlations of the kind that Davidson denies. If even then there would be no reason to count the physical level as authoritative, it will not be surprising that there are in fact no such correlations.

How convincing is the argument? It is neither complete nor completely knock-down. For completeness, it needs a fuller development of the analogy between psychological ascriptions and ascriptions of value: we should expect the two areas of discourse to have more in common than just this, if the analogy is reasonable. And even a proponent of the argument cannot regard it as completely knock-down. The position adopted in the ethical case seems itself to involve a moral decision, and accordingly is bound up in a less than decisive style of argument. The stronger the analogy, the more likely this is to hold in the case of believings. Nevertheless, in the absence of some motivation for physicalism which is independent of considerations about causality, enough has surely been done to make it plausible that we cannot verify the existence of believings without verifying the existence of the reactions they cause.

---

[7] "Mental Events", in *Essays on Actions and Events* p. 223.
[8] *Ibid.*, p. 222.

## VI

Let me summarise the argument so far. I suggested that (a) imposed a reasonable requirement on the verification of causes more strongly independent of their effects than (RI) or (IK) would permit. The failure of both psychological level and physical level verification to provide any access to believings which meets that requirement shows that believings are only Immanent causes with respect to the class of reactions in general.

But might there nevertheless remain an interesting special class of reactions with respect to which a stronger thesis could be maintained? The difficulty is that if we do not strengthen the conditions on the particularity of believings, believings seem to be Transcendent causes with respect to almost every special class of reactions, if these classes are specified without regard to the content of the belief.

Take a believing which in fact causes an action. If the subject had shown restraint, that believing might have caused no action at all. Suppose a believing in fact causes a reaction which is not an action; it does not seem impossible to imagine that if the subject's thought had been suitably interrupted, the believing might have caused an action, and nothing else. Take a believing which in fact causes only overt reactions; the same believing, it seems, might have caused only reactions which were not overt. An exception to this general rule seems to be that believings could not be Transcendent causes with respect to the class of reactions other than actions which result from deliberation; for a believing to exist in the absence of any such reaction, there would have to exist in addition, if believings are Immanent with respect to reactions generally, an action caused by that believing which resulted from deliberation. But any such action will be caused by some other reaction, involved in the deliberation, which will itself be caused by the believing. It is not clear, however, that this exception casts any further light on the nature of believings: it is simply the consequence of a special division of the class of reactions.

It seems that we can only rule out this liberality by revising our conception of the particularity of believings. The danger then will be that the causalist hypothesis may disappear as a substantive general thesis about believings.

## VII

I have tried to make plausible a view according to which believings are Immanent causes with respect to reactions generally, but Transcendent with respect to almost every interesting sub-category of reactions. Let us call this view the Diverse Independence view (DI-view). Much of the dispute between causalists and non-causalists can be seen as due to a failure to recognise this as an option. This has a general significance for the philosophy of mind which can be recognised in the positions this DI-view recommends on a number of central questions. The most obvious points can be made briefly.

(i) If the DI-view is right, we cannot treat all mental states uniformly. Pains, for example, seemed to be Transcendent with respect to the reactions they cause, while believings are not. This is why consideration of desirings was postponed. For while some desirings, like believings, are only Immanent with respect to reactions, others seem to be Transcendent. Transcendent desirings are those which are strongly associated with psychological states which they do not cause. Obvious examples are bodily desirings: if someone is thirsty, it seems to be *a priori* that he wants to drink. And it seems quite possible that someone should be thirsty and there be no reaction *caused* by the associated desiring. In line with what the DI-view would predict, the ascription of desirings like these does not commit the ascriber to a view about the rationality of the subject.

Associated with this metaphysical distinction between kinds of mental state, the DI-view will find an epistemological distinction. Transcendent states will be verifiable in the way required by premiss (a) of the argument in section IV: without verifying any caused reactions, by the subject himself; and by verifying an insulated indicator, by others. It seems likely that the DI-view will explain knowledge of Immanent states, on the other hand, by comparison with moral epistemology. The result is that there is no single problem of other minds.

(ii) If we adopt the DI-view, we will need to be cautious in talking about the spatio-temporal location of believings. A natural intuition suggests that believings always precede the reactions they cause. The DI-view cannot allow for this, for it would provide a way of constructing possible worlds to characterise independent existence which makes believings Radically Transcendent causes: the alternative worlds will be those which are like the actual world up to a certain time (the time of a believing), but differ thereafter. The same applies to parallel intuitions about spatial location: the DI-view does not invite the thought that believings are in the head. This does not mean that there can be disembodied minds. A believing cannot exist, on the DI-view, unless it causes some reaction; and it is plausible to think that reactions must occur in space and time. But there is no need to give a time to a believing except in a way that is parasitic upon the times of the reactions it causes. The temporal intuition which the DI-view opposes is easily explained: it arises from consideration of a limited class of reactions: those which are caused, and preceded, by other reactions which are also explicable by appeal to the same believings. It is unclear that there is any need to give believings spatial location.

(iii) The DI-view also denies that believings are essentially internal in any more metaphorical sense, opposed to being overt. For believings to be essentially internal, they would have to be especially connected with non-overt reactions. The DI-view denies this, without retreating to the excesses of behaviourism and insisting that believings be tied just to overt reactions. Believings are Transcendent with respect to both kinds of reaction.

(iv) There is room for a position intermediate between instrumentalism and realism, where realism is characterised by two theses: that the truth of ascriptions of belief does not just consist in their predictive efficiency, and that believings are Transcendent causes with respect to reactions in general.[9] The apparent dichotomy is borrowed from the philosophy of science, where it might seem appropriate. If it is appropriate there, this can only be because it is assumed that strong independence claims are essential to the relevant sciences: on that assumption, anyone who claims that (in some sense) there are not really such strongly independent entities as the sciences in question suppose there are, while holding that the statements of those sciences are true, must be something like an instrumentalist. But the DI-view precisely denies the parallel assumption in the psychological case: it is not essential to psychological discourse that believings be held to be so strongly independent. The DI-view can count as realist in a less question-begging sense, since it is not instrumentalist. But we should be wary of the reifying style of much talk about the mind; there need be no objection to it, but it at least encourages a conception of psychological states as independent of their effects in just the way which the DI-view denies that they are.

(v) The DI-view is compatible with some form of physicalism, but it denies at least one thesis which is plausibly seen as a central motivation for most physicalists. Causal sequences at the physical level can be seen as standing in some constitutive relation to causal sequences at the psychological level; but no more precise constitutive correlations can be made between items within such sequences at the two levels.

This has a consequence which conflicts with one of the most basic physicalist intuitions. We use the notion of explanation in both a weak and a strong sense. 'Explains why $p$' can be read weakly as "makes it unsurprising that $p$", or strongly as "makes it the case that $p$". The compulsion suggested by the strong sense is naturally explained in modal terms. For each replacement for '$p$' and '$q$' in a strong explanation of the form '$p$ because $q$', there will be some replacement for '$r$' which will make this schema true:

(i)   It is necessary that, if $q$ and $r$, then $p$;

[9] Of course, no one accepts the dichotomy in quite these terms. But it is implicit in D. Dennett, "Three kinds of intentional psychology", in R. Healey, ed., *Reduction, Time and Reality* (Cambridge, 1981), pp. 46 ff. It also seems to underlie B. Loar, *Mind and Meaning* (Cambridge, 1981), section 1.2, and C. Peacocke, *Sense and Content* (Oxford, 1983), chapter 8.

and if the replacement for '$r$' is not the same as the replacement for '$q$', we will also insist on this:

(ii) It is not necessary that, if $r$, then $p$.

It is natural to suppose that causal explanations in general are strong explanations in this sense, and plausible to hold that psychological explanations in particular are too. The DI-view can accept this as well as any other. What it does not accept is a fundamental physicalist intuition about strong explanations, according to which the modal connexion in causal explanations, expressed by (i), always holds in virtue of a corresponding modal connexion involved in a causal sequence at the physical level. In fact, it is not obvious what reason there is to accept this intuition. It might be supposed that instances of (i) could only hold in virtue of strict laws, and that the appropriate laws could only be found at the physical level. But what needs explaining about (i) is the modality, and an appeal to laws is no help here; for we would still need an explanation of the necessity of the laws themselves. Alternatively, we might suppose that an appropriate connexion with physics is built into the notion of a cause; but that is just linguistic stipulation. If we take satisfaction of (IE), (NAP), and (i) and (ii) to be distinguishing marks of causal explanation, the independent argument for the DI-view gives us reason to deny the fundamental physicalist intuition.

(vi) Finally, we should make something of a reassessment of behaviourism. Behaviourism can (perhaps charitably) be seen as making the radical claim that conceptual content is determined by facts about the reactions which believings are cited to explain. Classically, behaviourists restricted the class of reactions to overt reactions, and in some cases to motor responses, and insisted on excessively tight correlations between types of believing and types of reaction. But some version of the radical claim can survive the failure of such restricting conditions. Nevertheless it is incompatible with the view that believings are Transcendent with respect to reactions, on the plausible assumption that the belief believed is essential to a believing. For since, on the view that believings are Transcendent, a believing could have existed even if it had caused no reactions, facts about reactions cannot determine the content of what is believed: we are forced into an aetiological account of content. The DI-view does not itself conflict with the radical claim. Whether we accept the claim will depend upon our view of what it is to give an account of content.

The DI-view seems to give the non-causalist all he wanted; and I think it gives the causalist all he has reason to believe in. If we decide not to count the DI-view as causalist, that no longer matters. For in explaining how psychological explanation compares with more obvious kinds of causal explanation, Davidson's challenge to identify the pattern of explanation has been met. Of course, even if the DI-view is right, this is only a beginning: we still need some account of the necessity of psychological explanation, of the epistemology of belief ascription, and of conceptual content. But at least it will be a beginning from the right place.[10]

*University of Sussex*

[10] I am very grateful to Michael Woods for his comments on an earlier draft. I also have a great debt to David Charles, who has often discussed the issues raised here with me: this paper is the result of trying to get clear about the differences between us.

# MENTAL CAUSES AND
# EXPLANATION OF ACTION

## By Cynthia and Graham Macdonald

Non-reductive monism has recently been charged with leading either to inconsistency or to epiphenomenalism.[1] This dilemma is thought to arise from the fact that the position attempts to reconcile three apparently inconsistent principles. First, that there is causal interaction between mental and physical events, where the causal relation is understood as holding between individual events in extension. Second, the nomological character of causality, the thesis that where causal relations exist, there are (universal) laws linking events so related (but only under certain descriptions). Finally, there is the thesis that there are no causal laws linking mental events with physical events. (This feature is sometimes described as "the anomalism of the mental", and entails the non-reducibility of psychological theory to physical theory. Mental anomalism involves more than just the denial of psycho-physical causal laws; it denies the existence of *any* kind of psycho-physical law, and of pure psychological laws. Here we do not wish to be committed to the last two aspects of anomalism, so our use of the term is intended to capture that aspect most relevant to this paper – the claim that there are no psycho-physical causal laws.) These principles are reconciled by adopting a further thesis, viz. the claim that every token mental event is a physical event. Since it is understood that to be a mental (or physical) event is to be described in a certain way (e.g., in the vocabulary of propositional attitudes), this further thesis amounts to the claim that every mental event has a physical description and is thus "covered" by physical law. This, in so many words, is the view that every mental event is a physical event despite the fact that mental properties are irreducibly distinct from physical ones.

There are two main sources of the claim that such a view leads to epiphenomenalism; one has to do with the nature of causality, the other to do

[1] See, for instance, Ted Honderich, "The Argument for Anomalous Monism", *Analysis 42*, (1982), pp. 59–64 and "Psychophysical Lawlike Connections and Their Problem", *Inquiry 24*, (1981), pp. 277–304; Howard Robinson, *Matter and Sense* (Cambridge, 1982), esp. pp. 8–13; cf. also Jaegwon Kim, "Causality, Identity, and Supervenience in the Mind-Body Problem" in *Midwest Studies in Philosophy IV*, (Minneapolis, 1979), pp. 31–50 (esp. p. 47). For the classic statement of anomalous monism, see Donald Davidson, "Mental Events", in Foster and Swanson, eds., *Experience and Theory* (Amherst, 1970), pp. 79–101, reprinted in his *Essays on Actions and Events* (Oxford, 1980).

with a supposed link between causal efficacy and explanatory value. Disentangling these two objections is a tricky business, as their adherents often confuse them. However, the issue of causation must be kept apart from that of explanation, so we will deal with the objections separately.

## I

The argument for non-reductive monism appears to work because of the extensionality of the causal relation and the intensionality of nomologicality. If A and B are causally related events they are so however described. However the causal law under which A and B are subsumed is a law as a result (partly) of the descriptions embedded in it. The objectors admit that this may be true, but that it is only part of the story. Decomposing events thus causally related will reveal that there are some properties of those events which are causally irrelevant. An extended quotation from Honderich makes the point:

> It is not the age or (*sic*) the sheen of the teapot that is flattening the napkin, but its weight. It is not the weight of the door but its colour that makes it reflect the light. The most natural answer to the question of what caused something, then, is a property of an ordinary thing. What needs to be resisted immediately, however, is that what is in question is a general property, a universal. It is not the general property of weighing a pound, which is other or more than this teapot weighing a pound, that is flattening the napkin. That general property will exist if the weight of the teapot is changed and the napkin isn't flattened . . . We come to the idea, then, that what is flattening the napkin is *this teapot's weight*, an individual property of this teapot . . . It is not *all* of the teapot, or any individual property of it other than its weighing a pound, that is an instance of the general property of weighing a pound . . . causes strictly speaking are individual properties . . . [2]

The moral for mental causation is that if mental and physical events do interact, they must do so in virtue of certain (but not all) of their properties. These properties, the "causally relevant" ones, are, moreover, the prime candidates for properties that might figure in laws linking such events. In fact, Honderich claims[3], "The Principle of the Nomological Character of Causally-Relevant Properties" is required by any reasonable account of causation. Now this understanding of the relation between causality and laws causes trouble for anomalous monism. For the question arises, in virtue of

[2] Ted Honderich, "Causes and If p, even if x, still q", *Philosophy* 57 (1982), p. 292.
[3] In "The Argument for Anomalous Monism", op. cit., p. 62.

which properties does a mental event causally interact with a physical event? If the reply is, "the mental ones", the denial of anomalism would appear to follow, as it is expressions referring to these properties which would appear in the laws linking the causally related events. If, on the other hand, the reply is, "the physical ones", then the "mentality" of any given mental event would appear to cease being relevant to its interactions with other events, and epiphenomenalism would appear to follow.[4]

Let us assume that the relation between causality and laws is as depicted. Does psycho-physical lawlessness lead to mental inertia? Not without further argument, and we claim that the further argument rests on dualist prejudices. What has been overlooked is the crucial distinction between a property and its instance. Honderich insists, rightly, that it is the property *instantiated* (the "individual property") which is causally effective. However this seems to be forgotten when he turns to attack non-reductive monism. If we do insist that causality is a relation between token events, and that it is instances of properties associated with event types which are causally efficacious, then the "Principle of the Nomological character of Causally-Relevant Properties" should be amended so as to finish " . . . Causally-Relevant Instances of Properties". This amendment defuses the argument which is meant to lead to epiphenomenalism. Examples may help to see why this is so.

Associated with any event type, such as shooting, is a property, such as that of being a shooting. This property will be instanced by any event which is a token of that type. Indeed, the sense in which any token event "has" such a property consists in the fact that it is an instance of that property. Thus, for example, John's shooting of Joe at 12.00 p.m. on Sunday, 4 March, 1984, is a token of the type, *shooting*; and that event has the property of being a shooting by virtue of instancing it.[5]

Suppose now that a given mental event, say, Susan's desire for a drink, causes a physical event of Susan's body, say, a movement of her arm. Then it will be true that an event which is an instance of the property, being a desire for a drink (perhaps among others) is causally related to an event which is an instance of the property, being a movement of Susan's arm. But surely any

[4] Howard Robinson voices an almost identical crticism: ". . . interaction depends not upon some extensional causal relation but upon the intensional explanatory relevance of that feature in virtue of which the objects are supposedly interacting", op. cit., p. 12. Cf. also Kim: ". . . the pain is only a supervenient cause of the groan, and its causal role is dependent on that of its neural correlate which has a direct causal role with respect to the groan . . . in an important sense the pain has no independent causal power . . ." Kim's conclusion, however, is more positive than that of Honderich or Robinson. ". . . if this be epiphenomenalism", he says, "let us make the most of it"! Kim, op. cit. pp. 46–7.

[5] This parallel between event types and tokens, on the one hand, and the properties associated with such types and their instances, on the other, would seem to hold good irrespective of whether one endorses a Davidsonian or a Kim-type view of events. Both construe events as non-repeatable, dated particulars, and hence as individuals capable of possessing properties.

event may be an instance of more than one property. That is, different properties may be instantiated in the same "individual property" (to use Honderich's terminology). Susan's desire for a drink, for example, may not only be an instance of the property, being a desire for a drink; it may be an instance of the *distinct* property, being a desire for some water. John's shooting of Joe is an instance of the property, being a shooting; but it may well also be an instance of the property, being a movement of a finger, and of the property, being a pulling of a trigger.

The principle of the nomological character of causality requires that events bearing causal relations to one another be instances of the properties referred to by the expressions occurring in causal laws. It does not require that *every* property instanced by an event does so: indeed, Honderich's characterisation of "causally relevant" properties is in part intended to bring this point out. The principle of causal interaction requires that events that are causally related be so because of certain of their properties; and thus, that if any event which is an instance of the property, being a desire for a drink, causes one which is an instance of the property, being a movement of an arm, it must do so in virtue of certain of its properties. But 'property' here is ambiguous between properties and their instances. Since any event can be an instance of two or more distinct properties, it may well be the case that one and the same event is both an instance of the property, being a desire for a drink, *and* an instance of another, physical property, say, being a brain event, where being an instance of the former just is being an instance of the latter. That is to say, the different properties are co-instantiated; they, in this particular event, "share" the same instance. Their difference at the property-level is ensured by the two properties not being always co-instantiated. Now the instance of the property, desiring a drink (a mental property) will satisfy the principle of the Nomological Character of Causally-Relevant Instances of Properties; the instance is causally relevant because it is covered by a law.

In what sense does the "mentality" of any such mental event cease to be causally efficacious? In the sense that mental properties, like that of being a desire for a drink, fail to figure in laws linking the mental with the physical? This is simply to ignore the point that causality is a relation between token events, and thus that it is the instances of certain properties which do or do not link events causally with others. And instances of mental properties may well be causally efficacious. Indeed, if an instance of a mental property just *is* an instance of a physical one, then, despite the distinctness of the properties themselves, the anomalous monist is right to insist that the former can be both causally efficacious and be an instance of a property that is capable of figuring in causal laws. To insist otherwise, it seems to us, is tantamount to insisting that no event which is an instance of a mental property can be (i.e., be identical with) an instance of a physical one. And it is not clear that this is anything more than a dualist prejudice.

Now this response may fail to convince. The reason may lie in a tendency to suppose that in order for a mental property to be causally efficacious, any instance of it must be distinct from any instance of a physical property. Thus, if every mental event is a physical event, then the causal efficacy of any event *qua* mental would appear to require that it be both an instance of a mental property *and* a (distinct) instance of a physical property.

But why should we presume that this must be so? Suppose that mental properties supervene on physical ones in roughly the sense that if any two objects (organisms) are indiscernible with respect to the latter, they cannot diverge in the former.[6] Then it is reasonable to suppose that although mental properties fail to correlate systematically with any single physical property (let alone in any lawlike way), they may correlate with a disjunction (perhaps an infinite one)[7] of such properties. This encourages the following thought. Many physical properties, like that of being coloured, or being an animal, are plainly distinct from the many determinate forms which they may take (such as being red, or green, or being a tiger), since possession of a more determinate property (e.g., that of being red) by an object entails possession of the more determinable one (e.g., being coloured), but not *vice versa*. No one would suppose, however, that an object's exemplification of a colour, say, red, requires, first, that it be an instance of the property of being red, and second, that it be a (distinct) instance of a second, related property, viz. that of being coloured. To be an exemplification of the former just is, in this case, to be an exemplification of the latter, despite the distinctness of the properties themselves. Does this mean that colour is causally inefficacious? Of course not; for any causally efficacious case in which a more determinate form of that property is exemplified is a case in which the exemplification of colour *itself* is efficacious, by the extensionality of the causal relation (think of the property of having weight and that of weighing 2.3 kg.).

Similarly, it may be argued, mental properties correlate in a one-many way with physical properties (though in no systematic way), with the consequence that any instance of the former is an instance of one or another of some more determinate physical property. Just as to be red is to be coloured, one might say, to be an instance of the property, being a brain event B, can be an instance of the mental property, being a pain. Moreover, if an instance of the former is causally efficacious, then so is the latter. One might be tempted to

[6] This is how Kim characterises it in "Psychophysical Supervenience", *Philosophical Studies 41* (1982), pp. 51–70. See also *American Philosophical Quarterly 15* (1978), pp. 149–56. There are a number of difficulties associated with the concept of supervenience (see, for instance, Howard Robinson's discussion in *Matter and Sense*, op. cit.), but they are not central to the discussion at hand and we shall not address ourselves to them here.

[7] See Kim's "Supervenience and Nomological Incommensurables", op. cit., for example.

object that the red colour case is quite different from the envisaged brain event B/pain case, since in the former but not the latter, possession by a object (organism) of the subvenient (or "base") property (red) *logically* entails possession of the supervenient property (colour). But this, even if true, is beside the present point. Supervenience, as characterised here, is that relation between properties (or between a property and a (distinct) set of properties) such that if any two objects (organisms) are indiscernible with respect to the subvenient ones, they cannot diverge in their possession of the supervenient ones. The reason, or *grounds*, for the modal "cannot" may, however, differ from one case to another, as we make clear in section III.

We said earlier that once the epiphenomalist argument is supplemented in the required way, it could lead to the desired conclusion only by means of dualist prejudice. To insist that an instance of a mental property must be different from an instance of a physical property is to reveal such a prejudice. What was at stake was the consistency of anomalous monism. We believe that even if we grant the "Principle of the Nomological Character of Causally-Relevant Instances of Properties", we have shown it is consistent.[8] There is, however, a different route to the epiphenomonalist conclusion, one which detours through issues in the explanation of action. It is to this that we now turn.


II


It has been claimed that a denial of epiphenomenalism must depend upon "the intensional explanatory relevance of that feature in virtue of which the objects are supposedly interacting",[9] or "the conviction that an event as mental is an ineliminable part of any full explanation of an action".[10] These formulations suggest that there are two parts to this objection. The first is that mentalistic causal explanation is impossible; the second that even if it were possible, it would be redundant, hence eliminable. We will consider these objections in turn.

It may be thought that there is a fairly simple way in which the explanatory efficacy of the mental can be established, one which traverses the familiar "reasons are causes, so reason-type explanations are causal explanations"

---

[8] It is this failure to distinguish between properties and their instances which seems to us to lie at the heart of disputes between those such as Honderich and Smith. See Honderich, "Anomalous Monism: Reply to Smith", *Analysis* 43 (1983), pp. 147–9 and "Smith and the Champion of Mauve", *Analysis* 44 (1984), pp .86–9; and Peter Smith, "Bad News for Anomalous Monism?", *Analysis* 42 (1982), pp. 220–4, and "Anomalous Monism and Epiphenomenalism: A Reply to Honderich", *Analysis* 44, (1984), pp. 83–6.

[9] Robinson, op. cit., p. 12.

[10] Honderich, "The argument for Anomalous Monism", p. 64.

route.[11] Our claim will be that this can be endorsed only if a certain construal of singular causal explanation is accepted. The assumption that reasons are physical causes of actions is clearly not sufficient to justify the claim that reason-type explanations are causal explanations. One has to supplement that assumption by showing (a) that reason-type explanations *are* explanations, and (b) that they are causal explanations.[12] For our purposes it will suffice to concentrate on the issues surrounding causal explanation, specifically on whether mentalistic causal explanation is possible, and, if it is, whether it is not essentially redundant.

There are two different ways of going about providing a causal explanation; the first is by way of causal laws (nomological causal explanation), and the second is by way of singular causal statements (singular causal explanation). The epiphenomenalist objection clearly concentrates on the former. According to it, two causally related events, A and B, instantiate causal laws only under certain descriptions, $A^1$ and $B^1$. These descriptions form the antecedent and consequent of the conditional which specifies the law under which those events are subsumed. Roughly speaking, when one has an explanation of this type one will be entitled to expect that, whenever the causally relevant property of the event A occurs, then the "effect relevant" property of event B will occur. It will be canonical descriptions of these properties which fill the antecedent and consequent slots of the nomological conditional.

If this was all there could be to causal explanation, then it is clear that explanatory epiphenomenalism would be the result of a commitment to the denial of psycho-physical causal laws. It may be objected, however, that the above account of nomological causal explanation is too stringent; instead of $A^1$ and $B^1$ forming the antecedent and consequent of the law-like statement, one could have, so the objection would go, descriptions of A and B which are *approximately* those descriptions instantiated in the law. Thus, for example, brick-throwings can explain window shatterings, even though 'brick-throwing' and 'window-shattering' do not figure in law-like statements, if there is a relatively smooth transition from the vocabulary used in the explanation to that used in the strict statement of law. While we are happy to accept this amendment, it is unlikely to aid the anomalous monist, since it is the distinctiveness of the mental vocabulary which is often employed in arguments for the impossibility of reduction. Whatever "smooth transition" may mean, it is unlikely to encompass the sharp bump between intensional and

[11] Cf. Stephen P. Stich who asserts that "the claim that folk psychological explanations of behaviour are to be understood as ordinary *causal* explanations" is now "quite an orthodox view". See "On the Ascription of Content" in Andrew Woodfield, ed., *Thought and Object* (Oxford, 1982), p. 156. We deny this "orthodoxy".

[12] For somebody who thinks that showing (a) is sufficient, see Colin McGinn, "Action and its Explanation" in Neil Bolton, ed., *Philosophical Problems in Psychology* (London, 1979).

extensional vocabularies. One is forced to conclude that our monist must give up the claim that one can have mental *and* causal explanations of this type.

This result is unsurprising, since it is part of this monist doctrine that psycho-physical causal laws are unavailable.[13] However, it is possible that causal explanation can survive this result, since in singular causal explanation we might find sufficient extensionality to warrant the conclusion that this event, A, mentally described, explains why that event, B, physically described, occurs. To some extent a decision one way or another depends upon what one takes the term 'explanation' to be doing. If one expects all explanations to have a predictive capacity, then one is not likely to recognise this kind of singular causal explanation as genuinely explanatory. The reason for this is easy to see: the identity which the extensionality (more strictly, the referential transparency) trades on is a token-token identity. That is to say, the mental and physical properties are not identical, only their instances are. If expressions designating mental properties are not the type to figure in causal law-like statements, then specifying that this event (mentally described) explains why that event (physically described) occurred will not put the explainer into the position of being able to predict that when this mental property recurs, then that physical property will also recur. However, if one allows for explanation without prediction, then there is no reason to rule out this case as being genuinely explanatory. After all, it does what must be required of a causal explanation; it specifies which event caused the effect described in the explanandum. It also, crucially, licences the counterfactual that if the event mentioned in the explanans had not occurred, then matters would have turned out differently. It does this *because* the instance of the property mentioned (e.g. desiring a drink) is causally efficacious. Had this instance not occurred, then (barring cases of overdetermination) the event explained (her arm reaching for water) would have not occurred (or at least been less probable). This feature of singular causal explanation is shared by scientific explanation in general. In brief "We might say that scientific explanation, like singular causal explanation . . . is always explanation of why the actual outcome *rather than* certain other possible outcomes obtains; such explanations always proceed by showing that given the conditions that

---

[13] This is usually stated as a denial of psycho-physical laws. Not all laws need be causal, however, so our more limited denial doesn't by itself lead to full-fledged anomalism. One may want to hold that there are psycho-physical property-instantiation laws. This doesn't affect our argument.

actually obtained, the actual outcome was more favoured over these alternatives than it otherwise would have been."[14]

The temptation to regard this kind of explanation as lacking an essential ingredient often arises from the feeling that unless an explanation is justified, it is not really explanatory. Justification proceeds via prediction and regularity. Where this isn't forthcoming there is a temptation to think that we do not really have explanation. What needs to be justified in this case, however, is not the constant conjunction of the mental and physical properties, but the claim that this mental event caused that physical event. The latter claim, given monism, is obviously testable, regardless of the presence or absence of the constant conjunction of the mental and physical properties. Singular causal explanation is possible, then, even if the descriptions used in the explanation do not designate nomologically relevant properties.

It may well be felt that, even in this sort of explanation, not just any description of the cause in a given case will be explanatory. This is surely right, but doesn't by itself tell against the possibility of a genuine explanation singling out the cause by means of a relevant mental description. A description which would be irrelevant, and may well defeat the explanatory intent, would be one which specified the cause as, say, "The event my Grandmother thought of while munching her toast this morning". This is an essentially opaque way of singling out the cause, and one is hardly tempted to claim that the description gives us any insight into the nature of the causally relevant features of the event referred to. It could only be due to the pragmatic nature of explanation that this could ever be explanatory. We might count it as such if the person requesting the explanation had independent knowledge of the nature of the event referred to, and could identify it under the description given. However, even if we were tolerant enough to allow that, in this case, an explanation had been given, it would only work by courtesy of the independent knowledge available to the questioner. If mentalistic causal explanation conformed to this model it would indeed be suspect. But fortunately there is no reason to suspect that it does. The descriptions typically involved in such explanations give direct access to the properties whose instances are causally efficacious. Those seeking an explanation can be satisfied without recourse to independent knowledge of the nature of the cause. (They do not even have to know that the causally relevant instance is also an instance of a physical property.)

[14] James Woodward, "Singular Causal Explanation" *Erkenntnis* 21 (1984), p. 240. We accept this feature of Woodward's account of singular causal explanation, but reject his account of its extensionality, which depends on the notion of a sentence preserving "contrastive focus".

If the epiphenomenalist objection simply amounted to the claim that no mental causal explanation was possible, then the availability of singular causal explanation would be sufficient to defuse the objection. However, there remains the different form of the objection, one which allows for the possibility of such explanations but which insists that they are essentially redundant.[15] The redundancy is thought to arise from the all-encompassing nature of physical theory. For any future physical state, the best theory to predict that state will be physical theory, i.e., physics. Given monism, it looks as though physics is all we need, all other explanations of why the future state occurred being essentially eliminable.

It looks as though this objection could easily be defeated, as it appears to be of the following form: (a) mental explanation seems to be required to explain action, (b) physicalist explanation explains behaviour, (c) any action is identical with some behaviour, (d) therefore physicalist explanation can explain action, so (e) mental explanation is redundant. The move from (c) to (d) is, given the supposed intensionality of explanation, suspect.

The position is, however, more complicated. Some substitutions are allowable, even in classic deductive nomological explanations. In particular, it has been argued that substitutions (i) preserving property-identities, and (ii) involving nomologically correlated properties, may be legitimate.[16] It is clear that (i) will not present the required rationale for the substitution, and it looks as though non-reductive monists can avoid substitutions licensed by (ii) by their insistence that supervenience can be distinguished from reduction precisely because it aims to avoid such nomological connections between base and supervening properties. Whether it is successful in this aim, and indeed whether this *should* be its aim, is open to question, so it is to issues of supervenience that we must now turn.

III

Supervenience has been variously defined and it is beyond the scope of this paper exhaustively to survey all these definitions.[17] Our present interest is limited to the questions as to whether nomological connections are required in any reasonable formulation of supervenience, and if so whether

---

[15] Honderich (in "The Argument for Anomalous Monism") seems to take the line that mentalistic causal explanation is redundant, as does Kim in "Causality, Identity, and Supervenience in the Mind-Body Problem".

[16] Cf. James Woodward, "Explanatory Asymmetries" *Philosophy of Science* 51 (1984), pp. 421–442. Woodward is concerned with equalities of magnitudes, so our terminology is different from his.

[17] For an overview, and bibliographical material, the best source is *The Southern Journal of Philosophy* 21 Supplement, ed. T. Horgan (*The Spindel Conference 1983: Supervenience*), and Jaegwon Kim, "Concepts of Supervenience", *Philosophy and Phenomenological Research* 45, (1984), pp. 153–177.

this contradicts an important feature of non-reductive monism. The second issue may *seem* settled (against non-reductive monism) if it turns out that nomological connections are required; this seems to be the position of both Hare and Blackburn.[18] But the essential premises in Davidsonian anomalous monism are those which require lawlike support for causal interaction and assert that mental-physical causal interaction takes place, while denying that any mentalistic-physicalistic law is available. The type of law which is deemed unavailable is clearly *causal*, and it should be apparent that if there is a nomological connection between the base (the physical) and that which supervenes upon it (the mental), it is *not* a causal nomological connection. Our definitions of supervenience require that the mental be realised at the same time as the physical base; they do not envisage the supervening properties coming into existence as a result of an earlier configuration of physical properties.

Now it may well be the case that a derivative "temporal law" will be forthcoming if the mental and physical are nomologically connected. If we have nomological conditionals such that:

(1) $P1t^1 \rightarrow M1t^1$

(2) $P2t^2 \rightarrow M2t^2$

(3) $P1t^1 \rightarrow P2t^2$

then it would be possible to derive

(4) $P1t^1 \rightarrow M2t^2$

(where P and M refer to physical and mental states respectively, and $t_1 < t_2$).

The existence of such derived laws need not threaten the premises, as the "no causal law" requirement could simply be rewritten as "no non-derivative causal law", and the argument would go through (amending, of course, the causal law requirement to state that a non-derivative causal law is needed to support causal interaction). But one snag in this defence of non-reductive monism should be mentioned. Davidson's denial of the existence of mental-physical causal laws appeared to rest upon claims that told *generally* against mental-physical nomological connection (e.g. the holism of the mental, and that mental and physical terms answered to different evidential rules). If supervenience requires such a connection, then other grounds will have to be found for the repudiation of (non-derivative) causal laws linking the two. But does supervenience require nomologicality?

Our discussion will follow Kim's recent attempt to define two different concepts of supervenience. *Weak supervenience* is characterised as follows, with A and B being two non-empty families of properties:

[18] Cf. R. H. Hare, "Supervenience", *The Aristotelian Society Supp. Volume 58* (1984), esp. pp.15–16; and S. Blackburn, "Supervenience Revisited" (esp. pp. 58–61) in Ian Hacking, ed. *Exercises in Analysis* (Cambridge, 1985).

"A *weakly supervenes* on B if and only if necessarily for any x and y if x and y share all properties in B then x and y share all properties in A – that is, indiscernibility with respect to B entails indiscernibility with respect to A."[19]

The relevant point for us is that weak supervenience is too weak to provide us with any reason to believe that the physical determines the mental. As defined, it prohibits the possibility of two things agreeing in base properties but differing in supervenient properties only *within* any possible world. In other words, trans-world B indiscernibility permits trans-world A discernibility. This goes against our intuition that if A supervenes on B, then if any object were to become B-like, then it should become A-like. That is, any object in any world which has the relevant B properties should be indiscriminable, with respect to A properties, from all those other objects, in any world, which share those B properties. If this isn't the case we are left with a puzzle: why are the worlds thus segregated? As Blackburn puts it, why are there no "mixed" worlds?[20] There seems no plausible answer to this question, indicating that the definition of supervenience needs to be strengthened to something like the following:

"A *strongly supervenes* on B just in case, necessarily, for each x and each property F in A, if x has F, then there is a property G in B such that x has G, and necessarily if any y has G, it has F."[21]

The crucial difference between strong and weak supervenience lies with the second 'necessarily', and it is precisely this which leads to claims that supervenience requires nomological connectedness. It therefore also leads to the suggestion that (physicalist) explanations of behaviour are sufficient, that mentalistic explanation of action is replaceable. If in the above definition one takes 'G' to be a physical property (or a conjunction of physical properties) and 'F' to be an action-property, then an explanation of why something is G ought to explain why it is F. Or so the redundancy theorist claims.

Of course matters are never quite that simple. There are problems about infinite sets of properties in the supervened-upon base; whether one can perform Boolean operations on mental properties; and about what results from those Boolean operations (e.g. is the complement of a physical property itself a physical property? Do the conjunctions of physical properties form anything like a natural kind?). We will presume that these queries can be satisfactorily settled in order to concentrate on two related issues, that of the epistemology presumed and the nature of the necessity involved. We say these are related, because if the necessity is that of a scientific law, then it appears unproblematic that one will be able to "read off" the supervenient

---

[19] In "Concepts of Supervenience", p. 158.

[20] S. Blackburn, loc. cit.

[21] Kim, "Concepts of Supervenience", p. 165. We do not, in fact, believe that this definition is adequate, but its inadequacies are irrelevant to our present concern.

properties from knowledge of the base properties. This view is strengthened if one conceives supervenient materialism to operate like reductive materialism. In the latter, discovery of the reductions was intended to be the justification for the materialism; so it may be thought that the former materialism depends for its justification on *discovering* the supervenient dependencies.

Our claim is that this is incorrect, that supervenience is brought in to render consistent a materialism embraced for different reasons. The supervenient dependencies do not need to be discovered for the materialism to be justified. They are more likely to be stipulated on a priori grounds, which are fairly general and render supervenient materialism a plausible metaphysical thesis. We do not need to go into a discussion of the reason for the metaphysical thesis, but do need to note that if the above is a correct picture of the general orientation of supervenient materialism, then the type of necessity involved will be metaphysical necessity.

What bearing will this have on the question of explanatory redundancy? The force of the redundancy objection was that supervenience must lead to the eliminability of mentalistic explanation. That claim was rendered plausible on the supposition that, given we could physically explain all behaviour, we could explain that to which behaviour was nomologically connected. We have suggested that the substitutability assumption is justified only if the dependencies were knowable in the manner that they would be if these dependencies were scientifically lawlike. If they are not, and are in fact metaphysical, then the epistemological position is far less clear. It need not be the case that the mental properties can be "read off" from the physical base. If they are not, this renders the substitutivity argument far less potent. It leaves it an open question as to whether, some day, mental explanations will prove redundant.

## IV

Our discussion of the redundancy objection has proven less than conclusive. In closing we would like to draw attention to the power of this objection. It is tempting to think that if physical theory is more powerful than its mentalistic rival, then mentalistic explanation is simply a place-stopper for a physicalist explanation, forthcoming but temporarily unavailable as a result of present ignorance.[22] Now underlying this instrumentalist accusation is a residue of the positivist principle that the only possible attitude to adopt towards the special sciences is that either they deal in a subject matter different from that of physical theory (dualism), or else they are (in principle) reducible to physical theory, hence eliminable. But this would seem to prove

[22] This seems to be Dennett's view: see *Brainstorms* (Cambridge, Mass., 1978).

too much: it tells not only against the intended target, mentalistic explanation, but against all those sciences which claim some kind of independence from physical theory. In short, it imposes an instrumentalist interpretation on all those explanations which don't fit the nomological causal model, e.g., functionalist explanation in biological theory.[23] If, as seems likely, *any* science purporting to deal with properties supervenient on the physical (but not reducible to it) will be prohibited from employing nomological causal explanations, then *any* science of the supervenient will be charged with providing essentially redundant explanations.

Although the general issue of instrumentalism cannot be resolved here, enough has been said to indicate both the power (against all "supervenient sciences") and source (dualism or reduction) of the objection. Of course, the more tough-minded may be happy to claim that only physics provides us with genuine explanations, and that the other sciences must be, in principle, reducible to physics. To deride this as a positivist prejudice does nothing in the way of providing an *argument* as to why the middle ground is stable; why supervenient properties can be real, non-reducible, and not require a dualistic ontology. One has to justify the claim that a set of properties are not reducible but real; otherwise the position can be defeated, e.g. by explaining how supervenience can hold independently of the supposed reality of the supervening properties.[24] Given that the nature of the justification will differ depending on the kind of supervenient property at issue, a general justification seems unlikely. What we believe will be essential in such justifications, though, is the causal status of the supposedly real supervenient properties. What we provided in Section I of this paper was just such an account of how the causal status of the mental can be preserved against the epiphenomenalist objection. In the latter parts we have indicated that in denying genuine explanatory force to mentalistic explanation, the epiphenomenalist is just denying the possibility of a stable middle ground between dualism and reductionism. Such a compromise is clearly possible, but its actuality hás to be argued for case by case. What has been argued in this paper is that the case for nonreductive monism is not as weak as the epiphenomenalist objections would have us believe.[25]

*University of Manchester*
and
*University of Bradford*

---

[23] For a persuasive non-reductive view of some biological theory, see J. Dupre, "The Disunity of Science", *Mind* 92, pp. 321–46.

[24] See Simon Blackburn's account of the supervenience of moral properties, in *Spreading the Word* (Oxford, 1984, ch. 6).

[25] This article has benefited from comments by Roger Fellows, Richard Lindley, Philip Pettitt, and Leslie Stevenson.

# THE FAILURE OF LEWIS'S FUNCTIONALISM

## By Joseph Owens

Certain kinds of mistakes were characteristic of logical behaviourism and radical physicalism, and subsequent accounts of the mental have been formulated with these difficulties in mind. The logical behaviourist identified mental states with dispositions to overt behaviour, thereby flying in the face of the strong intuition that total paralytics, for example, share much the same range of mental states as we do, despite the fact that they exhibit virtually no behaviour. Such individuals posed no special problem for the radical physicalist who identified mental state-types (pain, belief, etc.) with physical *state-types* (e.g., types of neurophysiological states), states which the total paralytic could clearly instantiate. However, radical physicalism has proved even less attractive than logical behaviourism. Given the diversity of intelligent life, it is implausible to suppose, as the radical physicalist does, that there corresponds to each *kind* of mental state, e.g., pain, some particular *kind* of physical state. States such as pain are realized in organisms whose physiologies appear to have little in common. More importantly, even if it should be possible to provide physiological predicates (perhaps vast disjunctive ones) which are in fact co-extensive with mentalistic predicates, there is no reason to suppose that this co-extensivity would be law-like in character.[1] Given any such correlation, one can conceive of nomologically possible worlds in which the correlations fail to obtain; possible worlds in which there are individuals with familiar mental states but with non-standard neurologies.[2] These widely shared intuitions, of course, conflict with the physicalistic claim that kinds of mental states are to be identified with kinds of physical states.

In a number of influential and original papers David Lewis has defended, on *a priori* grounds, a functionalist account of the mental, one employing certain behaviouristic and physicalistic intuitions, but explicitly fashioned to avoid their twin pitfalls. Actually, over the years, he appears to have defended three different versions of *a priori* functionalism. The first version

[1] For discussion of these difficulties see Donald Davidson, "Mental Events", in L. Foster and J. W. Swanson (eds.), *Experience and Theory* (Amherst, 1970), and Hilary Putnam, "Psychological Predicates", in W. H. Capitan and D. D. Merrill (eds.), *Art, Mind, and Religion* (Pittsburgh, 1967).

[2] For the purposes of this paper, then, the radical physicalist is one who identifies mental state types $M_1 \ldots M_n$ with physical state types $P_1 \ldots P_n$, and, *in addition*, holds that these identities obtain in every possible world.

we may call "the strong Lewis theory", the second one, "token-function-alism", and the third one, "species-functionalism".[3] The strong Lewis theory, the one usually associated with him, was explicitly formulated to steer a course between logical behaviourism and radical physicalism. Though Lewis nowhere rejects his original formulation, the second and third versions are substantially weaker than the first, and they incorporate elements designed to circumvent difficulties in the first. His basic strategy remains the same, however, in these different accounts, and it is twofold in character. On the one hand, he develops a conceptual analysis of mental terms as abbreviating definite descriptions – descriptions which designate states satisfying functional conditions – and in formulating these descriptions he relies upon modified behaviouristic intuitions. On the other hand, he secures his materialism by arguing that these descriptions in fact designate physical states, so that mental states in fact are physical states.[4] These two components in his account are given a specific construal in his strong version (considered in Section I here), and they are modified in the second and third version (see my Sections II and III). In this paper I will argue that each of these accounts is defective; that, despite his claims to the contrary, none of these functional analyses provides for a way of steering between logical behaviourism and radical physicalism.

I

THE STRONG LEWIS THEORY

In his original formulation Lewis defended the claim that names of mental states abbreviate descriptions which characterize states in terms of their typical causes and effects; descriptions of the form: 'the state that typically is induced in such and such a fashion, which results in further mental states $M_1$ ... $M_n$, and which in turn results in this and that behaviour'. So, for example, a term such as 'pain' is taken to abbreviate a description such as: 'the state that typically is induced by damage, or danger of damage, to tissue; that results in feelings of self-pity, in crying out, in seeking help, in aversive behaviour . . . ' These descriptions specifying the characteristic causal role of the various psychological states are to be extracted from common-sense psychology, and they encapsulate the kind of knowledge one must acquire if

[3] The strong Lewis theory is elaborated and defended in his "An Argument for the Identity Theory", *The Journal of Philosophy* 63 (1966), pp. 17–25, and in his "Psychophysical and Theoretical Identifications", *The Australasian Journal of Philosophy* 50 (1972), pp. 249–58. He defends the token-functionalist view in his "Review of *Art, Mind, and Religion*", *The Journal of Philosophy* 66 (1969), pp. 22–7, and he opts for what I am calling species-functionalism in his "Mad Pain and Martian Pain", in N. Block (ed.), *Readings in Philosophy of Psychology* (Cambridge, Mass., 1980).

[4] For details see "An Argument for the Identity Theory", and "Psychophysical and Theoretical Identifications".

one is to be a competent employer of everyday psychological terms. The general idea here is that we would be reluctant to say of someone that he fully understood the term (or concept) 'pain' if he did not know that it was a state with certain kinds of characteristic causes and effects of the kind just mentioned.[5] In a more technical vein, Lewis elaborated and refined his treatment of everyday psychological terms by construing common-sense psychology as a theory, and then applying Ramsey techniques to define each psychological term (treating them as theoretical terms defined by the postulates of the theory).[6] For our purposes, however, we may ignore these technical details, except to note that this device allowed him to replace each psychological term with a definite description which specified a state in terms of its causal relations with other mental states, inputs and outputs, without employing any psychological vocabulary in the description. We will accordingly consider only intuitive functional specifications, such as the abbreviated one just given for 'pain', while keeping in mind that the mental terms which figure in such descriptions are theoretically eliminable.

In construing mental terms in this fashion, he attempts to allow, on the one hand, that the state designated by a given mental term $M_i$ may, on occasion, be instantiated while failing to play its characteristic causal role – as in the case of the nearly total paralytic. It is enough that the state *typically* plays this causal role. On the other hand these definite descriptions are descriptions of states in terms of their accidental causal roles, and thus they designate different kinds of states in appropriately different possible worlds, and thus he hopes to avoid the excesses of radical physicalism. In this section I will argue that, appearances to the contrary, this account is not adequate to this task. In particular, I will argue that the way in which he tailors this version of his account so as to allow for the possibility of the total paralytic

[5] Details may be obtained once again from the papers cited in note 4.

[6] Lewis provides this more technical account of mental terms in "Psychophysical and Theoretical Identifications", and in doing so he draws upon a general account of theoretical terms he earlier advanced in "How to Define Theoretical Terms", *Journal of Philosophy* 67 (1970), pp. 427–46. Very roughly, his claim is that psychological terms may be defined in the following fashion. Let $P(M_1 \ldots M_n)$ be a formulation of our common-sense psychological theory (the conjunction of everyday psychological platitudes), which is fashioned using the psychological terms $M_1 \ldots M_n$ (all of which are names). From $P(M_1 \ldots M_n)$ we obtain the open sentence $P(x_1 \ldots x_n)$ by uniformly replacing the psychological names $M_1 \ldots M_n$ by distinct variables $x_1 \ldots x_n$. Taking his cues from Ramsay and Carnap, Lewis then argues that the "empirical content" of the original theory $P(M_1 \ldots M_n)$ is simply a claim to the effect that there exists a unique n-tuple of states satisfying the open sentence $P(x_1 \ldots x_n)$. The terms $M_1 \ldots M_n$ respectively designate the members of this n-tuple if there is such a unique n-tuple (and designate nothing otherwise), and they are defined in such a way as to capture this intuition. They are defined as follows:

$$M_1 = {}_{d/f} \exists y_1 \exists y_2 \ldots \exists y_n (x_1) \ldots (x_n) (P(x_1 \ldots x_n) \equiv y_1 = x_1 \& y_2 = x_2 \& \ldots \& y_n = x_n)$$

Similarly for $M_2$, $M_3$, etc. In this way the psychological terms are replaced by definite descriptions which do not employ any mentalistic vocabulary though they do contain quantifiers ranging over mental states.

commits him to construing mental terms as non-contingently designating the same physical state in every possible world, and thus commits him to radical physicalism and all its attendant implausibilities.

On this account the mental term $M_i$ designates *the* state that happens to typically satisfy the relevant characteristic conditions $C_1 \ldots C_m$, and an individual in the actual world is in $M_i$ if and only if it is in the state that typically satisfies $C_1 \ldots C_m$ (in the actual world). It is not necessary that each token of the state designated by $M_i$ satisfy the causal conditions character-istic of $M_i$, and this fact is conveyed by the insertion of 'typically' in the description associated with $M_i$. Thus the paralytic and the non-paralytic may be in the same state, even though in the case of the former the state does not play its usual causal role. This is all very well, but one wants to know what Lewis counts as being in the *same* state in such instances – what kinds of states are these? One may admit that the total paralytic is in pain just in case he is in *the* state that plays the characteristic role of pain, but still want to know what kinds of conditions are necessary and sufficient for being in *this* kind of state. Obviously the causal conditions specified in the functional definition of pain do not of themselves provide the conditions in question, as instances of this state may fail to satisfy the causal conditions. The functional description characterizes the causal role of *typical* instances of the state; it picks out the state by an accidental feature, its causal role. Some care, however, is needed in understanding just how the account appeals to accidental properties. The claim is not one to the effect that two tokens $x$ and $y$ are instances of the same mental state if and only if they have some accidental feature in common, *viz.* that of playing the same causal role, for tokens of the same mental state may fail to play the same causal role. The reason for regarding them both as instances of the same mental state $M_i$ is that they are instances of some further *kind* of state, $N_i$, a state which is such that *its* instances typically satisfy the functional conditions associated with $M_i$. The suggestion is that when we use mental terms $M_1 \ldots M_n$, we use them with the presumption that there are (in the actual world) state-types, $N_1 \ldots N_m$, whose tokens typically satisfy the relevant functional descriptions. And, in the actual world any individual is in mental state $M_i$ just in case he is in the corresponding state $N_i$. This indeed is what justifies us in attributing mental states to the paralyzed individual.

So far as the nature of these state-types, $N_1 \ldots N_m$, is concerned, Lewis argues that we have good reason to think that they are neurophysiological; that it falls to idealized neurophysiological theory to specify the intrinsic character of these states (as opposed to the extrinsic characterizations of their causal roles).[7] Confident in the adequacy of physical theory to explain all physical phenomena, including behavioural phenomena, he envisions

[7] See papers cited in note 4.

idealized neurophysiological theory as providing us with intrinsic characterizations, $D_1 \ldots D_m$, of the states $N_1 \ldots N_m$; i.e. with intrinsic characterizations of the physical state types which happen to satisfy the functional conditions characteristic of mental states $M_1 \ldots M_m$. Given such a physiological theory, one could say that an individual in the actual world is in a given mental state $M_i$ just in case he is in the state satisfying $D_i$, i.e., just in case he is in $N_i$. No longer would we need to employ 'typically' in formulating the conditions, for we would have available the intrinsic charac- terizations of those states whose instantiations typically satisfied the relevant functional conditions. Idealized physiology would allow us to say what the state is that plays such and such a causal role, to say "what's there" even when it does not play the usual role, and thus it allows us to dispense with 'typically'.

But, of course, Lewis does not think of such physiological characteriza- tions as providing necessary and sufficient conditions for the obtaining of mental states in different possible worlds. He does not regard his analysis as committing him to that implausible kind of physicalism which would identify mental states $M_1 \ldots M_m$ with physiological states $N_1 \ldots N_m$ in every possible world. He claims that his analysis allows him, on the one hand, to identify $M_1 \ldots M_m$ respectively with $N_1 \ldots N_m$ in the actual world, while denying, on the other hand, that it commits him to making these identities in every possible world. He attempts to allow for this by construing each mental term $M_i$ as abbreviating a definite description of the form 'the state that typically plays causal role $R_i$'. $M_i$ thus designates in a possible world $W_j$ the state (in $W_j$) that typically plays causal role $R$; and since different physical states may satisfy this condition in different possible worlds $M_i$ will designate different physical states in different possible worlds.

What I want to question is whether he can plausibly analyse mental terms as contingent in this sense and at the same time envision idealized neurophy- siology as providing the intrinsic characterizations of the states designated by mental terms in the actual world. Suppose, for the sake of argument, that such physiological investigations were to proceed after the manner suggested by Lewis. That is, suppose we were to discover that individuals in this world are in pain if and only if their c-fibres are firing (or some such), that they have the thought that snow is white if and only if some specific neuronal configuration $N_i$ obtains, and so on for the various mental states. This, of course, is highly implausible, but I want to draw attention to a quite different problem. Suppose now, in the light of this very powerful and successful theory, that Alf, one of these neurophysiologists, were to boldly claim that it is simply not possible for anyone (in any possible world) to be in pain unless his c-fibres are firing. He is informed that he is clearly mistaken, that we can easily conceive of worlds in which individuals are in pain, even though there are no c-fibres in these worlds at all. However, he is not at all swayed by this apparent ability to conceive of such worlds, for he is only too well aware of the mistaken general tendency to construe theoretical (*a posteriori*) identities as contingent. It was, for example, not uncommon for individuals to think that they could conceive of worlds in which water failed to be $H_2O$. They conceived of worlds in which a colourless, odourless, potable . . . liquid was not $H_2O$, and they supposed that they were thereby conceiving of worlds in which water was not $H_2O$. They were mistaken of course, in that they were conceiving not of worlds in which water failed to be $H_2O$ but rather of worlds in which some liquid other than water ($H_2O$) had many of the surface features of water. True, *we* use these accidental features of water to pick it out, but it is neither a necessary nor a sufficient condition for something's being water that it satisfy these conditions. It has fallen to science to determine the nature of the stuff that satisfies these conditions, and we have determined that it is $H_2O$. Given that *this* is the nature of water, it is not possible that water should fail to be $H_2O$.[8]

Just as it fell to the chemist to determine the intrinsic nature of the stuff in the actual world designated by our term 'water', so, in our story, it has fallen to the physiologist to determine the intrinsic nature of the state designated by 'pain' (in the actual world). And we have in fact determined that 'pain' designates c-fibre firings. This is the state that satisfies the commonly employed functional conditions associated with 'pain', just as $H_2O$ is the substance that in fact satisfies the everyday conditions associated with 'water'. Prior to this determination, so long as one identified the state *only* by its accidental causal character, it seemed reasonable to speculate about 'pain' designating different kinds of states in different possible worlds. We simply didn't know what 'pain' *really* designated (*this* was not a prerequisite for being competent in the use of 'pain'), and so there appeared to be nothing odd about letting it designate state $N_i$ in possible world $W_j$, state $N_k$ in world $W_i$, and so on. However, now that we *have* determined the intrinsic character of pain, it is silly to think that it could be anything other than what it is, namely, c-fibre firings; just as silly as it would be to suppose that water could fail to be $H_2O$. In short, Lewis's efforts to avoid radical physicalism, by suggesting that the mental terms abbreviate definite descriptions which contingently designate different states in different possible worlds, seems to be undercut by the second element in his account, the claim that each mental term in fact designates a *kind* of physical state. Were physiological investigation to proceed in the manner envisioned by Lewis, the functional conditions

---

[8] For a defence of these kinds of "essentialistic" intuitions see Hilary Putnam, "The Meaning of Meaning", in his *Mind, Language and Reality: Philosophical Papers*, Vol. 2 (Cambridge, Mass., 1975). These intuitions are, I believe, intuitively plausible, and I will not attempt to provide any additional support for them here.

would cease to have the appearance of being necessary and sufficient conditions, and there would be little or no temptation to conceive of mental terms as abbreviating descriptions embodying these conditions. In Kripkean terminology, the descriptions would be more akin to reference-fixing than to descriptions of necessary and sufficient conditions.

If one is going to claim, as Lewis does in these early papers, that there is a particular kind of neurophysiological state designated by each mental term, a state whose intrinsic character is to be revealed by neurophysiological investigation, then I fail to see how one can avoid this objection. It certainly won't do simply to *claim* that functional descriptions are different from reference-fixing descriptions in that it *is analytic* that pain, for example, is whatever satisfies the relevant functional conditions. This is the very point at issue, and Alf can simply respond that his investigations throw doubt on this alleged analyticity. Moreover, he can claim to have history on his side. The only reason for thinking that it is in some way 'analytic' that pain is the state that satisfies certain characteristic causal conditions is that we would not say of someone that he had acquired the term or concept 'pain' if he did not know that pain was induced in this and that fashion, etc. But, then, consider the familiar term 'water' once again. Who could be said to understand this term unless he understands it to designate the stuff that fills our rivers, lakes, etc. It is required of an English speaker that he be acquainted with these kinds of commonplace features before we would attribute to him an under-standing of 'water'. However, though it is correct to say that a speaker must know something like this about water before he can be said to understand the term, it would be incorrect to infer from this that these kinds of conditions are necessary and sufficient conditions for something's being water. Prior to the scientific determination of the character of water, one might have been tempted to elevate these conditions to the status of neces-sary and sufficient conditions, to think that it is somehow analytic that something is water if and only if it satisfies these conditions. After all, when one learned the term 'water' one learned it *as* designating the stuff that fills our lakes, etc. It has fallen to scientific investigation to expose the inade-quacy of this proposal. Likewise, in the case at hand. Prior to our actual determination that pains are c-fibre firings, there was a certain plausibility in supposing that the causal conditions typically relied upon in identifying instances of pain were necessary and sufficient conditions for something's being in pain; indeed that it is analytically true that pain is whatever satisfies these conditions. Consequently, there was a plausibility in supposing that one could conceive of possible worlds in which 'pain' designated something other than what it designates in the actual world. However, as was evident in the case of water, one can be mistaken about what one can and can't conceive. In general, speculations as to the possibility of a given state having this or that different composition in different possible worlds are somewhat unfounded when made prior to the actual scientific determination of the character of the state. This investigation places limits on what one can and can't conceive. In the case at hand, we have *discovered* the common element between the total paralytic, the non-paralytic, and a dog, in virtue of which it is true to say of them all that they are in pain – in each case their c-fibres are firing. This is all it takes here, no more and no less; and this is all it takes in any possible world.

A more plausible line of defence appears to be at hand, however, for Alf seems to be ignoring a crucial distinction in treating the pain/c-fibre identification on the model of the water/$H_2O$ identification. He is simply mistaken in thinking that he can dismiss claims to be able to conceive of worlds in which pain fails to be c-fibre firing in the way in which he dismisses claims to be able to conceive of worlds in which water fails to be $H_2O$. One can dismiss claims of the latter kind by explaining how an individual might mistakenly suppose herself to be conceiving of worlds in which water fails to be $H_2O$. She conceives of worlds in which something other than $H_2O$ has the surface appearances of water and produces experiences qualitatively identical to our "water-experiences". One can conceive of such worlds, and though this is not to conceive of a world in which water fails to be $H_2O$, it is all too easy to suppose that it is.

But in the case of pain the story is quite different; one cannot dismiss claims to be able to conceive of worlds in which pain fails to be c-fibre firings in any similar fashion. One cannot undermine such a claim by arguing that though the claimant thinks she is conceiving of a world in which there is pain in the absence of c-fibre firings she is really thinking of something quite different: she is merely conceiving of a world in which someone has an experience qualitatively identical to the experience we have when we experience pain, a world in which this qualitatively identical experience occurs in the absence of any c-fibre firings. One cannot employ this strategy to dismiss such claims, for the simple reason that being in a state qualitatively identical to the state we are in when in pain *is* being in pain. Thus, conceiving of a world in which an individual is in a state qualitatively identical to our pain state despite the absence of c-fibre firings is, in fact, conceiving of a world in which that individual is in pain without there being any c-fibre firings. It would appear then that Alf cannot appeal to some simple analogy between 'water' and 'pain' to dismiss his opponents' claim that 'pain' does not necessarily designate c-fibre firings even though that is what it designates in the actual world; he cannot explain away his opponents' apparent ability to be able to conceive of worlds in which there is pain in the absence of c-fibre firings.

Such intuitions were, of course, used to great effect by Kripke in arguing against various kinds of identity theory, and they are, I think, quite convincing. Compelling though they may be, they are not available to a defender of Lewis style functionalism. One cannot opt for the functionalist analysis of 'pain' as abbreviating a description of the form: 'the state that typically is induced in such and such a fashion ... that is causally related to other internal states $S_i$, $S_j$, etc. in this and that way ...', *and at the same time* employ the semi-Cartesian intuition that an individual is in pain if he is in a state qualitatively identical to the state we are in when in pain. If the concept of pain is such that having a certain qualitative experience is a sufficient condition for being in pain, then it can't also be part of *that* concept that one is in pain only if one is in the state that typically satisfies a range of complex causal conditions. In general, once the theorist has opted for an account of the mental which removes introspectible qualitative characteristics from centre stage – for an account in which the issue as to whether an individual is in pain is ultimately determined by theoretical considerations rather than introspection – then that theorist can no longer employ the kind of Kripkean intuitions appealed to above. If being in pain is being in a state which satisfies certain complex causal conditions, then c-fibreless worlds in which an individual has an experience qualitatively identical to our pain experiences will *not* necessarily count as possible worlds in which someone is in pain despite the absence of c-fibre firings. Thus the functionalist cannot appeal to such Kripkean intuitions in response to Alf's plausible claim to the effect that physiologists have discovered the *real* nature of pain, viz, c-fibre firings.

It is worth noting, if only in passing, that the functionalist construal of mental states as theoretical states cuts two ways when it comes to providing a role for these kinds of Cartesian intuitions. The functionalist cannot use them to support the contingent character of his identity claims, but neither can Kripke use them, at least not without a lot of additional support, to undermine functionalist (identity) claims. The functionalist simply does not accept these intuitions, and will fail to be moved by any argument which makes undefended appeal to them. This last point, which has been noted by a number of authors, precludes our using Kripke style arguments in any simple fashion against a theorist such as Lewis.[9]

To repeat: the point of this story is to indicate the way in which Lewis's initial strategy for handling the case of the paralytic – by supposing that mental terms in fact designate physiological kinds – ultimately serves to undercut his analysis of these terms as definite descriptions contingently

[9] See, for example, W. Lycan, "Kripke and the Materialists", *The Journal of Philosophy* 71 (1974), pp. 677–89.

designating different kinds of states in different possible worlds. It commits him to radical physicalism and all its attendant implausibilities, a position he was intent upon avoiding.

## II

## TOKEN FUNCTIONALISM

In posing the above problem for Lewis's analysis we have assumed that he is a type/type identifier of sorts: identifying kinds of mental states with kinds of physical states in the actual world, while denying that these identities hold across possible worlds. Our concern was to argue that this position is untenable; that if one opts for such identities in the actual world one should retain them across possible worlds. Now it may be objected that this assumption is unwarranted, that his analysis does not really presuppose the existence of such type/type identities in the actual world. The suggestion is that even though he presents his account as an account of identity between types, this feature is rather accidental to his functional analysis and is best discarded. Indeed it is easy to modify the basic functional formulation so as to clearly avoid any commitment to such type/type identities. In our discussion of Lewis's position we have been accustomed to saying that an individual $x$ is in a given mental state $M_i$ (at some time $t$) just in case he is (at $t$) in *the* state that typically plays the causal role characteristic of $M_i$. What we should say, however, is that $x$ is in $M_i$ (at $t$) just in case he is (at $t$) in the state that *in him* typically plays the causal role characteristic of $M^1$.[10] Under this reading we leave the "surface analysis" of mental terms pretty much as before; 'pain', for example, still designates the state that plays a certain causal role. We simply shift the order of the quantifiers, and this distinction between the two formulations is one that might not be readily apparent in our ordinary employment of these terms. This kind of functional analysis accommodates materialistic intuitions, without requiring that individuals in the same psychological state be in the same physiological state; it is enough that there be in each of these individuals *some* state or other satisfying the relevant functional conditions; different states may satisfy these conditions in different individuals and the states identified are tokens, not kinds of states.

Furthermore, in responding to criticism by Putnam, Lewis seems to explicitly take this position, suggesting that such a "token-physicalism" is the only viable form of identity theory. He writes:

> Putnam argues that the brain-state hypothesis (and with it the functionally-specified-brain-state hypothesis) ought to be rejected

[10] The kind of functional definition mentioned in note 6 can, of course, be easily modified to obtain this result. For an example of such an explicit modification see Hartry Field, "Mental Representation", *Erkenntnis* 13 (1978), pp. 9–61.

as scientifically implausible. He imagines the brain-state theorist to claim that all organisms in pain – be they men, mollusks, Martians, Machines, or what have you – are in some single common nondisjunctive physical-chemical brain state. Given the diversity of organisms, that claim *is* incredible. But the brain-state theorist who makes it is a straw man. A reasonable brain-state theorist would anticipate that pain might well be one brain state in the case of men, and some other brain (or nonbrain) state in the case of mollusks. It might even be one brain state in the case of Putnam, another in the case of Lewis.[11]

It certainly here appears as though Lewis regards his own analysis as requiring nothing stronger than token-identities, for he surely regards his own position as viable. Does this, then, not undercut our earlier criticism which presupposed that he was a type/type identifier, committed to the claim that there is one brain-state common to all individuals in pain. The problem with this move, however, is that when the functional theory is so construed it no longer has the resources to account for the kinds of cases which had proven problematical to the logical behaviourist: cases of the perfect deceiver, the total paralytic, and so on. On the original physicalistic reading of the theory one was justified in attributing a mental state $M_i$ to such an individual on the grounds that he or she instantiated some physiological state $N_i$ – the state whose instances are such as to typically satisfy the relevant causal conditions. Now, however, we are no longer to presuppose that there is *any one physical state* satisfying these causal conditions in different individuals, and we cannot talk of *the* physical state whose instances typically play such and such a role. In the case of the total paralytic, we cannot say of him that he is in $M_i$ because he is in *the* state that typically plays the causal role characteristic of $M_i$ – there need be none. Nor, on the other hand, can we employ the modified Lewis definition to say of him that he is in $M_i$ because there is in him *some* physical state or other that plays the causal role characteristic of $M_i$. We can't say the former because we no longer subscribe to type/type identities, and we can't say the latter because in the case of the paralytic the mental state simply does not play its typical causal role – its role as specified by common-sense psychology. We can, of course, say that such an individual is in $M_i$ since he is in the *mental* state that typically plays the causal role that is characteristic of $M_i$, but this characterization is empty. It fails to provide any insight into the kinds of conditions which the paralytic satisfies, and in virtue of which he is in $M_i$. This revised version avoids commitment to type/type identities, but it does so at the cost of proscribing all appeal to common physical state-types. It fails thereby to provide any

---

[11] Lewis, "Review of *Art, Mind, and Religion*", p. 25.

non-mentalistic account of the conditions which are met by the paralytic and non-paralytic alike, conditions in virtue of which they are both said to be in the same state. So this weak version of *a priori* functionalism falls prey to one of the problems which wrecked the original behaviouristic programme.

## III

## SPECIES-FUNCTIONALISM

Faced with this difficulty, one might be tempted to opt for a revised version of the analysis which commits one to type/type identities, but of a more modest variety, to identities which are, so to speak, species-specific. What we functionally define is not pain simpliciter, but rather pain-in-humans, pain-in-dogs, pain-in-molluscs, etc., and likewise for the rest of the psychological states. Pain-in-humans, for example, is the state (presumably a physiological state) that *in humans* plays such and such a typical causal role R. As such, pain-in-humans is identified with a kind of physiological state, but there is no requirement to the effect that this kind of state be instantiated whenever dogs or molluscs are in pain. Having restored *kinds* of physiological states to the account, we can again allow for the total paralytic, and do so without falling prey to the difficulties mentioned in the first section. Given the relevant physiological differences between the kinds, there won't be any real temptation to think of the mental terms as rigidly designating kinds of physical states.

This brand of functionalism strikes me as being a device of desperation and as having little or nothing to commend it. Yet, this seems in effect to be what Lewis opts for in "Mad Pain and Martian Pain", his most recent effort to defend *a priori* functionalism. In this paper he recognizes that the central problem is that of steering between radical physicalism on the one hand, and behaviourism on the other – allowing for the possibility of pain in both the plastic Martian and the total paralytic (or madman). He argues that these two possibilities can be accommodated in a functionalist theory once we recognize a certain ambiguity in our use of psychological terms. He retains the central functionalist intuition that an individual is, say, in pain if and only if it is in the state that typically plays the characteristic role R of pain. But, since different physical states may play this role in men, dogs, and Martians, we should fashion our functionalist thesis to make this explicit. To be fully explicit, the functionalist claim should be cast in something like the following fashion: An individual of kind K (e.g., the human kind) is in mental state $M_i$ (e.g., pain) if and only if it is in *the* state that typically occupies causal role R (e.g., the characteristic causal role of pain) *in that kind*.[12] Thus a human is in pain if and only if it is in the physical state that typically occupies the causal

[12] "Mad Pain and Martian Pain", pp. 219 ff.

role characteristic of pain in humans; and it is on such grounds that we can speak of a total paralytic being in pain. A Martian, on the other hand, is in pain if and only if it is in the state that typically plays this role in Martians. Thus it would appear that one can, with a little ingenuity, fashion the functionalist account to steer the desired middle course.

This appearance is deceptive, however. For consider two individuals: Herman, a normal, non-paralyzed human, and Mary, a totally paralyzed Martian, both of whom are in pain. Herman is in the state that plays the characteristic role of pain in humans (call it $P_h$), while Mary is in a different physiological state, $P_m$, the state that plays the characteristic role of pain in Martians. They are both in pain, though they don't "directly" share any non-psychological characterization. They are different in their physical compositions, and in the actual causal roles of their respective states. Lewis would say that Mary is in the same psychological state as Herman since the state she is in ($P_m$) is the state that plays a certain characteristic role in typical members of her species (which is the same as the role played by $P_h$ in Herman and typical members of *his* species).[13] So Mary is in the same state as Herman (in pain) because of how things are with other members of her species. But, surely this is implausible. The issue as to whether they are both in pain or not, which is not an epistemological issue, is surely independent of the question as to how things are with Mary's fellow Martians. To put the matter in an intuitive, if somewhat crude, fashion: if Mary and Herman are both in pain, then they share some "internal state", and one simply cannot locate this sameness in the states of individuals other than Mary and Herman, in Mary's fellow Martians or whatever.

This difference is simply compounded when we look to a variety of different possible worlds; worlds in which Mary (or her replica) is ensconced in different communities, though her physiology remains constant. In some of these possible worlds $P_j$ plays the characteristic role of pain in her fellows, while in others $P_k$ plays this role. Are we then to say that she is in pain in the one world and not in the other, despite the fact that there is no physical difference in her across these worlds? While such intuitions are compatible with certain anti-realistic positions in the philosophy of mind, they are, I believe, clearly at odds with the kinds of realistic and materialistic intuitions espoused by Lewis and other functionalists (he is, after all, an identity theorist). These kinds of counterfactual considerations *do not* bear on Mary's physical or functional composition, and hence they *should not* bear on the issue as to whether or not she is in pain (which remember is not an epistemic issue). One final remark on this score: in allowing for the possibility that two

[13] Indeed, Lewis explicitly considers atypical Martians such as Mary and argues that they are in pain when they are in the physical state that plays the characteristic causal role of pain in their fellows ("Mad Pain and Martian Pain", p. 220).

physically identical individuals might differ in that one is in pain while the other is not, Lewis is clearly running counter to the doctrine of psychophysical supervenience, a doctrine that is close to the heart of most materialists.

Thus, while species-functionalism is fashioned so as to enable us to speak (i) of a common state (e.g., physiological) shared by typical and non-typical members of a species (including paralytics, madmen, etc.), and (ii) of a common state shared by individuals of different species (the functionally specified state), it does not, in a like fashion, provide for a sameness of state between typical members of one species and atypical members of another. It fails to provide any intuitive, non-psychological, account of how such different individuals as Herman and Mary might be said to be in the same psychological state of pain.

Lewis recognizes that there are difficult cases which do not seem to be decided by the account proposed. Thus he writes:

> But one case remains problematic. What about pain in a being who is mad, alien, and unique? Have we made a place for that? It seems not. Since he is mad, we may suppose that his alleged state of pain does not occupy the proper causal role for him. Since he is alien, we may also suppose that it does not occupy the proper causal role for us. And since he is unique, it does not occupy the proper role for other members of his species. What is left?

He goes on:

> I think we cannot and need not solve this problem. Our only recourse is to deny that the case is possible. To stipulate that the being in this example is in pain was illegitimate.[14]

Whatever we think of Lewis's response to this case, the difficulty we have posed is not of this kind. Our example is of two individuals who are both in pain on Lewis's own criteria. The difficulty is not that we do not know what to say, but that they do not share any common internal state (physiological or functional). In effect we seem to be saying that these two individuals are in pain even though *they* have nothing in common over and above being in pain. To find some non-psychological element in common we are told to look to the other members of the species. But surely any adequate reductive account of pain *must* provide for some non-mentalistically characterized property which is common to both, the possession of which does not turn on how things are with other members of the species.

I conclude, then, that each of these versions of *a priori* functionalism fails to do justice to commonsense intuitions about the mental which Lewis was intent upon capturing. And since there does not seem to be any further way

---

[14] "Mad Pain and Martian Pain", p. 221.

in which we might plausibly modify this functionalist programme, we should, I believe, reject the central thesis – the claim that commonsense psychology serves to "functionally define" our everyday psychological vocabulary. It is time to abandon once and for all the last lingering legacy of positivism, the search for "interesting", i.e. reductive, analyses of the mental.[15]

*The University of Minnesota*

[15] I wish to thank Tyler Burge for helpful comments on an earlier version of this paper.

# WITTGENSTEIN ON SENSUOUS EXPERIENCES*

By MALCOLM BUDD

I

It is in general true that whatever my judgements or assertions are about there are two possibilities: either they are justified (fully or partially) or they lack any justification. About most kinds of subject-matter I may or I may not lack sufficient reason, or even any good reason at all, for believing what I do. In these cases my judgement can be either well-founded or unfounded: I can possess or lack a justification for it. Furthermore, it can be either true or false. Accordingly, if my judgement is of this kind, I can have good reason for my belief and in fact be informed of the truth of the matter; or I can have good reason for my belief although it is actually false; or I can have no good reason, or insufficient reason, for a false belief; or, finally, what I believe can, fortuitously, be true even though my reasons are insufficient.

But there appears to be one subject-matter about which I always have, and cannot but have, the perfect justification for my judgements or sincere assertions and about which I cannot be mistaken: (the simple properties of) the intrinsic character of my present sensuous experience – my present sensations, sense-impressions, images and related phenomena.[1] For most kinds of assertion that I might make, what I say can be insecurely based. Such remarks can rest on illusion or various other forms of error, or can merely lack the evidential basis they require. It may be that I have no evidence for what I sincerely say or it may be that what I say goes beyond what I have evidence for: my evidence entitles me to say only so much, but I am led by the general structure of my beliefs and by my temperament to form a belief that is not merely a representation of my evidence, but instead a

---

*In the text I use the following abbreviations:
  BB   *The Blue and Brown Books* (Oxford, 2nd ed., 1960)
  PI    *Philosophical Investigations* (Oxford, 2nd ed., 1958)
  NFL  'Notes for Lectures on "Private Experience" and "Sense Data"' *The Philosophical Review*, 77 (1968)
  RFM  *Remarks on the Foundations of Mathematics* (Oxford, 2nd ed., 1978)
  RPP  *Remarks on the Philosophy of Psychology* (Oxford, 1980)
  Z    *Zettel* (Oxford, 1981)

[1] Although the qualification in parenthesis appears to be needed, it is not to my purpose to examine how the distinction between simple and complex properties of sensuous experiences might most plausibly be drawn. In what follows I ignore the qualification.

construction that is based upon but goes beyond this evidence. And, of necessity, this is hazardous. By going beyond my evidence I may fall into error: my construction may be a misconstruction. But if my remarks are restricted to the intrinsic character of my present "state of consciousness" they have, it seems, an absolutely sure foundation. My judgements about the intrinsic character of my present sensations, sense-impressions and images do not go beyond the evidence upon which they are immediately based, and, accordingly, I am always fully entitled to make them. My beliefs are about what is present to my consciousness and the contents of my consciousness are revealed to me if I direct my attention to them. And since I am directly aware of my present state of consciousness, if my beliefs are confined to its current condition they cannot be in error. This privileged position in which I stand to my present sensuous experiences is of course mine alone. For other people can never have as good reason for their beliefs about my present sensuous experiences as I have for my own beliefs about them. Their beliefs about my present sensations, sense-impressions or images must go beyond the evidence on which their beliefs are based, and so can never be as securely based as my own beliefs.

This conception that our beliefs about our present sensuous experiences rest upon an absolutely secure foundation is one of the principal objects of Wittgenstein's attack in his consideration of the concepts of sensation, sense-impression and image. And it is by reference to his rejection of this conception that his thought can best be understood.

II

Associated with this conception of the self-ascription of present sensuous experiences is, Wittgenstein believed, a certain play of the imagination – a certain picture we are liable to form: a picture of the items about which we have such perfect knowledge and of our relation to them. This picture is constructed on the model of the material world and our access to this world in perception. Thus: we might imagine that for each of us there is a "world of consciousness" (*RPP*, I 720), a "realm of consciousness" (*NFL*, p. 320), in which these items, when they are ours, occur and into which nobody but we ourself can gaze. Accordingly, there is an "external world" and a set of "internal worlds". Each of us is in the external world – at least, each of us is intimately connected with an object in the external world, the object we call our body – but each of us is the possessor of a world of our own, our internal world. And whereas the external world is built of one kind of material (matter), an internal world is built of another kind of material (mind). (*BB*, p. 47) The contents of a world of consciousness are not composed of matter, and a world of consciousness does not require the existence of matter to sustain it. The items in our internal world exist "inside" us, not in the sense in which physical events occur inside our bodies – for other people can (but usually do not) look into the interiors of our bodies, and the events that take place there are events in the external world and are composed of matter – but rather in a different sense that necessarily precludes others from observing these items. The "inner" object is necessarily hidden from everyone but the person in whose mind, in whose inner world, it exists. Whereas I can observe directly the contents of my own mind, other people can at most speculate about these contents on the basis of what they can observe – my body and its environment. My experiences, the objects in my world of consciousness (*RPP*, I 720, 733, 896) – the objects in my subjective space – are visible only to me. The "content" of an experience of mine is a "private object" that I observe within my consciousness and which another can never observe. (*NFL passim*, and especially p. 279, p. 316; *RPP* I 109, 440, 694)

This familiar picture, as so far outlined, is incomplete; but it is difficult to imagine how it could be finished in such a way as to render it attractive – and it is precisely its lack of finish that enables it to exert a malign influence upon us. The picture is designed to represent our sensuous experiences and our relationship with them. But, in the first place, it fails to delineate the connection between the external world – and, in particular, our body – and our internal world of consciousness. And if we should understand the nature of the link between a material object and an inner world of consciousness to be merely causal, this appears to open up two possibilities: that a human being might lack an inner world of consciousness and yet behave no differently from a human being who possesses an inner world, and that an inanimate object might "possess" an inner world. But it is not easy to make sense of these ideas. (*PI* 420 and surrounding sections, 281 and following sections)

A second respect in which the picture is incomplete is this: whilst it is designed to render intelligible one feature of the conception of the self-ascription of sensuous experiences that I have articulated, it contains nothing that would allow it to explain the other distinctive feature of the conception. It purports to explain why it is that a person's judgements about his present sensuous experiences are, and must be, better grounded than another person's judgements about them – for each person is supposed to have perceptual access only to his own inner world – but it does not make clear why these judgements cannot be mistaken. The picture represents them as being based on the deliverances of an "inner sense", whereby we look into our own mind and descry its contents. The idea that our judgements are not liable to error will be mirrored in the idea that our inner sense is not liable to defects, the medium of consciousness is fully transparent, the light of consciousness shines whenever our mind is active, no private object can block the view of another private object, and so on. The items in our world of consciousness must deliver their natures to us as soon as we attend to them – in fact, they exist only in so far as we are conscious of them – because our inner eye is ever vigilant, never malfunctions and is blessed with the power of perfect discrimination: as a result our consciousness is always represented to us as it is. But this idea of the flawless inner sense will be sufficient to explain the problematic feature of the conception of the self-ascription of present states of consciousness only if it is taken to mean not merely that our inner sense never does mislead us, but that it cannot mislead us. And the idea of a sense that is incapable of misrepresenting the world it provides information about is incoherent. Hence, the picture of a world of consciousness does not contain any material that would enable it to explain the alleged incorrigibility of avowals.

The introduction of an inner sense to provide access to the contents of a world of consciousness not only fails to guarantee the incorrigibility of a person's judgements about his present state of consciousness, but creates problems of its own. One such problem is this: if an inner sense provides us with our information about our sensuous experiences, it will itself involve sensuous experiences, which must be inhabitants of *an* inner world, perhaps another world within a world, watched over by its own inner sense, and so on.

However, it would be mistaken to believe that this second inadequacy of the picture of an inner world of consciousness, within which our sensuous experiences exist, stems from the inclusion of an inner sense by means of which we obtain our knowledge of the contents of our inner world of consciousness, and that the inadequacy would be removed – and the problems consequent upon its introduction would not arise – if we were to erase the inner sense. The image of an inner sense is an essential element of the picture even though it cannot fulfil the function it is intended to perform. For if we were to delete the inner sense and to add nothing in its place, the picture would not be improved: the disappearance of an inner sense would create a gap in the picture and would strip it of the power to offer any account – even an insufficient account – of how we acquire knowledge of the items in our world of consciousness. But nothing could be substituted for the inner sense which would guarantee that the contents of a world of consciousness are always faithfully represented to the possessor of that world of consciousness. And in fact the idea of an inner sense is an irreplaceable part of the picture: it exploits our familiarity with the senses as a means of acquiring knowledge of the world and thus encourages us to believe that we understand the picture of a world of consciousness.

A third respect in which the picture is incomplete is this: we are supposed to have perceptual access to the contents of our own world of consciousness, but not to the contents of any other world of consciousness. But nothing is offered in explanation of this restriction. If I am within my world of consciousness, why cannot another person also be within it? If I am not within my world of consciousness, why cannot another person share whatever kind of supposedly privileged access to it I possess? Without answers to such questions, the picture of a world of consciousness has too few details for it plausibly to masquerade as an adequate representation of its subject: it is merely an image, a metaphor, that attempts to present itself as though it were to be understood literally, but that disintegrates as soon as we try to grasp it in the intended manner. But let us set aside these difficulties for the idea of the inner world of consciousness.

III

The idea of the private object of internal observation leads, first of all, to the idea that words for sensations, sense-impressions and images must be taught *indirectly*. (*NFL*, p. 285) A person can learn the meaning of words that name or describe the intrinsic character of sensuous experiences only if he observes in his own case instances of what these words refer to: his inner sense must show him what a pain is, what an image of the colour red is, and so on. But we cannot directly observe, on any occasion, that the kind of private object we want someone to use the word as the name of is present to his mind. In consequence, our mode of teaching the meanings of words for sensations and other sensuous experiences is indirect, for we want our pupil to correlate such a word with something we do not observe on any of the occasions in question but which we hope he will observe within himself on those occasions.

But of course the situation quickly worsens. For if the contents of one person's mind are hidden from the minds of others in the radical way that is implied by the idea of the private object of internal observation, our conception of what we have reason to believe about other people's sensuous experiences and their understanding of the words they use to say what these are requires revision of an equally radical kind. This can be shown in the following manner. If we accept the idea of the private object of internal observation, the undeniable fact that the word 'pain' is the name of a certain kind of sensation is transformed into the idea that the word 'pain' is the name of a certain kind of private object. (A similar transformation will take place in the case of other words that we use to name or describe the intrinsic character of our sensations, sense-impressions and imagery.) Now consider the two propositions:

(1) For each person who uses the word 'pain' to ascribe pain to himself there is a certain kind of private object, instances of

which the person uses the word 'pain' to refer to in his self-ascriptions of pain.

(2) There is a kind of private object such that for each person who uses the word 'pain' to ascribe pain to himself, he uses the word to refer to instances of this kind.

It is clear that (1) does not entail (2): $(x)(\exists y)(x \; R \; y) \nrightarrow (\exists y)(x)(x \; R \; y)$. The natural thought that there is a common understanding of the word 'pain' and that each of us says the same of another person when we ascribe pain to him as we say of ourselves when we self-ascribe pain requires that we should be assured of the truth of (2). But it follows from the conception of the private object of internal observation that we could have no good reason to believe (2). Yet is it equally clear that nothing assures us of the truth of (1).[2] Hence, if we are to say only what we might be in a position to know, our claim should be personal and not plural:

(3) When I ascribe pain to myself I use the word 'pain' to refer to instances of a certain kind of private object.

For the idea of the private object of internal observation is such that all I can do is to speculate fruitlessly about the existence and nature of any private objects other than those that are or have been present within my world of consciousness. And yet it is these private objects that seem all-important in our understanding of the nature of consciousness. Words for sensuous experiences appear to stand for various kinds of private objects – at least, it is tempting for me to believe that I use them in this way in my own case. But there is no way in which anyone could know that another person uses such words in self-ascription to name the same kinds of private objects as he himself does, and, consequently, the idea that there is a common understanding of words for sensuous experiences is groundless.

IV

The set of ideas outlined in the first section of the paper – that we cannot be mistaken about our present sensuous experiences, that we have the perfect justification, the very best of reasons, for believing what we do about their intrinsic character, that our sincere remarks about their internal nature have an absolutely secure foundation – and the associated picture of sensations, sense-impressions and images as private objects of internal observation, were the principal targets of the sections in the *Philosophical Investigations* and Wittgenstein's other writings that are concerned with the concepts of sensation, sense-impression and image.

[2] Compare: "how can I generalize the *one* case so irresponsibly?", *Philosophical Investigations* 293.

Wittgenstein expressed his opposition to this way of thinking of states of consciousness in a number of connected remarks:

(i) I do not identify my sensation by criteria. (*PI* 290) (What happens is that I use the same expression.)

(ii) I cannot be said to learn of my present sensations. (*PI* 246)

(iii) Whereas a true sentence in the third person present that ascribes a sensation to someone transmits information, a true sentence in the first person present is akin to an expression (*Äusserung*) of sensation. (*RPP* II 63; *Z* 472)

(iv) When I say 'I am in pain' I use the word 'pain' without a justification. (*PI* 289)

(v) The verbal expression of sensation is not the report of (the result of) any observation. (*NFL* p. 319; *RPP* II 63; *Z* 472)

(vi) A sensation is not an object. (*PI* 304, 293: *RPP* I 1081–9; *BB* p. 47)

(vii) I do not derive the words in my verbal expression of a sensation from the sensation. (*NFL* p. 319)[3]

The basic thought that underlies these various formulations is easy to grasp. For someone to identify something by a criterion is for him to identify it by a method, the application of which he can cite in answer to the question 'How do you know it is . . . ?' or 'What reason do you have for saying that it is . . . ?'. (e.g., *PI* 239: *RFM* VII 40) The method provides him with a justification for his identification: he judges that something falls under a certain concept, and there is some other proposition that is his reason for believing what he judges to be true and which he accepts as a result of using some method for determining the truth of the matter.

Now it was Wittgenstein's view that 'I don't know whether I am in pain or not' – 'I know what "pain" means; what I don't know is whether *this*, that I have now, is pain' – is not a significant proposition. (*PI* 288, 246, 408)[4] Accordingly, someone who understands 'pain' has no means or method that he can use to find out whether he can truly say that he is in pain, the application or findings of which he can cite as his reason for believing what he asserts. For if there were a method that someone who understands 'pain' could use to find out whether it would be true to say 'I am in pain', it would be possible that he should fail to apply this method (hence the possibility of at least ignorance), or that something should go wrong in its application (hence the possibility of error). (*PI* 288) If he knows that he has not made

---

[3] I have omitted consideration of Wittgenstein's remark "It can't be said of me at all (except perhaps as a joke) that I *know* I am in pain", for the sake of brevity. I believe that nothing germane to the matter in hand is lost by ignoring the remark.

[4] Likewise the following is not a significant proposition: 'I know what "red" means; what I don't know is whether *this* image (or sense-impression) is an image (sense-impression) of the colour red'.

use of the method, or if he suspects that something might have gone amiss in his use of it, he could be in doubt as to whether he is in pain and it would be significant for him to say 'I don't know whether I am in pain or not'. Since this is not significant, someone who understands 'pain' cannot make use of a method for determining when he can truly utter the sentence 'I am in pain'. He cannot be in the dark as to whether he can truly say that he is in pain and resolve his uncertainty, come to learn what the truth is, by the application of some method of discovery. He does not learn or fail to learn of his sensations: he does not have some means that he can use to acquire information about their intrinsic characters ((ii) above).

The question 'How does a person know when he can truly say that he is in pain?', where this question is asking for the *basis* of the person's assertions, is misplaced if the person knows what the word 'pain' means. His assertions lack any basis. The answer to the question 'How does he know when he can correctly assert that he is in pain?' – where this means 'By reference to what, by the use of which method, does he find out that he is in pain?' – is 'By nothing at all'. He does not identify his sensation by criteria, but on the various occasions when he is in pain he uses, or is willing to use, the same expression – 'pain' ((i) above).

There is no intermediate step available to someone who understands the word 'pain' – a step such that if he takes it he is then in a position to assert that he is in pain – that would provide him with a reason for his self-ascription of pain and without which he would not know what to say: his apprehension of when he can truly say that he is in pain is unmediated. Without the employment of any method of discovery, he finds himself able sincerely to say 'I am in pain', as he can find himself groaning with pain. In this way his self-ascription of pain is akin to an expression of pain ((iii) above).

It follows that it is incorrect to maintain that the reason I have a right to be absolutely certain that I can truly say that I am in pain is that my remark has an absolutely secure basis, or that I have unshakeable evidence, or that I have an overwhelmingly good justification for what I say. My remark rests on nothing at all, in the sense that I have no reason that assures me of the probable or certain truth of my remark. My remark is ungrounded: in the self-ascription of pain I use the word 'pain' without a justification ((iv) above).[5]

[5] To assert that the reason I cannot be in error or in doubt about my being in pain is that I am *immediately aware* of the fact is to provide no explanation at all. To say that I am immediately aware of some state of affairs is merely to indicate the *end* of the chain of reasons. Hence, the picture of a world of consciousness would not be made more adequate by the substitution of the idea of immediate awareness for the idea of an inner sense: a private object of immediate awareness is no more acceptable as a model for a sensuous experience than is a private object of internal observation.

In particular, it follows that there is no kind of observation of anything, the result of which I report when I sincerely assert that I am in pain. The verbal expression of a sensation is not based upon observation of oneself ((v) above).

And *if* we conclude from this that a sensation is not the sort of thing that can be observed, and if we say that something is not an "object" unless it can be observed,[6] we can derive the conclusion that sensations are not objects ((vi) above).

This leaves just the last formulation ((vii) above) of Wittgenstein's underlying thought unexplained, and I now turn to this. The point is by now a familiar one.

## V

When I form an image and express in words what I have formed an image of, or when I have the experience as of seeing a certain colour and express the character of the experience in words, or when I have a sensation and express in words the nature of the sensation I experience, "the great difficulty here", Wittgenstein writes, "is not to represent the matter as if there were something one *couldn't* do. As if there really were an object, from which I derive its description, but I were unable to shew it to anyone". (*PI* 374) The thought that underlies his remark is the thought that it is mistaken to construe my expression in words of my present state of consciousness on the model of my description of a material object, by regarding my present state of consciousness as something that I, but only I, can observe – a "private object". This misconstruction involves crediting me with a reason for what I say when I express my image, sense-impression or sensation, a reason that justifies what I say, as I can have a reason that justifies my use of the word 'red' in a description of a material object. In this latter case, if I am asked to justify my description, one thing that I can do is to appeal to a colour chart that contains a sample of the colour correlated with the word 'red'. I can point to the sample and say "This colour is called red and this material object is, as you can see, the colour of the sample". I see a material object and I say that its colour is red. I could see something else that is agreed to exemplify the word 'red', and I could derive the word that I use to describe the material object from this second thing – this thing that correlates word and sample. Even when I don't in fact derive the word from the colour chart, I could justify my use of the word 'red' in this way by reference to a rule in

---

[6] "The description of the experience doesn't describe an object . . . The impression – one would like to say – is not an object . . . One can't look at the impression, that is why it is not an object. (Grammatically.)". (*RPP* I 1081–9)

accordance with which I use the word; just as someone who has been taught the word 'red' by reference to some particular thing that exemplifies the colour could explain why he used the word 'red' in some later case by referring to the sample and the claim that the object matches the sample. (*BB* pp. 14–15, 72–3)

Now – to take the case of the image first – my image of red is not something I observe and of which I have somehow been informed by others that something of this kind is called 'an image of red'. I don't learn that an image of the colour red *looks like this* or is *this sort of thing*. (*PI* 388) The fact of the matter is that I do not use any criterion to determine whether I have an image of the colour red. (*PI* 377) My verbal expression of my image is criterionless. When I render my image in words I cannot justify what I say by reference to an exemplary image: an image that can be seen to match the present image and that is agreed to be an image of red. The idea that I derive my description of my image from an object that only I can be directly aware of collapses: I could not apply any rules to derive from a private object the right words for my image. (*PI* 380)

We have already seen that the verbal expression of pain is not the report of an observation (of something only I can directly observe). When I assert that I am in pain I am not describing something I observe "within" myself. Hence, I cannot be said to *derive* my words from what I observe. I cannot derive my words from my pain, for this is not something I observe. When I am in pain and I say sincerely 'I am in pain', my utterance is not mediated by an observation of something or other from which I could derive the words I utter. (*NFL*, p. 319)

Finally, I cannot derive the word 'red' from my visual sense-impression as of seeing the colour red, but only from something that is red, i.e., from a sample of red. I cannot read off the description from something I observe. I cannot adduce the sense-impression as my justification for my utterance. (*NFL*, p. 319)

Hence, the self-ascription of sensuous experiences can be said to be underived ((vii) above).

## VI

It might be thought that the role that a sample of the colour red plays in the description of public objects could be played by a *memory-sample* of a private object of a certain kind in the description of private objects: so that if my image is thought of as a private object I could still derive my description of it from the image itself: if my pain is thought of as a private object I could derive my description of it from the pain itself by reference to a memory-image of pain, which functions as a sample does; and so on.

But this thought would be mistaken. For if I have forgotten or I am unsure what colour 'red' is the name of, I can look up a chart that correlates the word with a sample of the colour and thereby provide myself with a justification for using or withholding the word 'red' in my description of this public object that confronts me. But if I have forgotten or I am unsure what kind of private object 'S' is the name of – if I cannot remember which kind it is the name of – I could not look up a chart that correlates the word with a sample of the private object kind in order to regain assurance. The most I could do would be to form an image of such a chart. For such a chart correlating samples and words could exist only in my mind – in my memory or imagination – because the samples it contains are samples of kinds of private object. But my forming an image of a chart of this sort could not provide me with a justification for using, or for declining to use, the word 'S' in my description of the private object that is now present to my mind. (*PI* 265) A memory-image is not a sample that I can see but that others cannot see, and by reference to which I can establish that 'S' is, or is not, the right word to use for this private object. My appeal to a memory-image is not a matter of my looking up to see which sample is correlated with 'S'; it is, rather, my remembering, or my attempting to remember, which sample does go with 'S'. If I am unsure that 'S' is the right word to use for this private object, i.e., I am unsure what 'S' means, an appeal to a memory-image will not enable me to reach firmer ground; for I must remember which sample is correlated with 'S', i.e., what 'S' means, and this is just what I am in doubt about.[7]

It is therefore mistaken to believe that the role that a sample plays in the description of public objects could be played by a memory-sample in the description of private objects. Accordingly, the conclusion holds: I could not apply any rules to derive from a private object the right word for it.

## VII

We have now worked through a number of formulations of Wittgenstein's opposition to the idea of a sensuous experience as a private object of internal observation: an item that cannot be misidentified by the subject in whose consciousness it exists, and which provides the subject with a perfect justification for his beliefs about it. And we have seen that this opposition can be expressed in the thought that a sensation is not an object: my sensations are not the contents of a subjective space, into which only I can see. When I express my sensation in words I do not observe a private object, see it just as it is, and then render it in words. If my sensations were items that I observed with an internal eye, then when I express my sensation in words I would have

[7] Compare A. J. P. Kenny, *Wittgenstein* (London, 1973), pp. 192–3.

a reason, a justification, for what I say: the evidence of my inner sense. But the words I use to express my sensation I use without a justification: I do not identify my sensation by criteria. A name of a sensation is not the name of an object.

But if this is so, what is the right account of the meaning of names of sensations: how are they used? Immediately prior to his consideration of this question Wittgenstein announces the following conclusion – one he has reached as a result of his examination of the concept of following a rule:

> If language is to be a means of communication there must be agreement not only in definitions but also (queer as this may sound) in judgments. (*PI* 242: cf. *RFM* VI 39)

Now in a language that can be used as a means of communication words for sensations are, Wittgenstein insists, "tied up with" behaviour, which is the "natural expression of sensation". (*PI* 244, 256, 288) It is in virtue of this fact that our common words for sensations can satisfy the requirement that there should be agreement in people's judgements: we apply these words to each other on the basis of each other's behaviour and we apply them to ourselves in conformity with, although not on the basis of, the behaviour-criteria used to determine their application to another.[8] In a "private" language words for sensations are not tied up with behaviour, for the sensations they stand for do not have natural expressions. (*PI* 256) In fact, these words are used quite independently of the behaviour and bodily state of the user of the language. (*PI* 270) Accordingly, they cannot meet the requirement of agreement in judgements: the only basis available to another person for making judgements about the private language user's sensations is just irrelevant.

Now there are many connections between, on the one hand, the views Wittgenstein has developed in the *Philosophical Investigations* up to the point at which he begins his examination of how words refer to sensations and, on the other hand, the results of this examination. But I do not believe that it is possible to derive the conclusion of Wittgenstein's "private language" argument – that a "private language" for one's sensations is impossible – from the conclusion of his consideration of the notion of following a rule – that "obeying a rule" is a practice and, hence, that it is not possible to obey a rule "privately" (*PI* 202) – in the simple manner advanced by the "community interpretation" of Wittgenstein's discussion of rule-following. For the community interpretation of the idea of obeying a rule "privately" is wide of the

[8] The notion of behaviour, as Wittgenstein uses it, often includes the idea of the external circumstances in which the behaviour (in the narrow sense) occurs. See *RPP* I 314, II 148 ff. The vagueness of the idea that words for sensations are "tied up with" behaviour could not be completely removed, I believe, without attention to the role of the notion of causation in our understanding of such words. I consider this in the final section of the paper.

mark and its understanding of the idea of a "practice" is unwarranted. Accordingly, it misrepresents the nature of Wittgenstein's argument and credits it with a conclusion that it has not established.[9] In fact, the user of a private language can embrace the thesis that "obeying a rule" is a practice. He can agree that it is not what comes before his mind when he writes 'S' down that determines whether there is a rule that he is thereby obeying and what this rule is, but rather his use over time of 'S'. He can say that *if* others could be aware of what he is doing they would see, he hopes, that he is following a rule in his use of 'S' – they would react on each occasion as he does if they were to have what he has; and he can say that if they were to contradict him they would, perhaps, be right: he has made a mistake in his application of the term on some occasion or, more seriously, there is no regularity at all in his use of the term. The point is that others *cannot* be aware of what he does, and so they cannot know whether there is regularity or randomness in his behaviour – for others cannot be aware of the nature of the item (if any) to which he applies 'S' on any occasion. Since others can know only *at which times* he uses 'S' and never *what is true* at these times, they are never in a position to pass judgement on his use of the term.

The connection between Wittgenstein's assertion that it is not possible to obey a rule "privately" and the conclusion of his private language argument emerges when we focus on the real difficulty that faces the user of a private language. This arises from his intention to introduce a sign 'S' *as a name of a sensation* (in order to be able to record in words the recurrence of the sensation). (*PI* 258) And the difficulty is obvious. For if 'S' is intended to be the name of a sensation it must have the same "grammar" as a word for a sensation. Now this grammar has two essential components: that which is characteristic of the third-person use of names of sensations, and that which is characteristic of the first-person use. But in the case of the user of a private language there is no third-person use: nothing provides another with a good basis for using the term 'S' to describe the private language user's condition, and nothing provides the private language user with a good basis for using the term 'S' to-describe anybody else's condition. Hence, if 'S' has any claim at all to the title of a name of a sensation, it must be used in the way a name of a sensation is used in the first person – in particular, in the first-person present. And hence, when the private language user thinks 'I have S' he has no reason for believing that this is so: his self-ascriptions are criterionless: he uses 'S' without a justification: in order for him to know when to write down 'I have S' there is nothing he needs to find out about to underwrite his disposition to do so: his thought 'I have S' is groundless. But not only is this insufficient for 'S' to be granted the status of name of a

[9] See the discussion in my "Wittgenstein on Meaning, Interpretation and Rules", *Synthese* 58 (1984).

sensation, it is insufficient for it to be accorded the status of meaningful sign or word.

The private language user is someone who speaks, writes down or says to himself the sign 'S' at the same time as he concentrates his attention on a sensation – he gives himself a private ostensive definition of 'S' (*PI* 258, 268) – and then on certain later occasions writes the sign down again. Now his act of private ostensive definition does not give any content to the idea that it would be *correct* for him to write 'S' down on certain subsequent occasions and *incorrect* for him to write 'S' down on certain other occasions. For the combination of an act of attention to a sensation and the utterance of 'This is called "S"' does not determine the meaning of 'S': any ostensive definition can be variously understood. (*PI* 28) It is the way in which a sign is used, or is intended to be used, that determines its meaning, and the concentration of a person's attention upon a sensation as he speaks or writes down the sign implies nothing about how the sign is to be used. And the combination of an act of attention to a sensation and the utterance of 'This *sensation* is called "S"' likewise does not determine the meaning of 'S': the intention to use 'S' as the name of a kind of sensation of which *this* is an instance leaves indeterminate the nature of the kind in question. (Compare pointing to a coloured object and saying that 'C' is to be the name of *this* colour.) Furthermore, the intention to use 'S' as the name of a kind of sensation is coherent only if the intention is to use 'S' in the way in which words for sensations are used.[10] The only difference between the first and second styles of ostensive definition is that the second makes explicit use of the concept of sensation and thus shows what place in grammar is to be assigned to the word: it shows the post at which the sign is to be stationed. (*PI* 29, 257) Hence, the second style of definition merely makes explicit what is presupposed by the first style, namely that the private language user intends 'S' to be the name of a sensation. But this intention requires the private language user to use the sign according to the grammar of names of sensations, and this is something that he cannot do. As we have seen, his use of the word cannot be the same as the use of a word that is the name of a sensation. The most that the private language user can do is to use his sign 'S' in accordance with *part* of the grammar of the self-ascriptive use of names of sensations. And this implies that when he writes 'S' down he uses it without a justification: on each occasion when he writes 'S' down he has no reason to do so that justifies him in doing so.

It would be mistaken to think that an appeal to memory would provide the private language user with a justification for what he proceeds to do. We have already seen that a memory-image does not enable us to derive our

---

[10] "'To give a sensation a name' means nothing unless I know already in what sort of game this name is to be used". (*NFL* p. 201)

word for a sensation from the sensation itself in accordance with a rule. And the private language user's thought 'This is an S' receives no support of any kind from his thought 'This is the same as the one I called "S" previously'; for he must say that 'It is an S' is equivalent to 'It is the same as the one I called "S" previously' – the one thought is not on a different level from the other. Hence, all that his mastery of a private language comes to is the fact that he sometimes, without any particular reason, writes the sign 'S' in his diary. (*NFL*, p. 291) And since his use of 'S' is entirely unconstrained, 'S' is not a sign whose use is rule-governed.

This unfortunate consequence for the private language user's use of 'S', in which the abrogation of the normal language-game with the expression in behaviour is assumed (*PI* 288), does not hold for a sensation term in a common language. Although such a word in a common language is used in self-ascription without justification, this use is not unconstrained; for it must be used in general conformity with what is taken to be indicative of the occurrence of a sensation of the kind in question – the behaviour that is "expressive" of the sensation (to put the matter very loosely) – if the user of the word is to be deemed to understand what the term means. And so there are restrictions on the use of the word, even though in self-ascription the word is used without a justification: the groundlessness of self-ascription does not imply that there is no rule that is being followed when the word is used. It is precisely because the self-ascriptive use of a word for a sensuous experience is not viable in isolation that "an 'inner process' stands in need of outward criteria". (*PI* 580) For the self-ascription of an "inner process" will be criterionless; and without outward criteria a sign that supposedly stands for the "inner process" will not be rule-governed. This is why Wittgenstein insists that "if I assume the abrogation of the normal language-game with the expression of a sensation, I need a criterion of identity for the sensation". (*PI* 288)

The private language user is therefore impaled on the horns of a dilemma: either he intends 'S' to be a sign for something that others can have a conception of, or he does not. But if he does not, he is consigned to silence: there is nothing he can say that will make clear to others what kind of sign 'S' is supposed to be. If, on the other hand, he intends 'S' to be a sign which can be explained to others, either he intends it to be the name of a sensation or he intends it to be some other kind of word. But if he intends 'S' to be the name of a sensation, the most he can do is to use it in self-ascription in the way that a name of a sensation is used, and then his use is not rule-governed and he is not using 'S' as the name of a sensation. And he cannot escape from his predicament by retreating from his intention to use 'S' as the name of a sensation and resting content with a weaker intention to use it as some other kind of word, a name of something or other. For the words he uses to explain the nature of 'S' will be words in a common language and his entitlement to use these words requires him to provide a justification for using them that is acceptable to those who have a mastery of the language – and this is something he cannot do, or can achieve only at the cost of rendering his sign one that is not a word in a private language. (*PI* 261) Hence, the private language user's thought that he is using 'S' as a sign lacks any foundation.

The conclusion that the supposed use of 'S' as the name of a sensation in a private language amounts only to writing 'S' down from time to time, on each occasion for no justifying reason, enables us to make clear the connection between the two propositions:

> (i) It is not possible to use a word as the name of a sensation in a private language,

and

> (ii) It is not possible to obey a rule "privately".

For if the aspirant private language user merely writes 'S' down on a number of occasions, on each occasion only for the non-justifying "reason" that he considers it correct then to use 'S', there is only what is before his mind (the sign 'S') on the various occasions to give substance to the idea that he is obeying a rule in his use of 'S'. But, as Wittgenstein has shown, this is insufficient to give content to the notion of obeying a rule. For, otherwise, no matter what the set of occasions is on which someone uses the sign 'S', he will be following a rule in his use of 'S' throughout the series of occasions. And so if the person thinks he is following a rule in his use of 'S' – because on each occasion when he uses it 'S' is present to his mind in a certain way, i.e., 'S' seems to him to be the appropriate word for the occasion – he will be following a rule. But:

> to *think* one is obeying a rule is not to obey a rule. Hence it is not possible to obey a rule "privately": otherwise thinking one was obeying a rule would be the same thing as obeying it. (*PI* 202)

Accordingly, it is not possible to use a word as the name of a sensation in a private language *because* it is not possible to obey a rule "privately". For the use of 'S' by the aspirant private language user comes to nothing more than the sign's coming before his mind in a certain manner on the various occasions of use. And this involves his proceeding "privately", but not, thereby, obeying a rule.

## VIII

It can be seen, therefore, that at least these four considerations lie at the heart of Wittgenstein's private language argument:

(i) If language is to be a means of communication there must be agreement in judgements.
(ii) It is the way in which a word is used that determines what meaning it has, not what comes before a person's mind when he uses the word.
(iii) Words for sensations are "tied up with" behaviour.
(iv) A person does not identify his sensations by criteria.

And the last of these considerations is of crucial importance. Moreover, it provides one link between Wittgenstein's concern with the self-ascription of sensations and his more general concern with the concept of following a rule, and, in particular, with the notion of developing a series of numbers by the application of a formula. For he insists that a formula for performing a mathematical operation does not *compel* us to make use of it in the particular case as we do, in the sense that our reasons for doing so are not endless. But he believes that we are inclined to look for a justification of a certain kind – a logically conclusive reason – for our applying the formula as we do, and that we may be dismayed when we fail to find such an absolutely firm justification. And he believes that when we reflect on the self-ascription of present sensations we are liable to experience a similar temptation: we are inclined to look for a justification for our using the word that occurs in our self-ascription when there is no justification. (*BB* p. 73) And just as the lack of a perfect justification (as it were) for using a formula in a certain way is actually of no consequence, for in fact people react to instruction and training in similar ways and agree in their judgements as to how the formula is to be applied, despite the fact that the chain of reasons has an end; so the lack of a justification for our specification of our present sensation is also of no consequence, for in fact people react to "training" in the use of names of sensations in similar ways and self-ascribe sensations when others judge that it is true to say of them what they say of themselves. In both cases the requirement for the possession of words in a common language is satisfied – and it is satisfied because of our common human nature: we react in similar ways in response to similar exposure to, and training in the use of, language.

## IX

There is, however, one aspect of Wittgenstein's consideration of words that stand for sensuous experiences that is problematic: the virtual omission of any reference to, and no assessment of the significance of, the apparent fact that sensuous experiences are events that *cause* the behaviour in which they are "expressed". The sensuous experience that occupies pride of place in Wittgenstein's various discussions is bodily pain, and it is integral to the "language-game" that is played with the word 'pain' that a pain can be caused by something that happens to a person's body and, moreover, that a pain causes the movements of the body in which it is manifested. What does this feature of the language-game require of a pain: what must be true of a pain if it is to play the role assigned to it by the language-game – the role of that which brings about its natural expressions?[11]

Furthermore, a pain not only brings about its natural expressions, but also, it seems, the utterance that is the verbal expression of the pain (or the internal counterpart of the utterance: the awareness that one is in pain). Someone is said to understand 'pain' only if in general his readiness to ascribe pain to himself is in accordance with the behaviour-criteria on the basis of which pain is ascribed to another: there must be a general coincidence of his spontaneous inclination to behave in ways that are indicative of his being in pain with his being able sincerely to utter the sentence 'I am in pain'. Now it is natural to believe that this coincidence cannot be a mere coincidence: there must be some kind of causal connection between these phenomena that go together so regularly. And the nature of this causal connection, assuming that there is one, seems to be apparent: in the case of someone who understands the word 'pain', an instance of spontaneous pain-behaviour and the self-ascription of the pain responsible for that behaviour have a common cause – the pain that the person then feels. For I appear to be aware in my own case that this is indeed the fact of the matter: it is the pain that makes me limp and it is in virtue of my consciousness of the pain that I am in a position to say sincerely that I am in pain. When I sincerely declare that I am in pain I am in a position to do so only because, so it seems, I am aware of an event; and I am aware of this event *as* the immediate cause of my thought 'I am in pain' and as the object of my thought 'This is a pain'; and it is this event that causes both the verbal and the non-verbal behaviour in which the pain is expressed. But the requirement that my thought that I am in pain and the behaviour that reveals that I am in pain should be caused by my pain places a constraint on the correct account of the concept of pain. What must be true of a pain if it is to play the role of that which brings about its natural expressions, its verbal expressions and its unvoiced recognitions?

Now if one accepts this train of thought, it might appear that a presupposition of the language-game played with the word 'pain' is that each pain is

[11] It is clear that when Wittgenstein wrote *Philosophical Grammar* he embraced the view that a pain causes its natural expressions: "There isn't a further process hidden behind, which is the real understanding, accompanying and causing these manifestations in the way that toothache causes one to groan, hold one's cheek, pull faces, etc." *Philosophical Grammar* (Oxford, 1974), Part I 38.

identical with a physical event that occurs in the body of the subject of the pain. And since the causal considerations that apply to pain apply in a similar way to other forms of sensuous experience, the conclusion can be genera-lised: each sensuous experience must be identical with a physical event in the subject's body. If this were so, my sensations would not be "objects" to me, in as much as I do not observe them; but they would be observable in principle, even by me. A sensation would then be *something* (*PI* 293, 304), but not a something observation of which grounds self-ascription of the sensation. My self-ascriptions of sensuous experiences would be a form of sensitivity to the presence within me of something – something that has the property of being a sensuous experience of some kind or other; but the sensitivity, as far as my uninformed awareness of it reveals it to me, would be brute: I would not be conscious of how I know when to say that I am in pain, that I can see the colour red, and so on, in the sense that I would not be conscious of the causal mechanism that mediates between the sensuous experience and my consciousness of its presence within me. And the criterionless self-ascription of sensuous experiences would conform to this pattern: my self-ascription of S is a judgement or the verbal expression of a judgement that I am experiencing S; at a certain time I make or express such a judgement; I do not use any method to find out what is happening to me that would provide me with a reason to accept the judgement or that would support the judgement; a physical event that is identical with the instance of S in question causes the judgement and/or its expression (as well as the natural expressions of the experience). As soon as we abandon the concep-tion of sensuous experiences as the private objects of internal observation, we become free to conceive of them as physical events that occur in our bodies and that, although not observed by us, cause us to have beliefs – beliefs that are caused in a manner unmediated by perceptual experience – beliefs that are expressible in sentences of the form 'I am in pain', 'I can see the colour red', and so on.

Now it is hard to understand how the inherent suitability of sensuous experiences to play a causal role in the production of behaviour could be accommodated by Wittgenstein in any other way than by regarding them as being physical events in people's bodies – for he would have rejected recourse to Cartesian non-physical events as possible sources of the natural expressions of sensuous experiences and of our self-ascriptions of sensuous experiences. But whatever the merits of this suggestion, it is clear that Wittgenstein would not have accepted it. The suggestion that each pain must be a physical event in a creature's body derives, basically, from the thought that a pain causes the bodily movements in which it is manifested; but the train of thought I have developed has built into it a thesis that is specifically a thesis about the self-ascription of pain. Now the nature of the capacity to self-ascribe pain – what a correct understanding of this requires, and how we are inclined to misrepresent this to ourselves in false pictures that we conjure up when we are bewitched by our language – is one of the leading motives of Wittgenstein's investigation of the philosophical problem of sensation. If he had believed that the capacity to self-ascribe pain must be thought of as being founded in a causal mechanism, whereby a physical event in the body, the occurrence of which is required to make a self-ascription true, produces the inclination to self-ascribe pain, there would surely be some trace of this view in his various investigations of the concept of pain. But there is no such trace; and there is good reason why we should expect there to be no evidence of this kind of view in Wittgenstein's work. For although the postulation of a causal connection between a pain and the subject's self-ascription of that pain is compatible with the criterionless nature of the self-ascription of pain, the view that pains are events capable of causing self-ascriptions of pain is incompatible with the view, embraced by Wittgenstein, that it is senseless to suppose that someone might wonder whether he was in pain or be in error as to the fact of the matter. (*PI* 246, 288, 408) This can be demonstrated in the following manner. If a causal mechanism subserves the self-ascription of pain, so that whenever someone truly self-ascribes pain a physical event in his body, identical with his pain, sets in motion a causal mechanism that produces his self-ascription, it must be possible for this mechanism to malfunction. One way in which it might malfunction would be this: an event that would have produced a true self-ascription of pain if the mechanism had operated normally fails to produce any self-ascription at all. Since this event differs from an event that is a pain only in a respect that is inessential to an event's being a pain, it is not disqualified from being a pain by its lacking the property of causing a self-ascription of pain.[12] Accordingly, someone who understands 'pain' might properly wonder whether he is in pain, even though he has no inclination to self-ascribe pain. Another way in which the mechanism might malfunction would be this: the mechanism generates a self-ascription of pain although it has not been set in motion by an appropriate event. And this makes possible a situation in which someone is in error in believing himself to be in pain. Hence, Wittgenstein was not in a position to accept this view of the self-ascription of pain.

The train of thought I sketched insists that the natural expressions of a pain, and also the self-ascription of that pain, are caused by the pain; and it then argues that there is no viable alternative to thinking of this pain as being a physical event that occurs in the subject's body. Now we have already seen

---

[12] It is not of the essence of pain that it should cause a judgement in which it is self-ascribed – witness animals that experience pain and yet do not self-ascribe pain. And since the case involves only a malfunction of the mechanism that produces a self-ascription of pain, there is no ground for denying the person a perfect grasp of the concept of pain.

that Wittgenstein would have rejected the view that the concept of the self-ascription of pain requires us to think of a pain that is self-ascribed as being an event in the subject's body that causes the self-ascription. But would he have accepted the view that it is a requirement of the language-game played with the word 'pain' that each pain is identical with a physical event in the body of the person who experiences the pain? Did he believe that it is implicit in the concept of pain that on each occasion on which someone experiences pain a physical event must take place in his body with which that pain can be identified (or is in some way associated)? I believe that the answer to these questions is "No", and that Wittgenstein's reason for giving this answer gave him a further reason to reject the account of self-ascription we have considered.

It would have been entirely out of character for Wittgenstein to have believed that a language-game places a requirement of this kind on what happens inside people's bodies: it would have been foreign to his conception of the autonomy of language-games to have thought that when someone experiences a pain and this is manifested in the natural expressions of pain these natural expressions *must* be caused by a physical event in the person's body that possesses the properties the pain has. And I believe that this conception of language-games explains why he did not insist that the language-game in which 'pain' is used – and in particular the self-ascription of pain – presupposes that each pain is identical with a physical event in the sufferer's body; and why in his consideration of the concept of pain he emphasises the manifest causes of pain, the primitive natural expressions of pain, and various other manifestations of pain in people's behaviour. When Wittgenstein, in his discussion of "reading", maintains

> But in the case of the living reading-machine "reading" meant reacting to written signs in such-and-such ways. This concept was therefore quite independent of that of a mental or other mechanism. (*PI* 157: cf., *BB* pp. 120–1)

he appears to be expressing a certain conceptual thesis.[13] This thesis claims that if the criteria for the application of 'W' to something can be known to obtain without finding out that a certain proposition is true of that thing, the fact that 'W' applies to something does not require that that proposition should be true of that thing: the concept signified by 'W' is quite independent of the proposition in question. Since the criteria for the application of 'pain' to someone, and the criteria for someone to possess the capacity to ascribe pain to himself, can be known to obtain without finding out that a

---

[13] For further discussion of Wittgenstein's attitude to the concept of "reading" and to other related concepts, see my "Wittgenstein on Meaning, Interpretation and Rules", *Synthese* 58 (1984).

physical event occurs in the person's body that causes the behavioural manifestations of the pain and the person's readiness to self-ascribe pain, if we were to accept this thesis we would believe that neither the concept of pain nor the concept of the self-ascription of pain imposes the requirement that when someone experiences pain a physical event must occur in his body and cause whatever issues from his pain. Consequently, Wittgenstein's adoption of the conception of language-games articulated by this thesis would be a sufficient explanation of the fact that he does not insist that the occurrence of each pain requires a corresponding or identical physical event in the sufferer's body. And it would account for his not requiring that the explanation of a person's being able to acquire the capacity to self-ascribe pain – a capacity that someone has only if there is a general coincidence of his inclination to behave in ways that are indicative of his being in pain with his readiness to judge that he is in pain – must reside in the fact that when the person is in pain a physical event that causes the non-verbal behaviour that issues from the pain also causes the person's judgement that he is in pain. And it would also account for the flavour of behaviourism that is detectible in his examination of the concept of pain and other concepts of sensuous experiences. For his rejection of the Cartesian immaterial event and his refusal to acknowledge the necessity for an internal physical event to bring about the effects of a sensuous experience would preclude him from doing justice to the causality that is an integral element in our understanding of sensuous experience.[14]

*University College, London*

[14] A previous version of this paper was read to a graduate seminar on Wittgenstein given by Colin McGinn and myself at University College, London in the summer of 1982. I am grateful to Leslie Stevenson for his helpful comments on an earlier draft.

# KNOWING WHAT WE THINK

## By William Charlton

### I

Knowing what we think includes knowing not only what we know or believe to be true or false, but what we desire or are averse to, what we wonder, what we are glad of or regret – and no doubt the list could be extended. I shall concentrate on belief, desire and aversion, but I hope that my remarks will shed light on other modes of thought as well.

Descartes held that all thought is conscious. For reasons which will appear I am unwilling to go so far as that, but certainly some thought is conscious. Sometimes we know what we believe or want. We can know this, moreover, not by hearsay – as we might know we are secreting adrenalin, nor by perception – as we might know we are bleeding all over the carpet, nor by inference from things perceived – as we might know we are giving off an offensive odour. Some philosophers have seemed to deny there is such a thing as introspection, and others have protested that such a denial is perverse. It is indeed perverse to deny that we sometimes know our beliefs and desires by introspection if that simply means we know them without knowing them in any of the ways just mentioned. But the question then remains: how do we know them?

Or does that question remain? There are passages in the *Philosophical Investigations* in which Wittgenstein seems to be arguing that we cannot ask how we know what sensations we are experiencing because we do not, strictly speaking, *know* what sensations we are experiencing at all: may not the same arguments apply to beliefs and desires? Not all readers have been convinced that it is nonsense to talk of knowing what sensations we are experiencing. But even if Wittgenstein does succeed in showing this, his arguments can be extended to beliefs and desires only if beliefs and desires are like sensations. This has actually been held by some philosophers, for instance Russell. According to *The Analysis of Mind*, if I believe that there are crocodiles in the Nile, there are three items in my mind, a picture of crocodiles in the Nile, a sensation of assent, and a relation subsisting between the picture and the sensation, namely that of being assented to.[1] I know that I think there are crocodiles in the Nile through being aware of these items in just the sort of way in which I am aware of sensations of pain,

[1] Bertrand Russell, *The Analysis of Mind* (London, 1921), ch. XII, p. 251.

nausea and giddiness.[2] It seems to me very doubtful, however, that belief and desire are sensations in the way Russell suggests – I shall discuss his theory of desire below. Rather than linger, then, on arguments to show that the question 'How do we know what we think?' is unanswerable, I turn to answers that have in fact been given.

Locke says we know our thoughts by a capacity which:

> though it be not sense, as having nothing to do with external objects, yet it is very like it, and might properly enough be called "internal sense".[3]

Our knowlege of our beliefs and desires should be conceived on the model of our knowledge of the perceptible properties (and perhaps especially the visible properties) of objects we perceive. It is this view, not just that there is such a thing as introspection, but that it should be conceived on the model of seeing and hearing, which some followers of Ryle have wished to deny, and which D. M. Armstrong and D. H. Mellor, among others, wish to defend. I call this the "inner sense theory".

In "Conscious Belief"[4] Mellor says that the inner sense (which he calls "insight") resembles sight and hearing in the following ways: (1) It delivers not only "perceptions", sc. of our beliefs, but also "sensations", e.g. feelings of conviction; (2) We can develop it, get better at telling what we think and want; (3) Up to a point, at least, we can decide what to attend to with it; (4) But just as we cannot decide what colours we shall see, so we cannot decide what beliefs and desires we shall find we have. Of these points the fourth seems to me to require substantial modification in a way I shall indicate below; and the support for the inner sense theory provided by the first three seems slender in view of the objections to that theory.

Of these perhaps the most obvious is that there is no *organ* of inner sense. Suppose that instead of saying that we know what we think by inner sense, someone said we know because we are told by truthful spirits. We read of people who claim that all the actions they do, they do because they are told to do them by spirits; why not claim that all the thoughts we think we have, we think we have because we are told we have them by spirits? If someone claimed this we might wish to ask "How do the spirits tell us? Do they send written messages, or whisper in the ear, or what?" But just the same questions can be asked about the inner sense: how does it make the "deliveries" Mellor says it makes? Armstrong, as a professed materialist, would say that there are no spirits; but he also concedes that "there seems to be no sense-organ, no internal apparatus, to be manipulated in order to yield

---

[2] *Ibid.*, ch. VI.
[3] John Locke, *An Essay Concerning Human Understanding* II.i.4.
[4] *Aristotelian Society Proceedings* 78 (1977–8), pp.87–101.

introspective awareness".⁵ He adds that in spite of this "the materialist, at least, will assume that there are mechanisms". Why, then, should not the spiritualist assume that there are mechanisms?

In *A Materialist Theory of Mind*, Ch. 15, (a chapter to which Mellor refers us,) Armstrong says that introspection is a "self-scanning process".⁶ He gives no details, but he seems to think that it is merely a contingent fact that things inside the skull are not as follows. There is an area A of the brain consisting of tiny electric light bulbs, like those screens of light bulbs they have on motorways to advise maximum speeds. When and only when a person has a thought, a sentence expressing that thought lights up in area A. There is also a bit of brain B on a flexible and retractable stalk. This moves over A in a manner partly, though not entirely, corresponding to our desires to know what we are thinking. There is a lens in B, and light passing through it is projected onto a light-sensitive screen behind it, like the retina of the eye. We are aware of thoughts when and only when sentences expressing them are projected onto this screen in B. Inner sense theorists might ask: (a) If things were like this, would it not be reasonable to say that we know our thoughts by an inner sense? (b) Since it is merely contingent that things are not like this, may we not conceive our knowledge of our thoughts on the model of seeing and hearing? Mellor tells us flatly that the "mechanism" of inner sense "is in the brain. Whether it is in some definite part of the brain is a moot point, but a trifling one".

I am not sure that the point is trifling. If a person (either human or visiting from another planet) seemed to know the colour of things around him, but had no eyes or other organs sensitive to light, I should hesitate to say that it is by means of a sense that he is aware of the colours. Hence I am not sure I should answer "yes" to question (b) even if I answered "yes" to (a). But of course my answer to (a) would be "no". I know what thoughts *you* have, for the most part, because you tell me, either in your letters or in spoken words. When that happens a sentence expressing your thought is projected onto my retina, or reproduced in my inner ear. But I do not say that I know your thoughts by the sense of sight or hearing. By those senses I am aware, at best, only of sentences expressing your thoughts. Why then, if my brain were equipped with parts A and B, should I say that I know my own thoughts by a sense of which B is the organ?

"Because", an inner sense theorist might reply, "the lighting up of the sentences would actually *be* the thinking". Certainly the question whether it is by a sense that we are aware of our thoughts is more philosophical than neurological, and a critic of the inner sense theory may be invited to show

⁵ D. M. Armstrong and Norman Malcolm, *Consciousness and Causality* (Oxford, 1984), p. 112.
⁶ D. M. Armstrong, *A Materialist Theory of Mind* (London, 1968), p. 324.

that beliefs and desires are not the sort of things of which we conceivably could be aware by a sense. Philosophers have often been tempted to conceive thinking as a mode of speech or representation. Thinking that there is a bird in the bush is having a mental picture of a bird in the bush, and thinking that the bush is birdless is having the same picture with the caption 'This is *not* how things are'. Or if this seems too crude, thought is conceived as a kind of reflection of the world, like the reflection of water on the ceiling of a room overlooking a river, or a kind of emanation from the brain, like a mist rising from a marsh and assuming a succession of naturalistic shapes. Pictures, sentences, reflections and emanations are indeed things which can be apprehended by a sense. But believing, wondering, desiring and the like seem to be *modes* of apprehension, *ways* of being aware. This paper starts from the assumption that they are also in some way *objects* of awareness; but it is still difficult to believe that any outer object of perceptual awareness like a picture or a reflection will serve as a model by which we can conceive what it is to be aware of such an object.

Some time ago, R. B. Braithwaite proposed that we define belief roughly as follows:[7]

> *A* believes that $p$ = *A* entertains the proposition that $p$, and *A* is disposed to do what would be good or right if $p$.

Russell considers a similar account in *The Analysis of Mind*, ch. 12, and makes two objections. One is that we can have a belief which is completely unrelated to action, "which merely occurs in 'thinking'". Russell is hesitant about pressing this, and I think that apparent cases can be explained away. The second is that if entertaining a proposition does not issue in action whereas believing the same proposition does, there must be more to believing it than just entertaining it. Braithwaite's reply to this seems to me weak; but the objection disappears and his account is improved if we suppose that there is no such mental activity as entertaining propositions, no such thing, that is, as Descartes' *perceptio* or Hume's "reflecting simply".[8] We can then say:

> *A* believes that $p$ = for some action $\phi$ing, either for reason that $p$, *A* $\phi$s, or for the reason that $p$, *A* abstains from $\phi$ing.

This definition, like Braithwaite's, is intended to apply primarily to actual beliefs about the physical world, not to dispositional beliefs or beliefs about numbers, virtues or the validity of forms of reasoning. It needs modification to allow for the case where I believe that $p$ but act, not for the reason that $p$,

---

[7] "The Nature of Believing", *Aristotelian Society Proceedings* XXXIII (1932–3), pp. 129–46.
[8] Descartes, *Principles*, I.32; Hume, *Treatise*, I.ii.6.

but in spite of the fact that $p$. It also needs to be supported by positive argument, particularly as some people may wish to say that acting for the reason that $p$ presupposes, and cannot therefore constitute, believing that $p$. But I do not think I have to supply that argument here. Mellor allows that an account of belief like the one just proposed, an "action" account as he calls it, is basically correct.[9] Moreover, in what follows I need not hold that having the circumstance that $p$ function as a reason exhausts believing that $p$, but merely that it is an essential part of it, i.e. that belief is logically inseparable from action. I indicate two lines of reasoning to this less austere conclusion.

First, there is no way of dating beliefs except by the thinker's behaviour. *When* do I believe that your birthday is June 22nd? The question is not about the moment when I first learnt this or the period for which I believe it dispositionally, but about when I actually think it. I actually think it when I act accordingly. We cannot easily explain what we mean by "actually think-ing" as contrasted with "dispositionally believing" unless we speak of the belief as *operative*, and for it to be operative is for it to function as a reason.

But does not $A$ actually think that $p$ if he says that $p$ either to his friends or to himself? And may he not know (by inner sense or in some other way) that he is saying that $p$ to himself? However, saying, even sincere saying, does not imply believing but at best thinking you believe. In the eighteenth century many people said it would be better to have the Stuarts back, and thought they believed this, but their actions are good evidence that they did not. This brings me to my second point. How can anyone else know, how can I myself know, that I believe that $p$ rather than that not-$p$, or *vice versa*? How do I know that I think my car is *not* in the garage? If mental imagery plays any part, I may have the same imagery – a picture of my car standing in the garage – whether I believe it true or false that my car is there. I believe my car is *not* in the garage if I ask where it is, report it to have been stolen, do not, in order to get to places accessible by car, go to my garage, or the like (and have no reason for pretending my car is not there).

According to *The Analysis of Mind* ch. 3, a desire for an outcome $e$ is a feeling which is removed by $e$ and which causes action leading to its removal; Russell is undecided whether it has to have any intrinsic property of unpleasantness apart from this causal property. On this view if, for example, I want my daughter to marry George, I can be aware of the desire itself in the sort of way in which I am aware of bodily sensations, but to know what it is that I desire I must know what will remove this feeling (and know also, presumably, that it is causing me to act); and I know this by experience, induction or lucky guessing. Now it may be only by inference from my actual behaviour that I know of certain suppressed or long-term desires like a

[9] Op. cit. p. 88.

desire to sleep with my mother or a preference for quiet domesticity over power and fame. But surely we know some of our short-term desires not by inference or by reading Freud, but directly. Furthermore it is not clear that Russell can distinguish desire from aversion. My aversion to my daughter's marrying George presumably causes me to act; my action may result in just what I wished to prevent; and my feeling of aversion may evaporate when the worst has happened. It is true that our actions do not usually result in the opposite of what we want. Hume, however, says it is just a contingent fact about our makeup that the feeling of love is not regularly attended by a desire to harm.[10] Why, on Russell's showing, should not the feeling we now count as aversion to a certain outcome, regularly cause behaviour leading to that outcome, and the feeling we count as desire for it, regularly cause us to prevent it?

For these and other reasons I favour an account of desire similar to the account just offered of belief:

> $A$ desires that $B$ should become $f$ = for some action $\phi$ing, either in order that $B$ may become $f$, $A$ $\phi$s; or lest $B$ should not become $f$, $A$ abstains from $\phi$ing.

This definition, like the action definition of belief, is stronger than is required for my purposes here: it is enough if having $fB$ function as a purpose is part of what it is to desire $fB$. I may add that neither account implies anything about whether action which is for a reason or purpose can also be caused, rendered inevitable, by action on the agent. Jonathan Bennett[11] offers action accounts of belief and desire which up to a point are like mine. Beliefs must be reflected in behaviour, and what I desire (Bennett prefers the word 'intend' to 'desire') must function as a goal of my behaviour. But he also maintains that it is part of thinking that I believe or desire something to think that the relevant behaviour *is* causally explainable. This is a further thesis on which I express no opinion here.

The admission that action accounts of belief and desire are substantially sound is fatal to the inner sense theory. For to think that someone else believes that $p$ will be to understand his behaviour as being for the reason that (or despite the fact that) $p$. To think that I myself have a specific belief or desire will be to understand my own behaviour in this way. And understanding pertains to the intellect, not to the senses. The theory that we are aware of our beliefs and desires by a kind of inner sense goes with the idea that phrases of the form 'believes that $p$', 'desires $fB$', signify one-place predicates

---

[10] David Hume, *A Treatise of Human Nature*, II.ii.6, ed. C. A. Selby-Bigge (Oxford, 1888) p. 368.

[11] J. Bennett, *Linguistic Behaviour*, (Cambridge, 1976), chapters II–III.

or exemplifiable properties just as do 'is spherical' and 'is two feet long'. Once this idea is discarded, the inner sense theory becomes quite unrealistic.

## II

What, then, can we put in its place? How *do* I know what I think? Before postulating special psychological machinery of the *virtus dormitiva* type ("There is in us a capacity the nature of which is to tell us what we think"), we should see if this puzzling kind of knowledge is not conceived as inherent in some mode of thinking which is less problematic. Instead of assuming that being aware of beliefs and desires is being aware in an ordinary way of special objects, sc. mental activities or states, we should see if it is not being aware in a special way of ordinary objects.

Consciousness of thought needs to be seen in contrast to unconscious believing and wanting. If it is correct to say that my cat does not leave a certain spot because that spot is warm or sunlit, or that it moves in order to get away from a dog or to approach a mouse, then the cat has beliefs and desires of a sort. Does it also have and apply concepts? We find it natural to credit sagacious animals with some rudimentary sortal concepts, but less natural to say they have concepts of properties or spatial relations. But whether or not the cat applies concepts, surely it is not *aware* of any concept it applies or of any part of the content of its thought. For although it may perceive or think that there is a dog ten feet in front of it, we should be reluctant to say it knows what sort of thing it is which stands to it (it believes) in this relationship, or what relationship it is in which (it believes) this individual stands. If $A$ $\phi$s in order that $B$ may become $f$ or for the reason that $C$ is $g$, $B$'s $f$-ness or $C$'s $g$-ness enters into $A$'s thought: but *pace* Descartes this way of coming into thought does not automatically involve consciousness of thought.

I wish to suggest that a person is in some measure conscious of his thought in two kinds of case which, whether or not they are separable in fact, will be described separately in this section and in III. One is the case where he is exercising some kind of know-how. Suppose I know how to swim, or how to speak Turkish, or how to get from Paris to Rome by car, or how to make white sauce. In the first place, I could hardly apply such knowledge unconsciously. A dog, and still more a fish, might swim unconsciously, but a human being who swims must normally have some awareness that he is swimming. Next, awareness that I am applying such know-how must involve, and may be exhausted by, knowledge that I am effecting, or failing to effect, (or preventing or failing to prevent) definite changes. If I am applying knowledge of how to make white sauce, I must know, or at least have some idea or wonder, whether or not I am succeeding. A person can speak or swim without having any single overall purpose; he can swim or chat for fun. But even then he will have short-term purposes. The swimmer will know if he is getting across the current to the far side of the river, the speaker will know if he is asking when his Turkish friend's son is getting married. Being aware that one is exercising a skill often amounts, I think, to no more than being aware one is effecting something one knows how to effect. But, thirdly, this monitoring of the efficacy of one's action must surely involve awareness of the change one is bringing about or the property or relationship one is making something acquire. If I know or hope I am succeeding in making white sauce, I have some idea of the consistency I am imparting to the stuff in the pan. If I fear I am not causing my translation to the far side of the river I know what spatial relationship I am failing to give myself.

I said just now that we hesitate to say animals know what properties and relationships they are giving themselves. The reason, I suggest, is that although we ascribe purpose of a sort to animals, we hesitate to ascribe know-how. Although they can bring about certain changes when they want, they seem not to know how they bring them about, even in the nebulous way in which the unprofessional cook knows how he causes the contents of the pan to thicken (sc. by heating and stirring). On the other hand as soon as an agent can be said to have some idea what he is doing, he must have some consciousness of the content of his thought.

Does this consciousness involve the exercise of any special sense-like capacity? The preceding remarks were intended to fit any kind of technical expertise without restriction. Let us consider however, those kinds which involve coordination of sense-organs with causally active limbs: skills like cooking and driving rather than skills like finding cube roots and composing Greek elegaics. Driving involves coordination of eye, hand and foot; cooks use their feet less than drivers, but they may use their noses more. Now it is part of exercising such a skill to watch for and keep under observation factors relevant to the effectiveness of one's action. The driver watches for traffic lights and other road-users; the cook keeps his sources of heat and the contents of his pans under continuous surveillance. The skilled man is also aware of the position of the limbs he is using. The driver knows that his left hand is down or that his right foot is on the middle pedal. Is he aware of these things in addition to thinking he is making the car turn left, or failing to bring it to a halt? Does the cook have three distinct thoughts, that the gas is low, that his right hand is round the wooden spoon, and that he is making the sauce thicken? I suggest not. Those parts of his body the position of which the skilful man knows are the ones he is using in exercising his skill. His awareness of their position, then, is not separate from his monitoring of the efficacy of his action. And neither is his awareness of the factors relevant to its efficacy. Rather, his awareness of these factors *takes the form of*, or *constitutes*, on the one hand, awareness of the position of the limbs he is using, on the other, a causal appraisal of his success. But that being so, since awareness of the content of his thought is implicit in awareness of succeeding or failing, the only sensory capacities required for it are those required for observing the causally relevant factors: the familiar senses of sight, smell, hearing etc. Awareness of the position of his limbs and of the properties or relations which (he believes) he is causing things to acquire is a special, skilful application of these ordinary senses.

Other writers too connect knowledge of our thoughts with knowledge of the position of our limbs. But Armstrong connects them in a very different way. He thinks the driver knows the position of his hands and feet by a special sense called "proprioception", which depends on certain physiological hardware, such as Eustachian canals and receptors in the joints, in the way in which sight depends on the eye and hearing on the inner parts of the ear.[12] If a motorist sees a lorry emerge from a side-street and knows that his foot descends on the brake-pedal then he is aware (Armstrong would say) of two independent objects by two independent senses, the lorry by sight and the foot by proprioception. Taking this line, Armstrong can go on to model inner sense on proprioception: if the motorist is also aware of *seeing* the lorry and of *being averse* to hitting it, these are further objects of which he is aware by his further, self-scanning sense.

If the motorist is listening to an oboe concerto on his cassette-player, then the emergence of the lorry and the entry of the oboe are indeed separate objects of which he is aware by separate senses. But to assimilate to this his awareness on the one hand of other road-users and on the other of his hands and feet, is quite unrealistic. The driver *coordinates* hand and eye; his driving and his listening to the concerto are not coordinated but merely parallel. No doubt he would not be aware of the position of his limbs if he did not have the Armstrongian hardware. But it does not follow that the receptors in his joints play the same sort of role as eyes and ears: their role may be more like that of nerves and tendons. Without nerves and tendons I could not brake or swerve. Learning to drive is learning a new way of using these nerves and tendons, even though I may not know I have them. It is also, no doubt, learning a new way of using the receptors. But the receptors are used in driving, and it is rather because he can drive that the motorist knows the position of his feet than the other way round.

That sounds paradoxical. We are strongly inclined to assume that to be able to brake I must know where my feet are. Now I can, of course, know where my feet are independently of exercising any skill which involves using them. I may see where they are, or be told by someone else, or I may infer

---

[12] *Consciousness and Causality*, pp. 110–12.

their position from something else I perceive. But the kind of direct knowledge of the position of our limbs which is of greatest philosophical interest, (and which Elizabeth Anscombe probably had chiefly in mind when, in *Intention* and elsewhere, she spoke of "knowledge without observation"), seems to me inseparable from the skilful use of those limbs. The most elementary case, perhaps, is the use to avoid pain. A cat – I have to thank my colleague Mr. G. Midgley for the example – can be said to have some knowledge of the position of its tail, if it knows how to move its tail when there is danger of someone treading on it, and it exercises this knowledge. But if this is right, learning to use a limb does not presuppose being able to tell where it is; it is learning a new way of telling this. Nijinsky knows the position of his limbs better than a hobbledehoy.

If we try to make the skilled man's awareness of the limbs he is using and the change he is effecting something over and above his awareness of the objects he perceives around him, we shall find it hard to give a satisfactory account of the latter awareness. We cannot say that the driver's mental life is a succession of awareness of particular things, the position of this lorry, the swerve of that cyclist and so on. For there is no definite number of such objects of awareness. The driver has neither a finite nor an infinite series of thoughts of the form "$A$ is $f$" or "$A$ is $r$ to $B$". He is more or less continuously aware of a continuous (though shifting and not too sharply demarcated) causally relevant field. But what, then, holds this awareness together, and entitles us to say that he is aware of anything at all? The monitoring, surely, of the efficacy of his action, which renders his use of his sense-organs an exercise of know-how.

Our causal understanding probably starts with understanding changes we are ourselves effecting; but it does not stop there. If the cook is aware of the content of his thought in thinking that he is causing the sausages to become brown, the gardener will be aware of the content of his thought in thinking the sun is causing the tomatoes to turn red. And that being so, he will be aware of it in thinking that the tomatoes *are becoming* red. For to think that – or so I have argued elsewhere[13] – is to think something is making them red. If I am right about this matter, then whereas thinking that an object *has* a property need not involve knowing what property is coming into one's mind, thinking it is *acquiring* a property must. Hence a remark of the form "$A$ thinks $B$ is becoming $f$" may be construed as a report, not of an applying by $A$ to $B$ of a novel concept, that of becoming $f$, but as $A$'s awareness of a familiar concept, that of $f$-ness, which he is applying.

One further point before I leave the subject of causal understanding. I have argued that it involves some awareness of what one is thinking; but this awareness need not itself be conscious. I can know *what* I think is being

[13] W. Charlton "Causation and Change", *Philosophy* 58 (1983) pp. 154–60.

effected without knowing *that I think* it is being effected. The gardener can
know what colour is entering his thought without knowing that this colour is
entering it. The changes we think we are causing or preventing in the cases I
have been considering (cases where our judgement is not based on hearsay
or inference but is direct) are changes which we want to cause or prevent,
and it is questionable whether a change ever appears in our thought as a
causal *explanandum* if we are totally indifferent to it. But that being so, to be
conscious of our awareness of it we should be conscious of our desire for it
or our aversion to it. But to know that I desire the tomato, say, to become
red, is to go beyond causal understanding of its change of colour to a
teleological understanding of my behaviour.

Someone might, perhaps, insist that it is quite possible to think causally
about changes to which we are indifferent. But it is a consequence of action
accounts of thinking that any consciousness of thinking must involve teleological and not merely causal understanding. I come here to the second of
the two sorts of case I wish to discuss.


## III

According to our action accounts, believing that $p$ involves having the
supposed circumstance that $p$ function as a reason, and wanting $B$ to become
$f$ involves having $fB$ function as a purpose. It follows that if $A$ is aware of
believing that $p$ he is aware that this circumstance is functioning with him as
a reason; there is some action or inaction on his part that he understands as
being for the reason that $p$. If he is aware of desiring $B$ to become $f$, he
understands some behaviour of his as being for this purpose. The question,
then, 'How are we aware of our beliefs and desires?' becomes the question
'How do we understand our behaviour as being for a reason or purpose?' For
the present discussion it will be sufficient to concentrate on beliefs and
reasons – I think it could be argued that we know what we want, or what we
are trying to do, through knowing our reasons for action.

How, then, can I think that it is for the reason that $p$ that I am $\phi$ing? I must
be aware of the circumstance that $p$ as a reason. But if for the reason that it is
sunny I go out, I am aware of the sunshine as a reason in some way, yet I
need not (any more than a sun-loving cat) understand my behaviour or be
conscious of knowing that the sun is shining. For that I must be aware of the
sunshine as a reason in a further way.

I can be aware of a circumstance as a reason for action or inaction to
someone else. I can think of the sunshine as a reason for action or inaction to
you. I do that if I think that it is for the reason that the sun is shining that you
are going out. But what is it to think that? What is it for me to understand
someone else's behaviour teleologically? I do not think such understanding

can occur *in vacuo*, independently of any practical concerns I may have, or even independently of any friendly or hostile interest I may have in the person I am understanding. The historian's understanding of persons long dead, like the reader's understanding of people in novels, presents special problems; but I suspect that to say '*A* thought that it was for the reason that *p* that *B* was $\phi$ing' is generally to explain some benevolent or malignant action or desire on *A*'s part. However that may be, it is plain that thinking of a circumstance as a reason to a person is often acting *in order that* it may function (or, in the less standard case, that it may not function) as a reason with him. I may draw your attention to the sunshine as a reason for going out. I may remove an impediment to your going out because of it. Or, if I am malignant, I may make it hard for you to go out although it is sunny. In any such case my behaviour is intelligible only on the supposition that I am aware of a circumstance as a reason to you of which you are, or would do well to be, aware.

Similarly your behaviour can be intelligible only on the supposition that you are aware of something as a reason to a third party. That being so, to understand your behaviour I may have to realise that you are aware of some circumstance as an object of awareness to *me*: that you are acting, say, to make me aware of it. I suggest that this is how we first become conscious of ourselves, not as causal agents effecting changes in our surroundings, but as persons with beliefs and desires. Children realise that their parents regard them as persons. And this is also how we first become conscious of our beliefs and desires. The child becomes aware that it is averse (or that it is not averse) to the becoming muddy of its clothes when it understands that its parents are acting in order that it may prevent (or be careful not to cause) this change. I am aware of the sunshine as a reason in the further way we were seeking when I understand that you are acting to make me act because of it.

In the past, philosophers have imagined that we first, on the basis of inner sense, apply the notion of a person to ourselves, and that we later extend it to others only because their observed behaviour suggests they are like us. Although few adhere to this view today, many might still shrink from what I am proposing in its place, namely that one first applies the notion of a person with beliefs and desires to others, and later extends it to oneself because they seem to treat one as a person too. Yet this view is not without advantages.

One is that it enables us to see how awareness of oneself as a person could arise in a community. A child could get the idea of a person from its parents, even if they were not aware of themselves as persons. Language, at least on the Grice-Bennett view, involves consciousness. If I am to declare (or "non-naturally mean") that there is a snake nearby, I must not merely act in order that this circumstance may function as a reason with you. I must rely for success in this project on your divining that my performance has this purpose. This involves not just thinking of you as a purposive agent, but thinking of you as thinking of me as one. On the view I am proposing, parents could try to make their children aware of reasons, and children could teach their parents to speak.

An advantage which is more important for the present discussion is that our knowlege of our thoughts can be seen as the result less of discovery than of decision. Locke and Hume would have us "turn our reflection within our own breasts" and find we have desires or aversions, as we might turn our eyes upon our chests and find we have hairs or spots. On the view I am recommending, little Sebastian becomes aware of the becoming muddy of his clothes as an object of aversion to himself through understanding that others are acting in order that it may play this role in his behaviour: they want it to be one of the things he abstains from pleasurable action in order not to cause. But Sebastian then decides whether to give it this role or not. The virtue of consideration which parents particularly want to instil into their children is a disposition to be aware of circumstances as having practical significance for others. Mellor says we cannot decide what beliefs we shall find we have. It may be that I cannot decide whether I shall believe it true or false that there is a Mozart concert next Wednesday. Our powers of self-deception, however, are considerable, and I may be able to persuade myself that my wife would just as soon entertain my dull sister and her family as listen to Mozart; I can also decide up to a point whether or not to be aware of what concerts are in prospect when I am committing my wife to social engagements.

I am suggesting that we first become aware of ourselves as persons through realising that others want us to act for reasons. It does not follow that we can never be conscious of thinking that $p$ unless we think that someone else is trying to make us aware that $p$. Once I have learnt to think of myself as a person I can think of a circumstance as one I wish *myself* to be aware of, and proceed to act in order that it may function with me as a reason. Suppose I have drunk a whole bottle of wine. I might want myself to bear this in mind and abstain from driving because of it. In this particular case I might act as my own mentor: I might mutter "You mustn't drive, you sot, you've drunk a whole bottle". But whenever I am conscious of my reasons and purpose I act at least partly in order that I may act for these reasons and purposes. That is what it is to act on principle. It is to act because the circumstances make it right so to act, and at least partly in order to be the kind of person to whom these circumstances are reasons for this action or these desires. I am conscious, then, of believing that the pool contains crocodiles if I abstain from swimming not merely lest I be eaten, but in order to behave prudently and to abstain from bathing in pools which are crocodile-infested. My consciousness is not a mental episode distinct from behaviour. I am conscious of my belief in understanding my inaction, and I understand it in being inactive deliberately. Neither does my consciousness involve awareness of any special mental phenomena. To abstain deliberately from bathing I do not have to be aware of anything over and above the crocodiles. It is enough to be aware of their presence in a special way, as a factor which renders bathing not merely dangerous but foolhardy and irresponsible, and renders abstinence from bathing conduct befitting the person I wish to be.

"No doubt" it may be objected, "if you know that it is because there are crocodiles that you are unwilling to plunge in, you know that you think there are crocodiles. But you also know that you think countless other things: that $2^5 = 32$, that Caesar died in 44 BC, that Mars has two moons: where is the understanding and the moral responsibility in that?" These examples present a difficulty primarily for the action theory of belief. It is only because believing these things does not, at first, seem to involve action, that knowing we believe them seems independent of understanding action. I think that the action theory can cope with these examples, but I shall not argue the point further here.

My account requires a distinction between acting merely for a reason ($\phi$ing because $p$) and acting for the same reason on principle ($\phi$ing because $p$, and because that $p$ is a reason for $\phi$ing). It may be hard to decide in practice which explanation fits someone's behaviour, but the distinction is not one we can afford to discard. It was for the reason that she was handsome and available that Aeneas made love to Dido.[14] But the pious founder of Rome would never have subscribed to the principle that a foreign queen's being handsome and available is a sufficient reason for making love to her. Don Giovanni accepted that principle and worse. But had he been caught in the rain with Dido he might not have done anything noticeably different from Aeneas. How, then, would his behaviour be different? Would he utter his immoral principles to himself under his breath? Unlikely, and anyhow utterance would not be enough: he would have to believe them. We might say that for the infatuated Trojan awareness of Dido's charms simply took the form of a desire to make love to her. I say "took the form" because the relationship of awareness and desire in such a case is not that of cause and effect or premiss and conclusion, but rather of two aspects of a single piece of thinking. The calculating Don, in contrast, is aware of the lady's charms as providing an occasion for the sort of behaviour he considers worthwhile; his awareness takes the form of the judgement that it would be rational to act because of them. We might also say that insofar as one acts on principle, the acting is an end in itself, independently of the outcome. If the Good Samaritan acted on principle he would not consider his efforts wasted even though the victim of the mugging died; if he acted merely out of pity,

[14] Virgil, *Aeneid* I.496 ff., IV.160 ff.

for the reason that the victim was badly injured, perhaps he would. The suggestion I wish to make is that action on principle is differentiated by consciousness of the reasons for it. The Samaritan acts on principle only if he not merely acts because of the victim's plight but is consciously aware of it. (Similarly, of course, with sacrifice of principle, as distinct from mere thoughtlessness.)

It will be seen that I make our consciousness of our thought more restricted than philosophers sometimes suppose it is. Being conscious of thinking that $p$ involves a judgement on how good a reason this circumstance is for some action or inaction. I pointed out earlier that a man exercising a skill like driving is aware of factors relevant to the success of his action. He hardly judges these factors as reasons, and his awareness can hardly be conscious if there is no definite number of them – factors of which he is consciously aware will not be uncountable. But it may be thought that this involves a difficulty. For the skilled man can specify such factors if questioned. If I say to a driver "Why did you slow down a moment ago?" he may reply "Because there was a parked lorry and an on-coming bus". How can he give this answer if he is not aware of the vehicles?

My theory would not be undermined by an admission that the driver *is* conscious of seeing the lorry at the time, even though, unless a question or something else fixes the experience in his mind, he soon forgets it. But I doubt if his answer does prove he was conscious of seeing it. He knows, *ex hypothesi*, not only how to drive, but how to speak. To a motorist a lorry is (*inter alia*) a thing which can obstruct progress and make it necessary to brake by being stationed at the roadside. To a motorist who knows the word 'lorry', a lorry is a thing he can refer to in order to give a reason for slowing down. If, for the reason that there is a lorry, I can slow down, and yet not be conscious of seeing the lorry, then perhaps for the reason that there was a lorry I can say "I slowed because there was a lorry" without having been conscious of seeing the lorry. My answer proves I remember the lorry, but not necessarily that I remember seeing it.

## IV

I have argued that we are conscious of our thought in understanding changes causally, particularly those we are causing ourselves, and in understanding our own behaviour teleologically. These two modes of understanding are not, of course, mutually exclusive. The second normally entails the first. If I know for what reason I am swimming or stirring the contents of the pan, I must have some idea what I am effecting or failing to effect. The converse, however, is doubtful. A child might surely apply know-how and be aware of the change it is effecting without understanding its reasons or being morally responsible.

I have also argued that what we are conscious of in understanding causally is not the same as what we are conscious of in understanding teleologically. In the first case we know what properties and relationships enter into our thought, but it is only in the second that we are aware, strictly speaking, of their entry, and of believing and desire. I conclude by suggesting that consciousness of these two elements in our thought is consciousness of two aspects of ourselves.

It is hardly controversial that a human being is both a causal and a purposive agent. Clearly too we can be aware of ourselves as both, and aware not by observation, hearsay or inference but directly. Philosophers have given more attention to our direct awareness of ourselves as persons with beliefs and desires than to our direct awareness of ourselves as causal agents, but in fact both are puzzling. I said that in understanding causally the changes we are bringing about we are directly aware of the limbs we are using, and this, I suggest, is the elusive awareness of oneself as a causal agent. My direct awareness of myself as a thing which is causing (or failing to cause) some change is normally awareness simply of the part of my body I am using; but if I use the whole of my body, as I might to close the lid of an overfull trunk, I can be said to be aware of the whole of myself as a causal agent.

Knowing for what reason I am acting or refraining from action obviously involves being aware of myself as a person, but does the converse hold? I think so. Descartes says we cannot doubt our existence as persons, but in fact awareness of oneself as a person seems bound up inextricably with understanding what one is doing. I can think that it is *I* who am acting, and think of the action of my limbs as my own, only if I can see *why* I am acting. If a knife grasped by my hand plunges into a stranger, and I can think of no reason for killing this stranger, I say "Something has come over me: this cannot be *me*". And if I cannot see any reason for anything I do, if all my action and inaction is drained of practical significance, I begin to lose my grasp of my identity. We have a kind of knowledge of our identity which is infallible. I can be mistaken about my name or parentage, but I cannot be wrong about who I am in some more intimate way. But this identity which I know without a possibility of error is an identity I give myself. I know which person I am insofar as I decide what sort of person I shall be. If I cease to understand why I am doing what I do (I am envisaging a case not just for sympathy but for psychiatry), I cease to decide this; and then I no longer know who I am except by hearsay.[15]

*University of Newcastle-Upon-Tyne*

[15] I am grateful to the Editors of this issue of the *Philosophical Quarterly* for helpful comments on an earlier version of this paper.

# INCONTINENT BELIEVING

By Alfred R. Mele

'*Akrasia*', the classical Greek term that we translate as 'incontinence', denotes a lack of, or deficiency in, a certain kind of *kratos*, i.e. strength or power. The power in question is the ability to control oneself. This has traditionally been conceived as the power to act as one judges best, or to resist the temptation to act otherwise. But we can meaningfully speak as well of the power to *believe* as one judges best (and we need not conceive of believing as a kind of action). Some people, we say, fail to acquire certain beliefs which they take to be strongly supported by the evidence and better supported than competing propositions, or fail to abandon beliefs which they take to be less well supported than propositions with which the beliefs are epistemically at odds. Indeed, doxastic failures of this sort are commonly supposed to be centrally involved in self-deception, e.g. in the case of the loving, dependent husband who retains his false belief that his wife has always been faithful to him even though he recognizes that the evidence that she has been having an affair is much stronger than the competing evidence. In some such cases, a charge of *akrasia* may be in order: perhaps a *stronger* person would have acknowledged the unpleasant truth of the matter.

In this paper I shall attempt to characterize a central case of incontinent believing and to explain how it is possible. *Akrasia* is exhibited in a variety of ways in the practical or "actional" sphere; but in the full-blown and seemingly most challenging case the akratic agent performs an intentional, free action which is contrary to a judgment of what is better or best to do that he both consciously holds at the time of action and consciously believes to be at odds with his performing the action at issue. More precisely,

> in intentionally and freely *A*-ing at *t*, *S* performs a full-blown akratic action if and only if, at *t*, *S* consciously holds a judgment to the effect that there is good and sufficient reason for his not doing an *A* at *t*.

What I am after in this paper is an account of a comparable, full-blown variety of incontinent *believing*, and an explanation of its possibility.

## I

We say that incontinent action manifests the agent's weakness of will. Perhaps 'weakness' strikes us as too severe a charge in some instances of incontinent action. But in acting incontinently an agent shows at least that he is not perfectly self-controlled at the time. A perfectly self-controlled agent would not permit himself to be mastered by motivation which is at odds with his (all-things-considered) better judgement. Presumably we want to say something similar about incontinent *believing*. If it is *incontinent*, it should manifest some imperfection in the believer's self-control. This is not to suggest that our beliefs are under our direct voluntary control, i.e., that we believe at will. However, belief-acquisition and belief-retention often are subject to our *indirect* control – e.g., our (partial) control over how we gather data in a particular case.

The most detailed analysis of incontinent believing that I have encountered fails precisely because it ignores the weakness to which 'incontinence' refers. This is the analysis developed by John Heil in his otherwise instructive paper, "Doxastic Incontinence".[1] For a formal statement of the account, the reader should consult p. 65 of Heil's paper. The following passage provides a useful illustration of his view – viz. that to believe incontinently is to believe "*in the teeth of* the evidence" (p. 65):

> The incontinent believer is typified by the psychoanalytic patient who has acquired what might be termed an intellectual grasp of his plight, but whose outlook evidently remains unaffected. Such a person has failed somehow to integrate his appreciation of certain facts into his overall psychological state. He continues to harbour beliefs, desires and fears that he recognizes to be at odds with his better epistemic judgment. (p. 69)

I do not doubt that in some such cases beliefs which one recognizes to be at odds with one's better epistemic judgment are *incontinently* harboured. But must this always be so? Suppose that Fred, a psychoanalytic patient, judges that since the truth about certain aspects of his life may be very painful, he is, all things considered, better off holding the unwarranted beliefs that he now has about these things than he would be if he instead believed the propositions best supported by the evidence. Perhaps Fred is properly charged with epistemic irresponsibility for holding these beliefs;[2] but does he hold them incontinently?

Consideration of an analogous case from the practical or "actional" sphere should prove helpful. Suppose that Barney judges that the moral reasons for doing $A$ are better than the moral reasons for doing $B$ (both of which actions he knows to be open to him), but that he nevertheless intentionally does $B$

[1] John Heil, "Doxastic Incontinence", *Mind* 93 (1984), pp. 56–70. See also, Amelie Rorty, "Akratic Believers", *American Philosophical Quarterly* 20 (1983), pp. 175–83; David Pears, *Motivated Irrationality* (Oxford, 1984), ch. 4.

[2] On epistemic irresponsibility, see Hilary Kornblith, "Justified Belief and Epistemically Responsible Action", *Philosophical Review* 92 (1983), pp. 33–48.

(and does not do *A*). From this, we cannot infer that Barney has acted incontinently, for he may have judged that, all things considered, it was better to do *B* than *A*. Even if Barney places appreciable value on moral considerations, he presumably has non-moral values as well; and in some cases he may take moral considerations to be evaluatively overridden by other considerations. Similarly, a person who has epistemic values – who has a pro-attitude towards having only epistemically warranted beliefs – may take these values to be overridden by others in certain cases. Consider, for example, the undergraduate who sincerely states in the final exam for his philosophy of religion course that although he is now convinced that the bulk of the evidence supports the claim that the Christian God does not exist, he still finds himself believing that there is such a God and, what is more, sincerely maintains that, all things considered, it is quite *rational* for him to hold this belief, given that the strong evidence against Christian theism is not entirely conclusive and that he would be unbearably unhappy as an atheist or an agnostic. Such a person believes against his better *epistemic* judgment but in accordance with his better *all-things-considered* judgment. Therefore, although he may, from an epistemic point of view, believe irresponsibly, he does not believe incontinently (on the assumption that the all-things-considered judgment is not itself incontinently held). This point applies to Fred as well. Neither exhibits a deficiency (or imperfection) in *self-control* in believing as he does (unless *akrasia* is manifested in the better judgment itself).

The preceding paragraph suggests that there is, for our purposes, an important difference between the judgment that, all things considered, one's doing *A* is better than one's doing *B* and the judgment that, given all that is relevant to the epistemic warrant of *P* and *Q*, *P* is more warranted than *Q*. A person who holds the latter judgment may consistently judge that, all things considered, his believing *Q* is better than his believing *P*; but an agent who holds the former judgment cannot consistently hold that, all things considered, his doing *B* is better than his doing *A*. The explanation is that considerations of epistemic warrant constitute only a species of value, a species that can be evaluatively overridden, in the believer's opinion, by non-epistemic values.

Heil has, I think, identified an important variety of epistemically irresponsible believing, viz. believing "in the teeth of the evidence", against one's epistemic better judgment. However, such believing does not manifest incontinence if, in the agent's (non-akratically held) opinion, his pertinent epistemic values are evaluatively overridden by nonepistemic values of his. In that event, he no more exhibits *akrasia* than does someone who, in accordance with his all-things-considered better judgment, acts against his better moral judgment.

Two further points should be made in this connection. The first concerns responsibility. Suppose that Betty believes that $P$ is false even though she judges not only that there is much more epistemic warrant for $P$ than for not-$P$ but also that, all things considered, her believing $P$ would be better than her believing not-$P$. Suppose further, however, that she believes not-$P$ during $t$ only because a mad scientist, bypassing Betty's own belief-forming mechanisms, directly implanted this belief in her in such a way that no amount of self-control would enable her to dislodge it during $t$. Here again we do not have doxastic incontinence; for Betty's holding the pertinent belief during $t$ is not, *ex hypothesi*, due to any weakness on her part. Nor even is this case one of epistemic irresponsibility.

This is, to be sure, a highly contrived case; but it does have a point. We need, in a characterization of doxastic incontinence, to pin the responsibility for the crucial belief (at least in significant part) on the believer. Full-blown incontinent *action*, traditionally conceived, is *free* action; and the preceding case points to the necessity of finding a doxastic analogue. An attempt to construct and defend an account of the analogue – what I shall call "free* belief" – would take us too far afield, but a gloss on the notion is in order. As I shall use the term, the *freedom** of a belief during a period of time is a function of the degree and kind of control that the believer or his doxastic mechanisms had, or were capable of having, in the etiology of his holding the belief during the period in question.

The second point is about motivation. As incontinent action is typically conceived, the incontinent agent is defeated by motivation which opposes his better judgment. Standard analyses identify incontinent action as intentional action and therefore do not need to specify as well that it is motivated; for all intentional action is motivated. But the "motivatedness" of incontinent action is one of its defining features. This is true as well of incontinent believing. *How* it is motivated will be discussed in some detail below. *That* it is motivated is a purely conceptual matter. To *be* incontinent (in the pertinent sense) is, by definition, to be deficient in one's capacity to contain or restrain one's desires, feelings, etc.; and incontinent "behaviour", whether actional or doxastic, is a manifestation of this deficiency, or at least of an associated imperfection.[3]

The following characterization of full-blown incontinent belief, modelled after the above account of full-blown incontinent action, accommodates the preceding points and avoids the problems with Heil's analysis:

[3] Even a person who is very self-controlled (e.g., about sexual matters) may, in a particularly trying case, incontinently fail to live up to his pertinent standards. In acting incontinently such a person shows, not that he is *deficient* in respect of self-control, but only that he is less than perfectly self-controlled.

In believing that P during t, S exhibits full-blown doxastic incontinence (*FBDI*) if and only if the belief is motivated and free* and
during t, S consciously holds a judgment to the effect that there is
good and sufficient reason for his not believing that P.

By 'a judgment to the effect . . . ' I mean a judgment that *settles* for S the
matter of whether it is, all things considered, better to believe, or not to
believe, that P. My analysis does not suggest that the judgement violated in
*FBDI* must always, or even usually, be based in part on non-evidential
considerations. Indeed, I would surmise that in typical cases of *FBDI* the
subject takes evidential considerations alone to provide good and sufficient
reason for his not believing P. However, in cases in which the subject
"believes in the teeth of the evidence" but takes considerations of epistemic
or evidential warrant to be overridden by other considerations, my analysis,
unlike Heil's, does not entail that the subject believes incontinently; for in
such cases the subject does not consciously hold a judgment to the effect that
there is good and *sufficient* reason for his not believing that P. I do not wish to
deny that a believer's ranking non-epistemic considerations over epistemic
ones in a particular case may itself exhibit incontinence. However, doxastic
incontinence of this sort is beyond the scope of this paper and the above
analysis. My concern here, again, is with a single *species* of incontinent
believing.

Two points should be clarified before this section is brought to an end.
First, nothing that I have said depends upon the supposition that it is
sometimes *rational* to believe in the teeth of the evidence. Nor do I pretend
to have a formula for weighing epistemic against non-epistemic considerations. It is sufficient for my purposes that we can sometimes *take* our
believing in the teeth of the evidence to be rational (or best, all things
considered).[4] Second, although we expect agents to decide or intend to
perform actions of certain types on the basis of their all-things-considered
practical better judgments, I am not suggesting that people decide or intend
to *believe* certain propositions on the basis of their judgments about what it is
best or better to believe (though they may occasionally decide to *get themselves*
to believe certain things). Believing is not a kind of action. This point is
plainly compatible, however, with its being the case that our judgments about
evidence have an influence upon what we believe; and even judgments about
what it is best, *practically speaking*, to believe may be efficacious – e.g. the
person convinced by Pascal's pragmatic argument for belief in God may, by
conscientiously following the suggested programme, bring it about that he
holds theistic beliefs.

    [4] Interesting arguments for a stronger view are advanced by Jack Meiland in "What Ought
We to Believe?" *American Philosophical Quarterly* 17 (1980), pp. 15–24.

## II

I turn now to the question of the *possibility* of full-blown incontinent believing. I shall start by addressing a general reservation that some readers may have. It may be suggested that '*S* consciously holds a judgment that there is good and sufficient reason for his not believing that *P*' *entails* '*S* does not believe that *P*', so that full-blown incontinent believing is impossible. The underlying assumption would seem to be this: that to judge that there is good and sufficient reason for believing that *P is* to believe that *P* and, similarly, to judge that there is good and sufficient reason for not believing that *P* precludes one's believing that *P*. The assumption paints an attractive picture no doubt, but one that is overly optimistic about human rationality. Heil quite correctly observes (p. 69) that psychoanalytic patients sometimes harbour not only fears that they recognize to be unwarranted, but beliefs as well. And the literature on self-deception is filled with plausible examples of full-blown doxastic incontinence (some of which will be rehearsed below). Surely, we do not want to rule these cases out *a priori*.

In attempting to explain the possibility of full-blown doxastic incontinence it will be useful to distinguish between two cases of the phenomenon. First, there is the case in which the agent's judgment that there is good and sufficient reason for his not believing *P* is based on evidential or epistemic considerations alone.[5] I will call this *narrow incontinent believing*. This is to be contrasted with the case in which the judgment is based on both epistemic and non-epistemic considerations, what I will call *broad incontinent believing*.

That narrow incontinent believing is possible seems clear. Some cases of self-deception are instances of this sort of incontinence. Consider the stock example of the woman who judges, solely on evidential grounds, that there is good and sufficient reason for her believing that her husband is having an affair (and for her not believing that he is not having an affair) but who nevertheless believes, due in part to her wanting it to be the case that he has been faithful to her, that he has not been so engaged.

Broad incontinent believing may be more perplexing, but it too seems quite possible. Consider, e.g., the insecure, jealous husband whose initial suspicion that his wife is having an affair develops into a genuine belief, even though he knows that his evidence that she is being unfaithful is quite weak, that he has much better evidence that she is not having an affair, and that he would be much better off not having the belief in question.

In some cases of incontinent believing, both broad and narrow, an explanation of the possibility of the phenomenon is not far to seek. Brief consideration of an explanation of the possibility of full-blown akratic *action* should

---

[5] Here and hereafter I use 'the agent's judgment that there is good and sufficient reason . . . ' as shorthand for 'a consciously held judgment of the agent to the effect that there is good and sufficient reason . . .'.

prove useful. The better judgments against which akratic agents act are often formed on the basis of their *evaluations* of their reasons for action. But the motivational force of a reason may not be in alignment with the agent's evaluation of that reason (e.g. the motivational force of my want not to experience the pain of having a tooth pulled, or the reason for action in which that want consists, may be radically out of line with the low evaluative ranking that I give that want in judging it best to schedule a dental appointment). Thus, one who judges it best, all things considered, to do an *A*, may be more motivated to perform, and consequently perform, some competing action, *B*.[6]

The condition of at least some incontinent believers is quite similar. It is on the basis of his *evaluation* of (or evaluative attitudes toward) epistemic considerations that the person who exhibits narrow doxastic incontinence judges there to be good and sufficient reason for his not believing that *P*; but items which he takes to provide only weak evidence for *P* may, due to his conative condition, have a great deal of salience at the time at which he forms or acquires a belief about the matter. Because of the attractiveness of what they suggest, the bulk of his attention may be drawn to these items, and his apprehension of competing items may be quite pale by comparison. Since he consciously holds the judgment that there is good and sufficient reason for his not believing that *P*, he is in no position sincerely to justify to us his believing that *P*; indeed our pressing him for justification may well make it difficult for him to retain the belief if we manage to shift the focus of his attention to his reasons for not believing that *P*. But when he forms or acquires the belief that *P*, it presumably is not a concern for justification that is guiding him.

At least some cases of broad incontinent believing admit of the same sort of explanation. Suppose, e.g., that Wilma judges not only that the evidence that her twelve year old son, Basil, has been experimenting with narcotics is very strong and much stronger than the contrary evidence, but also that her believing that he has been doing so is much better supported by non-epistemic considerations than is her not believing this. She thinks that even if the epistemic evidence were significantly weaker it would be best, practically speaking, for her to believe that Basil has been taking drugs, for she fears that in the absence of this belief it would be very easy for her to fail to give him guidance that he may well need. To be sure, Wilma wants it to be false that her beloved Basil has been using drugs and she recognizes that believing that he has been doing so would be very painful for her, but she judges that the pain is outweighed by other practical considerations. Undoubtedly, many more details can be added to the story of Wilma's finally

[6] I develop this line of explanation in "*Akrasia*, Reasons and Causes", *Philosophical Studies* 44 (1983), pp. 345–68.

coming, on the basis of epistemic and non-epistemic considerations, to hold the judgment that there is good and sufficient reason for her not believing that Basil is innocent of drug use. However, let us suppose now, for the sake of brevity, that she does come to hold this judgment but that she nevertheless believes that he has not been using drugs.

Here again the salience of evidential items may properly enter into the explanation of incontinent believing. Because she very much wants it to be the case that Basil has not been experimenting with drugs, Wilma's attention may be drawn at crucial junctures to items suggestive of innocence: "Basil has always been a good little boy. Only a few weeks ago he was happily playing in the sand with his little brother's toy trucks in just the way that he played with his own toys a few short months ago. Can a boy like this be a drug user? He is only a *child*!" Wilma's (all-things-considered) better judgment implies that she should not let herself be swayed by reflections of this sort after having given the evidential items involved due consideration in arriving at her overall epistemic judgment. But it is not hard to understand how, when fondly entertaining a vivid image of her beloved young son playing innocently and happily in the sand, Wilma may not be on her guard against self-deception.

Of course, if this is to be a case of full-blown incontinent believing, Wilma must satisfy the free* belief condition. Now, Wilma's story can be told in such a way that the pertinent belief is unfree*: one can suppose that her attention is *irresistibly* drawn to items suggestive of innocence and that the influence of these items upon her is such as to preclude her having any control whatsoever over what she believes about the matter at hand. However, it surely is not necessary to tell the story in this way. We may coherently suppose that it was within Wilma's power to take measures which would have resulted in her not being unduly swayed by emotively charged images of an innocent Basil – e.g., measures such as forcefully reminding herself at appropriate moments of her low assessment of the evidential merit of the considerations in question while forcing herself to recall, with suitable vividness, memories supportive of the opposite hypothesis.

The previously mentioned case of the insecure, jealous husband seems, at least initially, more problematic. In the case of Wilma, there is on the side of incontinent believing what we might call, with David Pears, a "desirable goal".[7] Although Wilma judges that all things (epistemic and otherwise) considered it is best not to believe that Basil is innocent of drug use, there is still something substantial to be said, from her own point of view, for her believing that he is innocent. There is something significant to be gained by doxastic incontinence, even if this would result (in Wilma's own opinion) in a greater loss. But what does our jealous husband have to gain as a result of

---

[7] Pears, *Motivated Irrationality*, p. 42.

believing that his wife has been unfaithful? If we are at a loss for an answer to this question, we may be hard put to see what *motivates* his belief. And if we cannot get a grip on the motivational issue, can we understand his holding the belief in question? Furthermore, if the belief is not motivated, we do not have incontinence after all.

Pears, in his recent book, *Motivated Irrationality*, has suggested that in cases of the sort in question there is a "wish" for an "ulterior goal", namely, "the elimination of a rival". (p. 44) To be sure, the agent does not construct for himself a practical syllogism starting with a wish to eliminate rivals for his wife's affection and concluding – via a "minor premise" to the effect that his believing that his wife is having an affair would increase his chances of detecting and eliminating rivals – with a desire or decision to form the belief in question. But a subconscious analogue is quite possible; and the postulation of a goal-directed process of this sort does help to make intelligible our jealous husband's acquiring the belief in question.

It may seem that this explanatory retreat to the subconscious makes it difficult to interpret the case of our jealous husband as an instance of full-blown doxastic incontinence. If a subconscious process is operative here, one might think that matters are wholly beyond the agent's control, so that our jealous husband's infidelity-belief is unfree*. Indeed, Pears himself seems to suggest as much: he claims that when the wish for the ulterior goal is present, "nature takes over . . . and sets up an emotional programme that *ensures* its achievement". (p. 44, my emphasis)

This, however, is a stronger line than is called for or even plausible in many cases. Jealousy need not turn an agent into an automaton. A jealous husband may know that he is disposed to make unwarranted inferences where his wife's fidelity is concerned and may attempt to short-circuit the subconscious process in situations in which it seems to him likely to take effect if left unchecked. People may attempt in a variety of ways to resist *acting* contrary to their better judgment – e.g., by vividly representing to themselves the expected harmful consequences of acting on the pertinent competing desires, by picturing the tempting activity or object in a way that makes it unappealing, by refusing to entertain attractive images of the offending desire's object while focusing their attention instead on their reasons for not letting themselves be swayed by the desire.[8] Similarly, a jealous man, upon first entertaining the suspicion that his wife is having an affair, might try to circumvent the pull of subconscious forces by going to the woman at once for reassurance, or by relating to friends his suspicion and the flimsy grounds on which it rests, with a view to generating salient support for the fidelity-hypothesis. If the subconscious "emotional programme" is in

---

[8] Cf. William Alston, "Self-Intervention and the Structure of Motivation", in Theodore Mischel, ed., *The Self: Psychological and Philosophical Issues* (Oxford, 1977), p. 77.

fact such as to "ensure" the formation of the unwarranted belief, the belief would seem not to be free* – in which case a necessary condition of full-blown doxastic incontinence is not satisfied. But the suggestion is surely implausible that *no one* who holds a belief on the basis of the subconscious process that Pears describes had it within his power to take reasonable measures[9] such that, if they had been taken, the process would have been short-circuited.

Two possible sources of confusion should be removed. First, although I have appealed to Pears' suggestion as a helpful explanatory hypothesis, I certainly do not mean to be claiming that in all cases in which jealousy leads a person, via a subconscious process, to form the pertinent infidelity-belief, a wish to eliminate rivals does the motivational work. This work, I should think, may be done by a variety of wishes, including certain self-destructive wishes that have nothing at all to do with the elimination of rivals. What is important for our purposes is that we have some way of making sense of cases of the sort in question, and that it be sufficiently determinate to permit us to investigate the freedom* of the generated beliefs. Second, I have not taken a position on the extent and potency of the influence of motivation on belief, a subject of some controversy in psychological circles.[10] My analysis does commit me to the view that full-blown incontinent belief is motivated belief. But it is admitted on all sides that motivation has some influence on belief, and I have said nothing about the *prevalence* of doxastic incontinence. If the relatively "cold" attribution theories are correct (e.g. the one recently advanced by Nisbett and Ross),[11] there is much less doxastic incontinence than some motivation theorists may think; but disputes about the magnitude of the phenomenon affect neither my analysis of *FBDI* nor my explanation of its possibility.

## III

Although there is substantial overlap between incontinent believing and self-deception, I have said little about the latter. There is at least one point, however, that should be made: a person's being self-deceived in believing

---

[9] The distinction between reasonable and unreasonable (or non-reasonable) measures of resistance rests on considerations of utility. An agent who has it within his (physical and psychological) power to commit suicide as a means of preventing himself from holding a certain belief has a powerful method of resistance at his disposal. However, given the cost of the method, its use would typically be unreasonable. On the other hand, we may safely suppose that there are agents for whom the use of measures of resistance of the kinds described above would often be quite beneficial.

[10] See Richard Nisbett and Lee Ross, *Human Inference: Strategies and Shortcomings of Social Judgment* (Englewood Cliffs, 1980), pp. 231–48.

[11] *Ibid.*

that $P$ is neither a necessary nor a sufficient condition of his incontinently believing that $P$. I have attempted elsewhere to characterize self-deception[12] and will not do so again here. For present purposes it is sufficient to notice that as self-deception is typically (and, I think, correctly) conceived, the following points (among others) are true: (i) $S$ is self-deceived in believing that $P$ only if $P$ is *false*: (ii) non-epistemic considerations in favour of holding, or not holding, $P$ are irrelevant to the truth of the claim that $S$ is self-deceived in believing that $P$. In contrast, one may incontinently believe what is true, and (as I have shown) non-epistemic considerations of the sort in question are quite relevant to the truth of a charge of incontinent believing. The latter point opens up interesting possibilities which cannot be treated in detail here. First, cases are conceivable in which one is self-deceived in believing that $P$ but does not *incontinently* believe that $P$ – e.g. a case in which $S$ (non-akratically) takes the strong evidence that her husband is having an affair to be outweighed by non-epistemic considerations and ends up believing, falsely, but in accordance with her all-things-considered better judgment, that Mr. $S$ is not having an affair. There is also the converse possibility, cases in which one incontinently believes that $P$ but is not *self-deceived* in believing that $P$. An obvious example (given (i) above) is the case of an incontinently held *true* belief. But one can imagine examples to the same effect in which $P$ is false – e.g., a case in which $S$ judges (non-self-deceptively) that his evidence for $P$ (which proposition turns out to be false) is better than his evidence for not-$P$, judges (non-akratically) that he nevertheless has good and sufficient reason to believe that not-$P$, and incontinently believes that $P$, having been defeated by his attraction to (apparent) truth. Surely, a charge of self-deception is inappropriate here, since $S$ believes in accordance with what he non-self-deceptively takes to be the better evidence.

Much remains to be said about doxastic incontinence. In my attempt to come to grips with the full-blown case, I have left the bulk of the phenomenal terrain unexplored.[13] However, I shall be satisfied if I have given an adequate account of full-blown incontinent believing and contributed to our understanding of its possibility.[14]

*Davidson College*

[12] "Self-Deception", *Philosophical Quarterly* 33 (1983), pp. 365–377.

[13] For a partial map, see Rorty, "Akratic Believers".

[14] A draft of this paper was written during my participation in a 1984 NEH institute on human action directed by Robert Audi at the University of Nebraska-Lincoln. Thanks are due to the NEH for its support and to Robert Audi, Jim Montmarquet, Paul Moser, and Michael Smith for their comments on the earlier draft.

# RUSSELL'S DECEPTIVE DESIRES

## By George Graham

Few topics have elicited more controversy from philosophers than self-deception. The idea that people deceive themselves has wide acceptance, but no stable and received interpretation.[1] In this essay I shall try to extract, or at least construct, an interpretation of self-deception which may be found in a neglected section of Bertrand Russell's *The Analysis of Mind*. I think the particular account I give of his ideas in the context of the concerns of other philosophers will illuminate problems that may be found in the literature on self-deception: problems about its content, the difference between self-deception and wishful thinking, and the phenomenology of self-deception.

## I

Some philosophers puzzle over how to distinguish self-deception from wishful thinking.[2] Both the self-deceiver and the wishful thinker hold a belief because they want its content to be true. So, what is the difference? We can get an answer to this question from Russell.

In the concluding remarks of Lecture III ("Desires and Feelings") he writes:

> . . . self-deception arises through the operation of desires for beliefs. We desire many things which it is not in our power to achieve . . . But it is found that a considerable portion of the satisfaction which these things would bring us if they were realized is to be achieved by the much easier operation of believing that they are or will be realized.[3]

This says that self-deception should be analyzed in terms of desires for beliefs. Russell immediately identifies a contrasting desire which he calls the "desire for the actual facts".[4] The implication is that self-deception should

[1] For a worthwhile survey of most of the major sorts of interpretation of self-deception, see Béla Szabados, "Self-Deception", *Canadian Journal of Philosophy* 4 (1974).

[2] See Patrick Gardiner, "Error, Faith, and Self-Deception", *Proceedings of the Aristotelian Society* 70 (1969–70); Robert Audi, "Epistemic Disavowals and Self-Deception", *The Personalist* 57 (1976).

[3] Bertrand Russell, *The Analysis of Mind* (London, 1921), p. 74.

[4] *Ibid.*

114                          GEORGE GRAHAM

be analyzed in terms of desires for beliefs outweighing desires for facts.[5] That means self-deceptive beliefs are under the control of desires. But belief *should not* be under control of desires; at least in the sense that desiring should not be enough to cause belief.[6] Belief should be produced by evidence (warrant, facts, etc.). Why then does Russell contrast believing because one desires belief, with believing when one desires facts? His point may be that beliefs are controlled by desires, whether for beliefs or facts. However, talk of "desires for facts" is ambiguous. It can mean either that a person wants true beliefs; or that he believes something and wants that very thing to be true.

> (a) On the first interpretation, we have a person who believes something which he would *not* believe if confronted with contrary facts.
> (b) On the second interpretation, we have a person who believes something which he would believe if confronted with contrary facts.

I suggest that the first interpretation is Russell's notion of "believing from a desire for facts" and the second is his notion of "believing from a desire for belief". So understood, when one believes from a desire for facts, desire does not cause one to hold any particular belief; one merely wants true beliefs whatever their content turns out to be. On the other hand, when one believes from a desire for belief, desire does cause one to hold a particular belief; one wants something more than truth – one wishes something specific to be true, and desiring this makes one actually believe it.

So Russell does not hold that beliefs are necessarily controlled by desires. Some are; but some aren't. When a desire for belief leads, in some sense, to belief, belief is controlled by desire; the desire is causally responsible for the belief. However when a desire for facts leads, in some sense, to belief, belief is not controlled by desire but by evidence (facts, warrant, etc.). At most, desire is responsible for a person's respect for or sensitivity to the evidence. In other words, desiring $p$ when this produces *the belief that $p$* is "desiring belief".[7] Whereas believing $p$ when this is produced by evidence for $p$ is "desiring facts".

If this is right, it suggests an interpretation of the difference between self-deception and wishful thinking. In wishful thinking a person desires belief but not when this conflicts with facts or there is strong evidence against it. So

[5] Hereafter I shall omit the redundant 'actual'.
[6] This has been argued by a number of writers. For an important discussion see Bernard Williams, "Deciding to Believe", in *Problems of the Self* (London, 1973).
[7] Of course other things might be meant by a notion of desiring belief; see Terence Penelhum, "Self-Identity and Self-Regard", in A. O. Rorty (ed.), *The Identities of Persons* (California, 1976). I am explicating simply what Russell means by the notion.

wishful thinkers believe what they want, but not when confronted by contrary facts, only when contrary facts are indecisive or non-existent. However, self-deceivers believe what they want even when confronted with contrary facts. After all, says Russell, their desires for belief outweigh their desires for facts. We must therefore suppose that self-deceivers insulate themselves from the facts; mere wishful thinkers are sensitive to conflicting evidence.

To illustrate, consider Fred, who believes that he is not terminally ill because he wants not to be terminally ill. If he has not been confronted with good evidence of his terminal condition, he is just a wishful thinker. On the other hand, once really *confronted* with contrary evidence, were he to believe that he is not dying he would be self-deceived. Here desires for beliefs outweigh desires for facts; and lead him to believe something "which is not in (his) power to achieve".[8]

## II

I have extracted the following description of self-deception from Russell:

> S is self-deceived just when S believes what S desires to believe and does so when confronted with contrary facts.

And I have suggested that the idea of the self-deceiver believing in the face of contrary facts distinguishes self-deception from wishful thinking. To adapt Heil's apt term, self-deceivers are guilty of epistemic incontinence, whereas wishful thinkers are innocent.[9]

Two points of clarification. I assume that a central idea of Russell is that self-deception is caused by desires for beliefs; that is, $S$ has at least one desire for belief which explains in part both what he believes and why he believes this when confronted with contrary facts. It is not a matter of $S$'s being stupid or ignorant, etc., but of the relative weight of his desires for beliefs. As Szabados has said, "what one can be self-deceived about must link up with one's wants".[10] Russell certainly agrees. Second, when I speak of "contrary facts" which "confront" the self-deceiver I mean facts which the self-deceiver sees as contrary to his favoured belief. This is how I explain Russell's idea of desires for beliefs defeating desires for facts in self-deception.

It will help in understanding the notion of believing when confronted with contrary facts to draw distinctions here. First, we must distinguish between the *existence* of contrary facts, and perceiving or *knowing* them. It seems eminently reasonable to say that self-deceivers believe what is contrary to the

[8] Russell, op. cit.
[9] John Heil, "Doxastic Incontinence", *Mind* 93 (1984) p. 369.
[10] Szabados, op. cit., p. 67.

facts; so that if one is self-deceived one believes falsehood(s). But just because contrary facts exist does not mean that people know of such facts, or in any sense see them. Thus, in addition, the self-deceiver must know or perceive the facts contrary to his belief.

Another distinction grows out of the notion of knowing or seeing contrary facts. Let us say that one can know or see contrary facts under a description. When a person knows or sees contrary facts under the description 'contrary', he is, in the manner in which I wish to be speaking of this notion, confronted with them. For instance, Fred believes he is perfectly healthy. His doctor tells him that he is terminally ill; and Fred appreciates that this is contrary to what he believes. But one might see contrary facts and not appreciate that they are contrary. For example, Fred's wife, Edna, might overhear the doctor's remarks but not appreciate that they conflict with her own belief in Fred's good health. So we must differentiate between seeing or knowing facts which are contrary (to one's belief) and seeing or knowing them to *be* thus contrary.

I am saying that for Russell, self-deceivers see contrary facts and appreciate that they are contrary to their belief. They see them as contrary. This is what I mean when I speak of self-deceivers being confronted with contrary facts.

### III

Presumably some process explains the production of belief by desire for belief, when self-deceivers are confronted by contrary facts. Against their desires for facts, self-deceivers might put contrary facts out of mind, manipulate evidence against the contrary facts so as to reduce their contrariety, inflate evidence for the favoured belief, and so on.

Russell has an empirical hypothesis about the process. It is that self-deceptive belief formation is accompanied by feelings of "discomfort" or "restlessness": by which he seems to mean doubts, qualms, suspicions, misgivings, and the like.[11] We can refer to such feelings as "cognitive discomfort". Moreover, according to Russell, these feelings arise from the dissatisfaction or incomplete satisfaction of self-deceivers' desires for facts. Someone who is self-deceived believes what he wants but not with the truth he desires.

Russell's hypothesis is important. For one thing, it suggests a plausible distinction between self-deception and closely related self-delusion. For another, it meshes well with other models of self-deception. I have in mind so-called cognitive conflict models, which insist that self-deception implies

[11] Russell, op. cit., esp. pp. 72–4.

such conflict states as believing something and disbelieving it, or believing both one thing and some opposing thing. Cognitive conflict models are popular with theorists who assume self-deception is very similar to other deception.[12] I shall briefly discuss each main point in turn.

Self-deception may change into self-delusion, and the passage may be gradual. But we need to distinguish the two. Self-delusion exists, I propose, only where cognitive discomfort is absent. Someone who is self-deluded believes what he wants when confronted by contrary facts, and in some unconscious sense appreciates that facts are contrary, but this appreciation never occurs in consciousness. Delusional mechanisms eliminate any sort of doubt, suspicion, or discomfort from the person's awareness. He is, as it were, beyond mere self-deception; just as the self-deceiver is, as it were, beyond mere wishful thinking.

To illustrate, consider Rex, a cowardly soldier who wants to be brave and therein believes he is, in the teeth of numerous marks of cowardliness. But Rex never doubts. In fact, neither qualm nor query quibbles his consciousness. He is self-deluded.

Compare Rex with Tex, an unknown actor who wishes to be famous and therein believes he is, in the face of numerous signs of mere obscurity. But quibbles fleck at Tex. He harbours nagging doubts or suspicions about whether he is famous. He is discomforted. This shows that Tex is not so *deluded* that his appreciation of contrary facts never enters consciousness. He is simply if sadly self-deceived, because some sort of appreciation of contrary facts enters awareness in the form of discomfort. Or as Russell might put it: enters in the form of the felt dissatisfaction of desires for facts. But Rex is sadly if simply self-deluded because no sort of appreciation of contrary facts enters his consciousness. He doesn't feel the dissatisfaction of his desires for facts.

It may be thought, however, that discomfort is not required of self-deception either; that someone might be *peacefully* self-deceived. But I think we must be very careful here. We must ask what we want to designate as self-deception and self-delusion. I assume that we wish the concept of self-delusion to mark a sort of cognitive pathology which is more impervious to contrary facts than self-deception, and unlike self-deception can have psychotic forms. Someone can be psychotically self-deluded but not psychotically self-deceived. The natural next step, then, is to look more closely at the degree of imperviousness involved in self-delusion. My hypothesis is that absence of discomfort (doubt, suspicion, qualm, or query) is one way of identifying that degree. People who are self-deluded are so seriously

---

[12] See, e.g., John Turk Saunders, "The Paradox of Self-Deception", *Philosophy and Phenomenological Research* 35 (1975); Jeffrey Foss, "Rethinking Self-Deception", *American Philosophical Quarterly* 17 (1980).

deceived that they don't even feel discomfort; so that if someone is peaceful in his own deception, this is more like self-delusion than self-deception.

Now to the second point. As said, cognitive conflict models take self-deception to require logically some sort of conflicting beliefs. Perhaps these beliefs are part of the confrontation with contrary facts. Perhaps they are necessary if self-deception is genuine deception. Russell is mute on whether self-deception requires cognitive conflict. Not every theorist agrees that it does.[13] But this is not the place to discuss the merits of the thesis; the only point I want to make concerns the possibility of discomfort, given cognitive conflict.

The supposition that self-deception requires cognitive conflict can help to account for the discomfort of self-deceivers. This is what I meant earlier when I said that Russell's discomfort hypothesis meshes well with cognitive conflict models. One such explanation would go like this: Since self-deceivers are in cognitive conflict, their desires neither for facts nor beliefs are completely satisfied. They thus feel discomfort. Tex, for example, wishes and thereby believes he is famous, which helps satisfy his desire for belief. In facing contrary facts he also doubts or disbelieves he is famous, which helps satisfy his desire for facts. But neither desire is completely satisfied because of the existence of the opposing belief; so Tex feels discomfort. He grows restless in the teeth of contrary facts. The discomfort hypothesis thus seems to be reinforced by the thesis that self-deception requires cognitive conflict. With cognitive conflict, discomfort can be expected.


## IV

Many other interpretations of self-deception recognize that self-deception arises in part from people believing what they want. But Russell is the only theorist, to my knowledge, who holds that desires for facts also play a role, and that self-deception arises from desires for facts being defeated or checked by desires for beliefs. Also, whereas conflicting beliefs are important to other theorists, conflicting *desires* are important to Russell, though this is compatible, I have argued, with requiring conflicting beliefs of self-deception.

Desires for facts are sometimes called by epistemologists and others 'epistemic desires'. These are desires for truth – evidence, warrant, and the like, but detached from nonepistemic considerations. It is an exercise of some intellectual dexterity to isolate the domain of the epistemic; but assuming this can be done, Russell's desires for facts fall within the domain. The dissatisfaction or partial satisfaction of such desires he takes to be the source of discomfort (doubt, etc.) in self-deception.

[13] See, e.g., David Kipp, "On Self-Deception", *The Philosophical Quarterly* 30 (1980), p. 121.

One can, thus, extract an interpretation of self-deception from Russell. The interpretation comes from the Russell of Neglected Passages. But it lights the passage to self-deception by illuminating self-deception's content, phenomenology, and location on the continuum of epistemic maladies, which has wishful thinkers at one end, self-deluded persons at the other, and self-deceivers in the middle.

*University of Alabama at Birmingham*

# DELIBERATION AND THE PRESUMPTION
# OF OPEN ALTERNATIVES

## By Tomis Kapitan

By *deliberation* we understand practical reasoning with an end in view of choosing some course of action. Integral to it is the agent's sense of alternative possibilities, that is, of two or more courses of action he presumes are *open* for him to undertake or not. Such acts may not actually *be* open in the sense that the deliberator would do them were he to so intend, but it is evident that he *assumes* each to be so. One deliberates only by taking it for granted that both performing and refraining from any of the acts under consideration are possible for one, and that which is to be selected is something entirely up to oneself.

What is it for a course of action to be presumed as open, or for several courses of action to present themselves as a range of open alternatives? Answering these questions is essential for an understanding of deliberation and choice and, indeed, for the entire issue of free will and responsibility. According to one common view, a deliberator takes the considered options to be open only by assuming he is *free* to undertake any of them and, consequently, that whichever he does undertake is, as yet, a wholly *undetermined* matter. Built into the structure of deliberation, on this theory, is an indeterministic bias relative to which any deliberator with deterministic beliefs is either inconsistent or condemned to a fatalistic limbo. An unmistakable challenge is thereby posed: is there an alternative conception of the presuppositions underlying deliberation more congenial to a deterministic perspective yet adequate to the data? Convinced that there is, I develop a partial account of deliberation which, though highly similar to the aforementioned view, diverges at a critical juncture.

## I

### THE POSTULATE OF FREEDOM

That a deliberator presumes himself to be free to undertake any one from a range of alternatives seems undeniable. While such an attitude might not involve the agent's *knowledge* that there are undetermined actions, choices or deliberations, it is often thought to include his *belief* to this effect. Perhaps Kant had this in mind when he set forth his celebrated postulate of freedom:

> It [Reason] must regard itself as the author of its principles inde-
> pendent of foreign influences. Consequently, as practical reason or
> as the will of a rational being it must regard itself as free, that is to
> say, the will of such a being cannot be a will of its own except under
> the idea of freedom.[1]

This passage has been interpreted as implying that agents must adopt an
indeterministic stance with respect to their own practical thinking, or some
portion thereof, that this is essential to the conviction that their choices are
their own.[2] If freedom and agency are so mated within practical reason, it
follows that any deliberator who also believes his future acts and choices to
be (already) determined is *ipso facto* inconsistent.

My object is not an exegesis of Kant. Many contemporary philosophers *do*
advocate this interpretation of the presumption of open alternatives, for
example, Hector-Neri Castañeda, who writes:

> One of the fundamental facts about practical thinking is that it
> hinges on the agent's *presupposition* that he can choose from several
> alternative courses of action open to him. This does not, of course,
> imply, as Kant firmly stressed, that the agent is free in the sense that
> his acts, or his volitions, are uncaused. Perhaps the presupposition
> is just a dialectical illusion (to use Kant's term) of practical thinking.
> If it is, the universe is *ugly*: given the biological and psychological
> primacy of practical over contemplative thinking, we are, thus,
> condemned to presuppose a falsehood in order to do what we think
> practically. We *must* in any case include the presupposition of
> freedom in our analysis of practical thinking . . . [3]

But what falsehood is it (if the universe is "ugly") that an agent is condemned
to presuppose in order to engage in practical thought – that he can choose
from among open alternatives, that he is free, or that some of his own acts or
volitions are uncaused? In the passage cited these disjuncts are conflated;
Castañeda evidently holds that if someone assumes he can choose then he is

---

[1] Immanuel Kant, *Fundamental Principles of the Metaphysic of Morals* (Bobbs-Merrill, 1949),
p.65, translation by T. K. Abbott of *Grundlegung zur Metaphysik der Sitten*, originally published
in 1785.

[2] This interpretation is strongly suggested by what Kant says elsewhere in the same work, for
example, pp. 63, 69–79, 73–78, and various commentators have urged this reading, e.g., H. G.
Paton in the introduction to his translation of the *Grundlegung* (New York, 1964), pp. 46–48.

[3] Hector-Neri Castañeda, *Thinking and Doing* (Dordrecht, 1975), pp. 134–5. Again,
on p. 312 of this work, he writes that ". . . to the consciousness of an agent making deliberations: (i) he appears free to choose from alternative courses of action; (ii) his choices appear
uncaused . . . "

committed, *qua* rational being, to the presupposition that he is free and, thus, that some of his choices are uncaused and undetermined.

Richard Taylor and others arrive at the same conclusion by focusing on agency; one who deliberates about what to do must assume that his eventual undertaking is *his* to choose, "under his control" or "up to himself". Were he to suppose that his choice will be the outcome of antecedent conditions over which he has no control, he could not take his eventual act to be up to himself. Taylor is insistent, in short, that assuming the latter is to suppose one's choice *alone* will determine the undertaking, not some other conditions existing prior to choice. Consequently, a deliberator must take his choice to be undetermined.[4] With a slightly different emphasis, Nicholas Denyer argues that since determinism entails the future to be fixed and necessary, but that one deliberates only about what is taken as contingent, it follows that "a deliberator cannot then consistently believe that his actions are determined by events prior to his deliberations."[5] Denyer stresses the modality embedded within the presupposition of freedom; to hold that one is free, that one both *can* perform an action and *can* refrain from performing it, is to assume that one's future undertaking is as yet a *contingent* matter. This assumption, he claims, conflicts directly with the belief that one's choices and actions are already determined by past or present conditions. Reflecting both approaches, Peter van Inwagen concludes that since we all believe in our own freedom,

> ... to reject free will is to condemn oneself to a life of perpetual logical inconsistency. Anyone who rejects free will adopts a general theory about human beings that he contradicts with every deliberate word and act.[6]

That a deliberator does not view himself at the mercy of an indifferent causal network is, to an extent, *unquestionable*; his assumption of self-agency, of his power to choose, is at once a recognition of his partial independence

---

[4] Richard Taylor has frequently advocated this position, e.g., in *Action and Purpose* (Englewood Cliffs, 1966), pp. 178–182 and in *Metaphysics* (Englewood Cliffs, 1974) 2nd edition, pp. 53–55. See also his "Deliberation and Foreknowledge", *American Philosophical Quarterly* 1 (1964), pp. 73–80. Similar views are espoused by Carl Ginet, "Might We Have No Choice?", in Keith Lehrer, ed., *Freedom and Determinism* (New York, 1966), pp. 87–104; J. M. Boyle, G. Grisez and O. Tollefsen, *Free Choice* (Notre Dame 1976); and J. W. Lamb, "On A Proof of Incompatibilism", *Philosophical Review* 86 (1977).

[5] Nicholas Denyer, *Time, Action & Necessity: a proof of free will* (London, 1981), p. 5, and see also pp. 39–42 and 65–6. Central to his position is a denial of true future contingents, so that even if one does φ at time *t* (when this is a result of his choice) it is not true beforehand that he will φ at *t*. Cf. my review of Denyer's book in *Noûs* 18 (1984).

[6] Peter van Inwagen, *An Essay on Free Will* (Oxford, 1983), p. 160.

from the flow of events and of his ability to shape an indeterminate future. The Kantian postulate of freedom, coordinating agency and contingency, is well-grounded in the phenomenon of choice, and there is no intent to oppose it here. Yet, what this presumption of freedom amounts to is not something which the data unequivocally reveal. The reading so far encountered, henceforth labeled the "Standard Interpretation", must be measured against the overt dissent of those who, while deliberating, take their actions to be caused by their volitions, and these volitions, in turn, to be terminal points of deliberations whose every phase is determined. To believe in free will while taking it to be an illusion is not a comfortable position to be in. But for this very reason, the presence of deliberating determinists, while not refuting the Standard Interpretation, motivates development of and interest in a rival account.

## II

## THE PRESUMPTION OF EFFICACY

To fix intuitions, let us consider an example of a man on a leisurely hike through the countryside who unexpectedly comes to a fork in the path and stops to deliberate about which branch to follow. Suppose, as he looks down each path and weighs the advantages and disadvantages of taking it as opposed to the other, a companion asks him about what he is thinking. We can imagine the following exchange:

> *Companion*: Do you feel that you can take either of the two paths?
> *Hiker*: Certainly, I can take either of the paths, depending upon which one I choose.
> *Companion*: Can you tell, at this stage, *which* path you will eventually take?
> *Hiker*: No, not now; I've not yet made up my mind on the matter.
> *Companion*: Are you aware of anything which will *cause* you to take, or to choose, either the path to the right or the one to the left?
> *Hiker*: Well, I hadn't thought about that, but now that you ask I guess that I must say no, I am unaware of any such thing; as far as I can tell it is entirely up to me which path I take.
> *Companion*: Would you say, then, that you are *free* to choose either the path to your right or the one to the left?
> *Hiker*: Indeed, haven't I just told you that I can choose either?

Let us assume the hiker's responses to be typical of what one might expect from a normal deliberator satisfying at least minimal conditions of rationality, and so let us exploit the example as a springboard for conjectures about deliberation. His response to the initial question, for instance, immediately suggests an underlying attitude; he takes each alternative to be *open* only because he feels that he would perform it if he chose to and that, otherwise, he would refrain from so doing. That is, he assumes his will to be both necessary and sufficient for the action, *viz.*, that his choice would be *efficacious* in bringing about his performance or non-performance of any of the considered options. Generalizing, we propose a schema attributing what can be called a *presumption of efficacy*:

> (PE) an agent presumes that his φ-ing is an open alternative for him *only if* he presumes that he would φ if and only if he were to choose to φ.

A schema of this sort conceals much. A more detailed version would require temporal indices fixing the times of the presumption, choosing and doing, and, in many cases, probability qualifiers on the biconditional within the scope of 'presumes', when the agent does not think his intentional efforts will be guaranteed success. The term 'choose' may give way to 'decide', 'intend', 'undertake', 'try', etc., though in using 'choose' I assume that choice is a species of *intending to do* something or other. In addition, the occurrences of 'he', 'his' and 'him' within attitudinal scope should be taken to convey the agent's self or first-person reference, and hence are limited as to their possible substituends.[7] For the present, these refinements can be left implicit.

The embedded biconditional in the consequent of (PE) poses no special problem, whether construed subjunctively or indicatively. Obviously the assumed linkage between φ-ing and choosing to φ is not purely logical, but causal, and thus context-bound. That is to say, the agent takes his φ-ing to be consequent upon his choice *given* circumstances as they are, a qualifier implicitly within attitudinal scope which could be more precisely exhibited by a restricted universal quantifier over circumstances. This reading allows the

---

[7] I am assuming, thus, that the presumptions are to be taken in what is sometimes called a *de se* sense, see David Lewis, "Attitudes *De Dicto* and *De Re*", in his *Philosophical Papers* (Oxford 1983), pp. 133–59. A view that I find congenial is Castañeda's where the latter occurrences of 'he' in (PE) are *quasi-indicators*, that is, devices we have for attributing indexical reference to others. See his "He: A Study in the Logic of Self-Consciousness", *Ratio* 8 (1966), pp. 130–57; "Indicators and Quasi-Indicators", *American Philosophical Quarterly* 4 (1967), pp. 85–100; and "Reference, Reality and Perceptual Fields", *Proceedings and Addresses of the American Philosophical Association* 53 (1980), pp. 763–822. He has argued in these and other papers that quasi-indicators cannot be replaced by third-person designations and, thus, that first-person reference is irreducible to third-person reference.

agent to be mistaken in his presumption of efficacy without saddling him with suppositions he might recognize to be inconsistent – as would be permitted on an external reading of the qualifier. An important feature of (PE), of course, is that the deliberator takes his choosing to be an *essential* factor in causal chains leading up to either his doing or refraining. This is crucial to the sense of agency; that the action is under his control stems partially from the supposition that he would do it *only* through his own conscious effort.

A word about 'presumes'. It would be incorrect to think that a deliberator is always conscious, via some propositional attitude, that the alternatives he is weighing are open to him. More likely, certain dispositional states are involved, e.g. beliefs. But since 'belief' has calcified in the lexicon of some to imply an ability to articulate the content, perhaps what we want are lower-level doxastic states – better conveyed by terms like 'feels', 'assumes' or 'takes for granted' – states for which corresponding linguistic abilities may be lacking. For convenience, 'presumes' shall be used to indicate doxastic attitudes generically, allowing the character of the relevant dispositions to fluctuate among various doxastic levels.[8]

III

## THE PRESUMPTION OF CONTINGENCY

At first glance, (PE) might be thought to be all that there is to the presumption of open alternatives. Recalling the conditional analysis of freedom championed by G. E. Moore and others, why not say that a deliberator takes a course of action to be open just in case he believes it *possible* that he perform it and *possible* that he refrain, with the modalities unpacked conditionally as indicated by the consequent of (PE)? Unfortunately, even if one accepts the equivalence, the conditional analysis no more provides for the agent's *sense* of freedom than it does for an account of freedom itself; to take a course of action as possible in that one would do it if one chose will not suffice for taking it as *open*. Nadia, upon entering the local ice cream shop, might believe that she would eat chocolate ice cream if she chose, but may also realize that if she did she would break out in a horrible rash. She might even dislike the taste of chocolate and have formed a belief that because of this and her fear of a rash she will be caused not to choose chocolate ice cream. Believing that her not eating chocolate ice cream is already determined, therefore, she no longer considers it an open alternative

---

[8] Compare Castañeda's illuminating discussion of the locution 'feels that' in "Philosophical Method and Direct Awareness of the Self", *Grazer Philosophische Studien* 7/8 (1979), pp. 1–58.

despite her acceptance of the conditional.[9]

It is tempting to say that a deliberator must also assume that it is possible for her *to choose* a considered alternative, and it is precisely this that Nadia lacks. It is evident, however, that applying the conditional analysis to this sense of possibility would merely postpone the difficulty besides raising familiar problems about choosing to choose.[10] Perhaps such reflections have led some to suggest that if an agent deliberates about φ-ing then he assumes that his φ-ing is still a *contingent* matter and that, consequently, nothing *yet* determines his choice either to φ or not to φ. Nobody, as Aristotle emphasized, deliberates about that which is impossible or necessary. Of course, to avoid a facile refutation of determinism it is essential to view the modality as within attitudinal scope, so that we have,

(1) an agent presumes that his φ-ing is an open alternative for him *only if* he presumes that his φ-ing is contingent,

which implies that he also takes his *not* φ-ing to be contingent.[11] Alternatively, one could speak of his choosing (intending, undertaking, etc.) φ as contingent, and again add that the schema is to be qualified by temporal parameters, i.e., the agent assumes, while deliberating, that his φ-ing at *t* is, *as of yet*, contingent.

The problem now is to give some account of the modality in (1), for it is certain that not just any sort of contingency will do. Mere logical contingency is not sufficient, nor, for that matter, any other sort of contingency fixed *solely*

[9] The literature on the conditional analysis of freedom is copious. Besides Moore's classic work *Ethics* (Oxford, 1912), ch. 6, echoing longstanding views of John Locke, Jonathan Edwards *et al*, there is also J. L. Austin, "Ifs and Cans", *Proceedings of the British Academy* 42 (1956), pp.109–132; R. Chisholm, "J. L. Austin's Philosophical Papers", *Mind* 73 (1964); K. Lehrer, "An Empirical Disproof of Determinism", in Lehrer, ed., *Freedom and Determinism*; K. Lehrer, "Cans Without Ifs", *Analysis* 29 (1968), pp. 29–32; D. Davidson, "Freedom to Act", in his *Essays on Actions & Events* (Oxford, 1980), pp. 63–82; and A. E. Falk, "Some Modal Confusions in Compatibilism", *American Philosophical Quarterly* 18 (1981) pp.141–8. It is generally conceded that Moore's attempt to construe 'I can' in terms of 'I shall, if I choose' fails, though it is disputed what this means for the larger questions of determinism, compatibilism and freedom.

[10] See Wilfred Sellars, "Thought and Action", in Lehrer, ed., *Freedom and Determinism*, who mentions not only the threat of a regress that such an analysis engenders but also that it mistakenly construes volitions as actions to be brought about by yet further acts of will. See, however, Lehrer's treatment of the regress in "Preferences, Conditionals and Freedom", in van Inwagen, ed., *Time and Cause* (Dordrecht, 1980), pp. 187–201, as well as Krister Segerberg's discussion of Lehrer in "Could Have But Did Not", *Pacific Philosophical Quarterly* 64 (1983), pp. 230–41.

[11] Aristotle, *Nicomachean Ethics* 1112b, and see Richard Sorabji's endorsement of this reading in *Necessity Cause and Blame: Perspectives on Aristotle's Theory* (London, 1980), pp. 228 and 245. Compare Denyer, *op. cit.*, pp. 30, 40–2, and R. Burton, "Choice", *Philosophy and Phenomenological Research* 42 (1982) pp. 581–6. In speaking of *P* as contingent I mean, throughout, the conjunction of the possibility of *P* with the possibility of not-*P*.

by reference to a body of laws of nature. Instead, a modality which includes reference to the actual course of events, to the world of particular objects and conditions, is required, *viz.*, a relativized, concrete modality. Let us say that a state of affairs (event, proposition, etc.) *P* is *contingent relative to* a set of conditions *S* just in case neither *P* nor not-*P* is a consequence of *S*. The contingency is *concrete* if *S* contains particular facts or conditions, and *unqualified* with respect to time *t* if *S* contains all conditions existing prior to and at *t*.[12]

For Taylor and Castañeda, the contingency in (1) is, at least, *causal* in that the agent assumes that there do not exist, nor have existed, conditions causally sufficient for his φ-ing at the time in question. One could, alternatively, drop mention of causation, as van Inwagen does, and say that the agent assumes his φ-ing is not a consequence of any set of conditions (plus laws of nature) antecedent to and including the time of deliberation. In either case, the agent takes the contingency to be fixed with respect to *all* standing conditions, past and present. Denyer, even more strongly, opts for a type of *absolute* contingency; in *no* sense is the agent's φ-ing taken as necessary or impossible, or, in other words, it is not a consequence of *any* set of truths. A deliberator must, he contends, assume that neither the proposition that he will φ nor the proposition that he will not φ is already true, so that no truth about what happens in the future entails a proposition to the effect that he will φ or that he will not φ.

Each of these construals of (1) is a variant of what I have previously called the Standard Interpretation. In the present context its claim is that one who takes his φ-ing to be open assumes it to be contingent relative to *all* conditions (facts, events, propositions) existing (obtaining, occurring, being true) prior to and including the time at which the assumption is held. This unqualified modality requires the deliberator to consider his φ-ing to be, as yet, undetermined by those same conditions, hence, undetermined *simpliciter*.

To minimize complexities, define determinism broadly as the doctrine that each state of the world is fully determined by antecedent states, where *P*

---

[12] This notion of a relativized modality must be handled with some care to avoid unnecessary confusion. My preference is to construe the relation of *consequence*, employed in the definiens, in a *generic* sense, not to be restricted to the narrower concept of logical consequence unless otherwise specified. This has a great deal to do with whether *S* includes laws or nomological propositions *or* laws are principles underlying the consequence relation. I refer the reader to my "On the Concept of Material Consequence", *History and Philosophy of Logic* 3 (1982), pp. 193–211, for an extended discussion of extra-logical consequence. For more about relativized modality, see Hans Reichenbach, *Elements of Symbolic Logic* (New York, 1975), p. 396; T. Smiley, "Relative Necessity", *Journal of Symbolic Logic* 28 (1963), pp. 113–34; and I. L. Humberstone, "Relative Necessity Revisited", *Reports on Mathematical Logic* 13 (1981), pp. 33–42. J. W. Lamb, *op. cit.*, and others have used the term 'categorical' instead of 'unqualified' in discussing a deliberator's assumption of freedom, though with much the same meaning.

is *determined* by $Q$ just in case the existence (obtaining, occurrence, truth) of $Q$ is sufficient for the existence of $P$. Following Denyer and van Inwagen, determinism implies that at any instance there is just one possible future – in the unqualified or causal sense of 'possible'. Of importance is the fact that

> (2)  a determinist assumes that whatever he will do (choose, under-
> take, etc.) is already determined.

To locate an inconsistency within the beliefs of a deliberating determinist now seems easy; for as a deliberator, by (1), he takes his future act to be yet undetermined, but as a determinist, by (2) he assumes the very opposite, that it is already determined.

But matters are not so simple. To say that a determinist who deliberates about a range of actions $\phi_1, \ldots, \phi_n$ supposes that whatever he will do is already determined is *not* to imply that he takes his $\phi_i$-ing to be determined, for any $i$, $1 \leq i \leq n$. The quantifier 'whatever' in (2) falls *within* the scope of his assumption, so that he need not believe of any specific action that *it* is already determined. We cannot, then, automatically attribute to the deter-minist who deliberates about whether to $\phi$ the bald inconsistency of both believing that his $\phi$-ing is determined *and* that it is not.

One could argue from the claim that it is impossible to deliberate about what one *knows* one will do.[13] If one knows one will $\phi$ then there is no point in deliberating about whether to $\phi$; the issue is already settled and $\phi$-ing is no longer open but closed. Indeed, *if* this is so it seems fair enough to generalize to *belief* as follows:

> (3)  an agent presumes that his $\phi$-ing is an open alternative for him
> *only if* he does not yet believe that he will $\phi$.

Now it is implausible that the consequent of (3) be satisfied if one believes one's $\phi$-ing is determined, that is, for minimally rational agents, (3) yields:

> (4)  an agent presumes that his $\phi$-ing is an open alternative for him
> *only if* he does not yet believe that there are conditions sufficient
> for his $\phi$-ing.

So, the argument goes, satisfying the consequent of (4) renders inconsistent any determinist who believes he will undertake at least one of the alternatives about which he deliberates. But this reasoning is also deceptive. Schema (3) is plausible only if negation has larger scope than the attitude within the consequent and, if so, it ascribes *no belief at all* to a deliberator. (4), however,

---

[13] See Section IV below. R. Taylor in "Deliberation and Foreknowledge" and again in *Action and Purpose*, pp. 174–6, has contended that one cannot *know*, while deliberating, which course of action he will eventually undertake, a claim also endorsed in C. Ginet, "Can the Will Be Caused?", *Philosophical Review* 71 (1962), pp.49–55; A. N. Prior, *Papers on Time and Tense* (Oxford, 1968), pp. 47–8; A. Goldman, *A Theory of Human Action* (Englewood Cliffs, 1970), p. 195; and Denyer, *op. cit.*, p. 48. Taylor's argumentation, in particular, supports the stronger claim that a deliberator cannot have a *belief* that he will perform this or that alternative, as he himself realizes in "Deliberation and Foreknowledge", p. 77.

generates the inconsistency only when negation has smaller scope, in which case it derives no support from (3). The confusion stems from the fact that expressions of the form 'he does not believe' are used to express both disbelief and nonbelief – an unfortunate ambiguity, but devastating for the argument at hand.

At the same time, this argument indicates where the inconsistency is to be found, if the deliberator is minimally rational and believes he will undertake one of the alternatives. For, by (1), he assumes of each alternative that his undertaking it is contingent and, thus, that there is, or will be, *a* future undertaking which is, as yet, undetermined. This consequence, *on* the Standard Interpretation, involves a belief which *does* conflict with that ascribed in (2), and the ascription of an inconsistency to deliberating determinists is secured.

A showdown with the Standard Interpretation over (1) is inescapable. That deliberation is wedded to a sense of contingency is manifest in our example of the hiker. But examine his response to the companion's third question. Taken literally, the words 'as far as I can tell' suggest an interpretation of (1) in terms of *epistemic* contingency; a deliberator assumes his φ-ing to be contingent relative to what he knows. However, more seems involved. I may, for instance, believe I will *not* fly to Copenhagen tomorrow and thus I do not deliberate about so doing, yet I may not know what I believe (perhaps some unforeseen emergency will call me to Copenhagen). The action is impossible relative to what I *believe* and so does not appear open to me, though it is contingent with respect to what I actually know. The words 'as far as I can tell', in fact, point to a broader construal of the modality in terms of *doxastic* contingency so that (1) would give way to something like

      (5)  an agent presumes that his φ-ing is an open alternative for him *only if* he presumes that his φ-ing is contingent relative to what he then believes,

where 'then', occurring before 'believes', refers to the time of presumption. (5) says, simply, that the agent takes no set of his beliefs to be sufficient for his φ-ing or for his not φ-ing.

As a necessary condition on deliberation (5) appears uncontroversial, but before judging whether it captures the full flavour of (1) a further issue must be addressed. Given that the modality falls within attitudinal scope is the same to be said for the qualifier 'relative to what he then believes'? If it has an *external* occurrence then the modality would be fixed by the entire body of the agent's beliefs with the consequent of (5) reading: for every subset $S$ of x's beliefs, x presumes that his φ-ing is contingent relative to $S$. The problem here is that since no one consciously rehearses all his beliefs while deliberating he may overlook what they entail or even what he believes they entail. Suppose at 10 a.m. Mr. Hawkins, having decided to take his son bowling at 3 p.m., acquires the belief that he will take his son bowling then. At 2 p.m., temporarily overlooking his earlier resolve, he deliberates about playing golf at 3 p.m.. Given *all* that he believes (dispositionally) at 2 p.m. it is not true that he assumes it possible that he play golf at 3 p.m. and, so, (5) would fail to formulate even a necessary condition. Weakening the consequent to refer to only *some* subsets of x's beliefs would saddle the condition with the same insufficiency that affected epistemic contingency. An external occurrence of the qualifier, in short, renders (5) unsuitable.

A solution is to insist upon an *internal* occurrence. This allows us to take the hiker's response at face value; by using the words 'as far as I can tell' he relativizes the modality to *what he then takes himself to believe*. As such, the occurrences of both 'he' and 'then' in the qualifier function in just the way that 'his' does within the scope of 'presumes', namely, as devices for attributing self-reference to the agent (see note 7).

A residue of ambiguity lingers. There are questions whether the scope of 'what he then believes' is to include that of the modal operator and whether 'what' indicates a quantifier occurring outside or inside the scope of 'presumes'. The first, I think, can be answered affirmatively since the qualifier specifies the character of the modality. The second turns on a choice between, roughly, (i) x presumes that if $S$ is any set of his beliefs then his $\phi$-ing is contingent relative to $S$, and (ii) there is a set $S$ such that x presumes that $S$ is the set of his beliefs and his $\phi$-ing is contingent relative to $S$. (i) bears a structural accord to the Standard Interpretation where quantifiers implicitly occur within attitudinal scope; its satisfaction is a minimal requirement. (ii), on the other hand, would seem to imply that a deliberator consciously reviews all that he takes himself to believe whenever the dispositional presumption ascribed in the consequent of (5) is activated. Though (ii) is perhaps not to be ruled out, (i) is a more cautious reading. We arrive, thus, at a version of (5) which can be labeled the *presumption of contingency*:

> (PC) an agent presumes that his $\phi$-ing is an open alternative for him *only if* he presumes that if $S$ is any set of his beliefs then his $\phi$-ing is contingent relative to $S$.[14]

[14] Peter van Inwagen has suggested that the variable '$S$' in a principle like (PC) be restricted to sets of beliefs the agent takes to be consistent "since not everyone will be willing to assume that his own beliefs are consistent, and since, presumably, no proposition is contingent relative to an inconsistent set of beliefs," (in comments at the American Philosophical Association meetings (Western Division) April 1984). I have two reservations about accepting this qualification: (1) While it may be that there is someone who is not willing to assume his own beliefs to be consistent, it does not follow that he takes them to be inconsistent. He may simply be in a state of suspending judgment on the consistency of his own beliefs since few, if any, can rest content with a recognized inconsistency. (2) I do not rule out considerations of *relevance* in a proper account of logical consequence, thus, am reluctant to accept the view that every proposition is a consequence of an inconsistent set.

It follows immediately from (PC) together with (PE) that anyone who takes his φ-ing as contingent relative to his beliefs thereby takes his *choosing to* φ to be similarly contingent, assuming, once again, minimal rationality.

What, then, can be said to favour this *doxastic* interpretation over the Standard Interpretation of (1)? The issue is largely empirical, and a full-fledged defence of (PC) must await the presentation of additional proposals which *as a body* are to be measured against the data (see section VI). But three minor considerations merit attention here. First, (PC) does provide *a* sense of contingency useful for explaining some cases of non-deliberation, e.g., that of Nadia and the chocolate ice cream. Second, one must avoid defending the Standard Interpretation by appealing to (3) and its supposed derivative (4), even if these are conditions on deliberation. The derivative guarantees only that a deliberator *does not believe* his φ-ing to be determined, not that he assumes it to be undetermined, and a confusion over the scope of negation in (3) and (4), I suspect, is one reason for the initial appeal of the Standard Interpretation. Finally, the very existence of deliberating determinists who deny holding indeterministic beliefs constitutes *some* evidence that they do not. Of course, this observation must be tempered by the notorious difficulty of establishing non-belief, particularly in this manner, but as inconsistencies are not to be lightly ascribed, it shifts the burden of proof to the opposition.[15]

IV

THE ANALYSIS

Both (PE) and (PC) formulate necessary conditions for a course of action to be presumed as *open* by an agent; jointly, they are sufficient. With temporal parameters implicit once again, we have:

> (PO) an agent presumes that his φ-ing is an open course of action for him *if and only if* (i) he presumes that he would φ if and only if he were to choose to φ, and (ii) he presumes that if $S$ is any set of his beliefs then his φ-ing is contingent relative to $S$.

In yet other words, an agent takes his φ-ing as open just in case he assumes that his will is efficacious and that he both can φ and can refrain from φ-ing. From this basic analysis the other properties of the presumption of open alternatives can be derived (see sections V and VI below).

Nothing has been said about the underlying action theory that a principle like (PO) might require, specifically, about what a *course of action* is. The

---

[15] None of the mentioned adherents of the Standard Interpretation, Taylor, Ginet, Castañeda, Denyer and van Inwagen, has, to my knowledge, seriously considered or, at least, directly discussed, an alternative explication of the modality involved in a deliberator's sense of an open alternative.

schematic letter 'ϕ' is intended to have expressions designating what are often called "action-types" as substituends, whether simple or compound. However, for a theory admitting compound courses of action though not compound action-types, (PO) is limited, and any attempt to extend or adapt the proposals would require more groundwork. An appraisal of (PO) must bear this in mind, but two points can be made here. First, if we view x's not ϕ-ing at $t$ as the *complement* of x's ϕ-ing at $t$ then it is not difficult to see that (PO) yields the desired result that a course of action is presumed as open by an agent if and only if its complement is as well. Second, it is plain that deliberation can also be *hypothetical*, as when one contemplates what to do if some condition $P$ holds, e.g., whether to complain if one loses.[16] Courses of action deliberated about on the supposition that $P$ holds may be said to be open-relative-to-$P$. It is easy enough to construct an analysis of this notion, in turn, along the lines of (PO) with the obvious adjustments in both of the clauses (i) and (ii). Once accomplished, and we acknowledge conditional intentions, then the following should be a targeted theorem: x presumes that his ϕ-ing is open-relative-to-$P$ just in case x presumes that "his ϕ-ing if $P$" is open for him.

Where $(A_1, \ldots, A_n)$ is a set of $n$ distinct courses of action, then the central principle on the presumption of open alternatives is no surprise:

> (POA)   an agent presumes that $(A_1, \ldots, A_n)$ is a range of open alternatives for him *if and only if* (i) for each $A_i$, $1 \leq i \leq n$, he presumes that $A_i$ is open for him, and (ii) he presumes that not all of $(A_1, \ldots A_n)$ are conjointly realizable.

Concerning (ii), it is allowed that an agent takes some of the members of the range to be conjointly realizable, e.g. one might debate whether to go to the butcher's, go to the baker's, or stay home while believing the first two to be compossible. Reference to the totality of the elements in the range is presupposed. If by *deliberative content* we understand a set of courses of action about which one deliberates, then a main assumption throughout has been: a set of courses of action is a deliberative content for an agent only if

---

[16] See, for example, van Inwagen, *op. cit.*, p. 155. The existence of hypothetical deliberation suggests that intentions and, thus, courses of action, can be conditional in form, a point that has long been urged by Castañeda. See, for instance, his *Thinking and Doing*, pp. 160ff., and also his "Reply to Sellars", in *Agent, Language, and the Structure of the World* (New York, 1983), ed., J. E. Tomberlin, pp. 419–33, and compare D. Davidson, *op. cit.*, pp. 92–4. This underscores the previous assertion about the limited nature of (PO) in the form given. I might add that, according to the way (PO) is stated, the very item that is presumed open and deliberated about seems to be the same as that which is said to be contingent in clause (ii). I do not wish to be committed to this. Instead, I am inclined to accept Castañeda's distinction between practical and contemplative thought-contents, *viz.*, between *practitions* and *propositions* to use his terminology, wherein the thing deliberated about is a practition and the thing viewed as contingent is a proposition. See Castañeda's *Thinking and Doing, passim*.

he presumes it to be a range of open alternatives for him. The converse does not hold; a sense of the relative significance of the included items seems required to secure a place in any deliberative content. That is, the presumption of open alternatives is only a necessary condition for deliberation.

Some fine points can be touched upon. For one thing, it may be erroneous to speak of *the* deliberative content if an agent can carry on several deliberations simultaneously. Also, adjustments concerning temporal parameters are needed to cover cases where a course of action comes to be dropped from deliberative content during deliberation. Content can fluctuate and what appears open at the onset of a deliberation may lose this character as the process unfolds (or vice-versa). The failure of the main assumption mentioned in the previous paragraph shows that inclusion of a course of action in deliberative content does not guarantee inclusion of its complement. That is, one can deliberate about two "positive" acts, say, whether to study French or Arabic, without consciously considering the complements of either. (PO) demands only that if a course of action appears open then so does its complement, *not* that if it is deliberated about then so is its complement.

## V

### INDECISION AND UNCERTAINTY

With (PO) and (POA) we have an analysis of a deliberator's presumption of open alternatives. The similarity of this account to the Standard Interpretation is apparent, but there is a fundamental divergence in the way each handles a deliberator's sense of contingency. It remains to be seen whether (PO) and (POA) can be used to explain other features of deliberation, specifically, a deliberator's state of uncertainty and his sense that he is free to choose. First, we consider the former.

Taylor, Ginet and others have argued that one cannot deliberate about doing something if one already knows one will do it (see note 13). Our hiker, for example, does not deliberate about the disjunctive act of taking the path to the right or the one to the left if this is something he has already decided upon and takes for granted he will do. His denial that he can tell which path he will take and his words 'I've not yet made up my mind' point not only to his ignorance or lack of belief about which alternative he will undertake but also to his state of indecision. More directly, there is a connection between deciding and believing what one will do which indicates that (3), if acceptable, should be accompanied by:

> (6) an agent presumes that his $\phi$-ing is an open alternative for him *only if* he has not already decided to $\phi$.

Initially, states of ignorance and indecision appear obvious as antecedents to decision and, thus, as ingredients in the presumption of open alternatives. However, objections have been raised against a requirement of ignorance and, *mutatis mutandis*, against proposals like (3) and (6).[17] For example, it might be thought that a person could decide upon a given course of action, believe he will succeed in his endeavour, and yet deliberate about it. The hiker, having made up his mind to go left, may continue to reflect upon his choice by considering likely benefits of going right or by attempting to locate justificatory grounds for his preference. Though still engaged in practical reasoning, he is no longer deliberating about *whether* to go left; taking the left path, by supposition, has already been settled. On the other hand, his subsequent thought *may* cause him to doubt the wisdom of his choice, deliberate anew about the action, or even abandon his previous decision. This possibility shows, at least, that (3) and (6) cannot stand in the form given. Modified versions might insist that one cannot take $\phi$-ing as open while at the *same* time intending to $\phi$ and believing one will $\phi$. But even these amendments face difficulties. Take the case of Mr. Hawkins who at 10 a.m. not only decides to take his son bowling at 3 p.m. and acquires a belief that he will do so but also instructs his secretary to remind him of this at 2:45 p.m. At 2:44 p.m., preoccupied with the day's business and having temporarily overlooked his earlier resolve, he suddenly deliberates about whether to play golf or to treat his son to a few games of bowling at 3 p.m. Has he abandoned his previous decision? Not necessarily; that he sustains his intention is evidenced by his ready acceptance of his secretary's reminder at 2:45 p.m., which reveals his existing dispositions not only to *affirm* that he will take his son bowling but to have a *volition* to do so. Plainly, the contrast of occurrent with dispositional states applies to intentions as much as to beliefs and, when coupled with the fact that agents can overlook or forget what they have previously accepted, this renders (3) and (6) open to such counterexamples.[18] Schema (4) falls prey to these as well insofar as Hawkins, by satisfying (PE), views his decision as a determining factor, and, with further modifications, the example casts doubt upon the more restricted ignorance requirement.

[17] Ginet's advocacy of the ignorance condition in "Can The Will Be Caused?", for example, has spawned a number of critics including J. Canfield, "Knowing About Future Decisions", *Analysis* 22 (1962), pp. 127–9; J. W. R. Cox, "Can I Know Beforehand What I Am Going to Decide?" *Philosophical Review* 72 (1963), pp. 88–92; and M. Stocker, "Knowledge, Causation and Decision", *Noûs* 2 (1968), pp. 65–73. Richard La Croix has also advocated the ignorance condition in "Omniprescience and Divine Determinism", *Religious Studies* (1976), pp. 365–81, but Phillip Quinn has argued to the contrary in "Divine Foreknowledge and Divine Freedom", *International Journal for Philosophy of Religion* 9 (1978), pp. 219–40. I have also discussed the issue in "Can God Make Up His Mind?", *International Journal for Philosophy of Religion* 15 (1984), pp. 37–47, particularly as it bears on the La Croix/Quinn debate.

[18] In this context a distinction must be drawn between *formulating* a decision, i.e., making up one's mind, and *rehearsing* that decision, viz., consciously affirming an intention already held. Castañeda's work on intentions is especially relevant here, see *Thinking and Doing*, pp. 275–8.

How, then, are we to interpret the hiker's response to the second question? That a decision terminates a period of *in*decision seems beyond doubt and lends immediate credence to Ginet's claim that decision involves change from a state of uncertainty into a kind of knowledge.[19] Restricting (3), (4) and (6) to *occurrent* beliefs and intendings might appear the best that can be hoped for. However, a different sort of problem follows upon this suggestion. The consequents of the conditions so modified still embody negation with larger scope than the (occurrent) attitude. Ascribing no *positive* attitude to deliberators, therefore, they add nothing to the content of the agent's sense of openness and, consequently, are of no assistance in analyzing the hiker's awareness that he has not yet made up his mind, i.e., his feeling of indecision. To capture the latter we need, not (6), but a more complex *presumption of indecision*:

> (PI) an agent presumes that his φ-ing is an open alternative for him *only if* he presumes that he has not yet decided whether or not to φ.[20]

This condition does not do full justice to the hiker's admission of ignorance. Being undecided falls short of a more encompassing state of uncertainty, for it is conceivable that a person might predict his own future undertaking without having yet decided upon it. Recalling our previous observations, a deliberator's prediction cannot be ruled out when construed dispositionally, and the mere exclusion of an occurrent attitude contributes little in analyzing the attitudes identified with a *state* of uncertainty. *Feeling* uncertain, while extending beyond a state of indecision, is not simply a condition of ignorance, and, for that reason, (3) is deficient. A more suitable means of accommodating the hiker's second response is a *presumption of uncertainty*:

> (PU) an agent presumes that his φ-ing is an open alternative for him *only if* he presumes that he does not yet believe whether or not he will φ.

So, we can avoid the difficulties attending (3) and its suggested modifications, yet provide an immediate account of the hiker's professed ignorance. What is essential to realize is that the consequents of (PU) and (PI) describe a state of uncertainty which, being sensitive to cases like those of Mr. Hawkins, preserves the core of Ginet's insight about decision.

---

[19] Ginet, "Can The Will Be Caused?", p. 51. Brian O'Shaughnessy in *The Will: A Dual Aspect Theory* (Cambridge, 1980), p. 297, also endorses a claim of this sort saying that a necessary condition of decision is that it resolves a state of uncertainty about what to do.

[20] I take it as obvious that the phrase 'whether or not' occurring in (PI), and also in (PU) below, indicates a conjunction of denials of belief falling within the scope of 'presumes'.

These proposals are not unrelated. A minimally rational agent understands that if something is or will be caused to occur then it will occur and, thus that if he does not yet believe that it will occur then he does not believe that it is or will be caused to occur. That is, on the rationality proviso, (PU) yields:

> (PS) an agent presumes that his φ-ing is an open alternative for him *only if* he presumes that he does not yet believe that there are conditions sufficient for his φ-ing or for his not φ-ing.

By satisfying the consequents of both (PS) and (PE), in addition, a deliberator realizes he is not committed to the existence of conditions sufficient for his *choice* to φ or not to φ. If, by (PU), he presumes he does not believe (know) that he will φ, then, by (PS) and (PE), he presumes he has not yet decided to φ. That is, on the proviso, not only is (PS) a consequence of (PU), but (PI) follows from (PU) together with (PE).

What about (PU) itself; can it be established on the basis of (PO)? The answer, I think, is yes, assuming, once again, minimal rationality. Suppose that a deliberator satisfies (PC); if he takes his φ-ing not to be contingent with respect to a set $S$ then he will not regard $S$ as a set of his own beliefs. Since he is rational, he does not think his φ-ing to be contingent with respect to the set consisting solely of the proposition *that he φs* at the time in question. So, he does not view the latter as a set of his own beliefs, that is, he believes that he does not believe he will φ at that time. Therefore, he satisfies (PU), and the sense of uncertainty emerges as a dimension of the contingency assumption.

What we have with (PU) and its derivatives (PI) and (PS), in sum, is not a deliberator's ignorance or indecision but, more cautiously, his disposition to affirm his own *non-commitment* to a specific alternative. This in no way implies that one who is conscious of being committed to φ-ing feels *compelled* to φ; he may correctly assume that he is able to refrain from φ-ing in that he would refrain were he to so choose. But while his φ-ing may be seen as a *possible* alternative in this conditional sense, he still might not take it as open. To see this, we need only to remind ourselves of the frequent claim that one *cannot* do a certain thing because one has already decided to do something else, and not because one's will would not be efficacious as regards that act.

Finally, a new light is cast upon the hiker's statement that he is unaware of anything causing him to choose one way or the other, indeed, that he is "free" to undertake either; his presumption of freedom includes recognition *of* both his own uncertainty and lack of intentional resolve. As such, (PU) codifies an additional feature of a deliberator's assumption of an open future and causal independency from the past – without the more sweeping imputations of ignorance and indeterministic beliefs. That it is a consequence of (PO), given a modest assumption of rationality, is an indication of the latter's strength.

## VI

## FREEDOM TO CHOOSE

The largest hurdle remains; does the foregoing do justice to Kant's insight that a deliberator's presumption of open alternatives is an assumption of *freedom*? Much depends upon what precisely is meant by 'freedom' here, but (PO) and (POA) *do* embody elements central to any reliable account of practical freedom, specifically, (i) of *ability* to act, (ii) of *contingency* of the *eventual* undertaking, and (iii) of *non-commitment* to a particular alternative. It is a deliberator's *sense* of (i)-(iii) – within a context fixed by what he himself takes to be the case – that *is* his presumption of freedom and self-agency. In this way, the above account presents a genuine philosophical contrast to the Standard Interpretation which construes freedom in terms of undetermined choice. Nevertheless, more is needed to show that the agent thereby takes himself as *free to choose* from among the alternatives before him.

It has already been remarked that (PO) explains certain cases of non-deliberation, e.g., why Nadia does not deliberate about eating chocolate ice cream, or, why a compulsive truth-teller – aware of his irresistible desires – does not consider lying to his best friend. In both, the agent takes himself as unable to choose, and it is failure to satisfy (PC) and (PS) that makes the difference. In other cases both (PC) and (PS) might be satisfied but (PE) not: consider a man in a room with a single door he believes to be locked but who knows that at 11 a.m. it will either be flung open or remain locked; he cannot deliberate about whether to open the door at 11 a.m. since he does not envision his will as efficacious in the matter. Van Inwagen describes a man in a room with two doors, one of which he believes to be locked and the other unlocked though he does not know which, suggesting that he cannot deliberate about which door to leave by. Failure to satisfy (PE), once again, can account for this, though it need not prevent the man from deliberating about which door to *try*. On the other hand, if deliberating about trying to φ is, by that very fact, deliberating about φ – thereby disputing the example – then the probability qualifiers implicit in (PE) lend it a desired flexibility.

How do we characterize the deliberator's presumption that he is free to choose, that he has both the ability to choose to φ and the ability to choose not to φ (or, to refrain from choosing φ)? Consider Nadia who, having ruled out chocolate, is still faced with a decision about which of the remaining 32 flavours to order. Suppose that she satisfies both (PE) and (PC) as regards each alternative; does she, therefore, find herself *free to choose*? If at all adequate, our analysis must sustain an affirmative response. But here comes a challenge. Imagine that Nadia consciously believes what the local astrologer told her, namely, there is a certain flavour such that it is already determined she will not choose it, though she has no idea which flavour this is. Assume, moreover, that she is not so irrational as to also believe her not choosing this flavour to be undetermined. Can she deliberate about which kind of ice cream to order? We come to a critical parting of ways; Nadia's deliberation is permitted as far as (PO) is concerned, but the Standard Interpretation must rule it out. That is, since Nadia now fails to believe of each alternative that not choosing it is undetermined, she does not take it as unqualifiedly contingent, and so, by the Standard Interpretation, her deliberation would be *pointless*; realizing that her choice is not entirely "under her control", Nadia must remain without ice cream.

This latter assessment seems unreasonable. Why shouldn't the following thoughts convince Nadia, and ourselves, that deliberation here *does* have a point? Look, I am hungry for ice cream and I want to select a kind that is both tasty and filling. I have definite likes and dislikes and I know I will order a given flavour just in case I choose to do so. Moreover, I will choose a flavour only *through a conscious effort on my part*, even if it is already determined, by the stars or whatever, that I will not choose one of them, whichever it might be. As far as *I* can tell the matter is entirely under my control: I *can* choose any one of the 32 flavours even though, at this stage, I am undecided as to which. I must, in any case, try something and it is only through deliberation that I will make the best choice.

In attributing to Nadia the belief that she is already determined not to choose one of the flavours we are not supposing that she will be, or believes she will be, *prevented* from so doing, i.e., that she would fail were she to somehow try to choose one of the flavours. At the same time, in analyzing her claim that she takes herself as *able to choose* we cannot simply ascribe a belief that there is no obstacle preventing her from carrying out her will, and in this, ability to choose differs from ability to *do* (which does involve such a belief). But certain analogies persist. That X *can* $\phi$ is equivalent to its being possible that X $\phi$s, and it is essential that what is said to be possible is an *action of X's*, as distinct from a mere bodily movement where agency is not so implied. Similarly, to say X *can choose* to $\phi$ is to say that it is possible that X chooses to $\phi$ and, with this, X continues to be viewed as an agent, a *maker* of choices, and not merely a passive object in some event or state-of-affairs.

The substantive claim concerns not agency but modality; when Nadia assumes it *possible* that she chooses any of the 32 flavours, the doxastic interpretation suffices to unpack the modality. Notice that her situation is not akin to one who feels he "has no choice" in the usual sense that his will would not be efficacious, e.g., one who does not deliberate about hovering unaided above the floor. Nor is it that of the compulsive truth-teller who finds himself unable to lie to a friend; thinking that he cannot choose to lie because of his own internal condition he fails to satisfy the consequent of (PC). Nadia, on the contrary, retains a sense of an open future to be partially completed by actions resultant upon choices which she yet takes as contingent given circumstances *as she understands them*. Her sense of an ability to choose consists in her presumptions that (i) her choosing to order any of the 32 flavours is contingent relative to what she then believes; (ii) she does not believe of any flavour that there are conditions sufficient for her choosing it or for her not choosing it; and (iii) her choosing *is* a conscious effort of *her own*. Both (i) and (ii) follow directly from (PO), while (iii) is a result of her having a concept of what a *choice* (an intention) is. More briefly, Nadia's sense of the contingency of what she is to choose, together with her conception of a choice as a conscious effort on her part, *is* her presumption of an ability to choose. Coupling this with her belief in the efficacy of her will and her desires to have the future completed in this way rather than that, we have all that is needed to give deliberation a "point".

This conclusion remains in force even if Nadia assumes that her choosing precisely one of the flavours, whatever it might be, is already determined, *viz.*, even if Nadia is a full-blown determinist. At this point, no doubt, we arrive at a vivid clash of intuitions, perhaps, to a conflict that can only be settled by appeal to experimental psychology. But, at this level, the leap to the unqualified sense of 'can', or absolute contingency, has been premature. The doxastic characterization of the modality embedded in a deliberator's sense of ability cannot be disqualified if it has yet to be articulated and subjected to proper test.[21]

[21] It might be charged that I have dealt unfairly with the Standard Interpretation inasmuch as its adherents do offer arguments in its favour. Arguments yes, but arguments whose inadequacy is due to a failure to explore alternative explications of 'possible' and 'determined'. In "Might We Have No Choice?" Ginet, for instance, has argued in the following manner: a deliberator must believe that his eventual choice is *effective*, i.e., that he "has" a choice (pp. 92–93); determinism, however, entails that our choices are always ineffective (pp. 90, 93); hence, anyone who believes in determinism either cannot choose at all or else is aware that he is constantly deluded – an "implausible" if not "impossible" condition to be in (pp. 93, 104). What is the meaning of 'effective' and 'has a choice' in this argument? From his examples of the prisoner and the child in an amusement park, one's choice to φ is ineffective if one's choice is not an essential factor in determining whether one will φ. But a determinist need not believe his choice is ineffective in *this* sense; if he satisfies the efficacy assumption then he obviously thinks that his intentions *are* essential components in causal chains leading up to his actions, and this is compatible with the belief that his intentions and actions are already determined. On the other hand, if an ineffective choice is, by definition, an *undetermined* choice, as the discussion on pp. 90–92 suggests, then it is the initial premise of Ginet's argument that demands further defence. In either case, the argument as it stands poses no obstacles to the proposed theory. On the contrary, since the position to which the deliberating determinist is forced by the Standard Interpretation is indeed implausible, it is a *virtue* of our proposals that they rescue the determinist from this doxastic quagmire.

Principles (PO) and (POA) can also be used to explain a deliberator's *awareness* or *feeling* of freedom. Of course, this feeling is not an invariant companion of deliberation; it emerges only when a measure of contemplative thinking overlays the process of practical reasoning, of deciding what to do, or how, or when to do it. This does not negate the fact that the feeling is *of* something that permeates deliberation all along. Of what? Not the act of choosing, for this is precisely what terminates awareness of indecision, contingency and an open future.[22] Instead, the agent's focus is now upon his ability to think and act within a context fixed by his own doxastic and intentional states; the feeling *is* the activation of the dispositions ascribed in (PO) and (POA).

Like its competitor, the doxastic interpretation preserves the indeterminacy of the future. More than this; it comprehends a factor that the Standard Interpretation cannot. A person who deliberates about whether to eat an apple, an orange or a peach may claim to be conscious that nothing causally necessitates his choice. Is there not some sense in which he is epistemically *justified*, by his experience, in saying that he is free to eat any of the fruit? An affirmative response not only provides grounds for distinguishing between the experience and the mere rehearsal of belief, it nicely explains the universality and conviction with which the assumption of freedom is held. This is no brute endorsement of indeterminism; the deliberator who says he is free *as far as he can tell* may very well be justified in so doing, for the contingency is there, detectable within his experiential content. But there is no reason to suppose that he can similarly be justified – by his experience – in claiming that he is free with respect to *all* past and present conditions, even if this latter claim is true. It is the doxastic interpretation that is on firmer footing here, and *if* the deliberator's choice is determined, then it is *this* view which avoids the uncomfortable conclusion that his *experience*, not just his belief, is purely illusory.[23]

## VII.

## CONCLUDING REMARKS

Although the preceding discussion has centered on deliberation, it is likely that the proposals culminating in (PO) and (POA) have a wider applicability.

[22] Here I go against the suggestion offered by Douglas Browning in "The Feeling of Freedom", *Review of Metaphysics* 18 (1964), pp. 123–46, who writes: "The long sought feeling of freedom is no other than the experience of the act of choice itself as it is performed, as it must be performed, within the practical stance" (p. 145). Compare, Boyle, Grisez and Tollefsen, *op. cit.*, pp. 18–20.

[23] Boyle, Grisez and Tollefsen, *op. cit.*, pp. 20–3, are also careful to distinguish the *experience* of freedom from the *judgment* that one is free. That an awareness of freedom would be virtually impossible if freedom is analyzed in terms of unqualified contingency has been emphasized by J. W. Corman and K. Lehrer in *Philosophical Problems and Arguments*, (New York, 1968), pp. 131–47.

For one thing, they seem to pertain to all *choice*, even that which does not emerge from conscious deliberation, insofar as decision involves a selection among presumed alternatives. Perhaps they govern all *intention* as well; what is the point of intending something which is not taken as open at some time before intending it? If so, then each intention is a choice, minimally, between a course of action and its complement, and we can appreciate anew Kant's insistence that a presupposition of freedom underlies all practical thought. Additionally, the proposals imply that an omniscient being cannot deliberate, choose, or perhaps, intend – a consequence of no small theological importance if creativity, perfection, or omnipotence necessitate such abilities.[24] It remains to be seen what relevance they have for the overall free will controversy, though there is every reason to suspect a firm and fruitful linkage.

The spectacle of a determinist who deliberates is at first perplexing. What is the point of deliberating if whatever one chooses and does is already determined? What difference can one's own deliberations possibly make? Faced with such questions, some conclude that we are, by our very nature as rational agents, indeterminists – an idea which can only disturb the determinist who takes his actions and volitions to be the outcome of antecedent factors while retaining a passion for consistency. Agreeing that an agent has a sense of the contingency of his own future, I have urged that the modality is indexed to what he himself assumes to be the case; it need not be a presumption of the non-existence of any determining conditions whatever. No more is required to give deliberation a point than the agent's ends, his belief that those ends will not be realized except through his own intentional activity, and his sense of freedom based, in part, upon his incomplete grasp of the future. If forgetfulness, as Nietzsche once wrote, is a precondition of action, an imperfect conception of what will be is no less essential. Practically-minded determinists, haunted by the spectres of inconsistency and fatalism, can be encouraged by this account of the matter.[25]

*Birzeit University*

[24] I refer the reader to the papers by La Croix, Quinn, and myself listed in note 17 above.

[25] I am indebted to Hector-Neri Castañeda for the valuable comments and criticisms he has provided during the development of this paper, to J. Christopher Maloney who years ago first kindled my interest in deliberation, and to Robert Audi, Robert Good, Hugh Harcourt, Steven Lee, Al Mele, Ron Miller, George Nakhnikian, Mark Pastin, Lynn Stephens, Eric Stiffler and Leslie Stevenson for their helpful comments on earlier versions.

# DISCUSSION

## VAN INWAGEN ON FREE WILL

### By John Martin Fischer

Recently, Peter Van Inwagen has presented a family of three arguments for the incompatibility of causal determinism and human freedom.[1] Here, I wish to focus on what he calls the "First Formal Argument". I shall contend that it is not convincing because it employs a premise which is highly controversial, and the evidence adduced in support of this premise does *not* support it over weaker premises which are consistent with compatibilism. I do not plan to argue that Van Inwagen's argument is obviously unsound; rather, I intend to show that it is not decisive, because it is incomplete in an important sense.

## I

## VAN INWAGEN'S ARGUMENT

The argument can be presented as follows. Determinism is defined as the conjunction of the following two theses:

> For every instant of time, there is a proposition that expresses the state of the world at that instant;

> If $p$ and $q$ are any propositions that express the state of the world at some instants, then the conjunction of $p$ with the laws of nature entails $q$. (p. 65)

Also, the following symbols are used. '$T_o$' shall denote some arbitrarily chosen instant of time earlier than J's birth; '$P_o$' shall denote the proposition that expresses the state of the world at $T_o$; 'P' shall denote the proposition that expresses the state of the world at T (it implies that J did not raise his hand at T), and 'L' shall denote the conjunction into a single proposition of all the laws of nature (pp. 69–70).

Van Inwagen's "First Formal Argument" consists of seven propositions, the seventh of which is alleged to follow from the first six (p. 70):

---

[1] Peter Van Inwagen, *An Essay on Free Will* (Oxford, 1984); page references hereafter are to this work. Van Inwagen first presented similar arguments in: "A Formal Approach to the Free Will Problem", *Theoria* 40 (1974), and "The Incompatibility of Free Will and Determinism", *Philosophical Studies* 27 (1975), pp. 185–99.

(1) If determinism is true, then the conjunction of $P_0$ and L entails P.

(2) It is not possible that J have raised his hand at T and P be true.

(3) If (2) is true, then if J could have raised his hand at T, J could have rendered P false.

(4) If J could have rendered P false, and if the conjunction of $P_0$ and L entails P, then J could have rendered the conjunction $P_0$ and L false.

(5) If J could have rendered the conjunction of $P_0$ and L false, then J could have rendered L false.

(6) J could not have rendered L false.

So  (7) If determinism is true, J could not have raised his hand at T.

This argument is powerful and disturbing. In evaluating it, it is crucial to understand the key phrase 'S can render P false'. Consider the following account: "S can render P false just in case it is within S's power to arrange or modify the concrete objects that constitute his environment in some way such that it is not possible "in the broadly logical sense" that he arrange or modify these objects in that way and P be true" (p. 67). Roughly speaking, I can render P false, on this account, insofar as I can affect my environment in such a way that my doing so would *entail* that P is false. Let us call this definition "account I".

Although Van Inwagen earlier presented this as adequately capturing the intuitive concept of being able to render a proposition false, he now recognizes that this account is unacceptable.[2] He says:

> Let us suppose that in 1550 Nostradamus predicted that the Sphinx would endure till the end of the world. And let us suppose that this prediction was correct and, in fact, that *all* Nostradamus's predictions were correct. Let us also suppose that it was within Gamel Abdel Nasser's power to have the Sphinx destroyed. Then, I should think, it was within Nasser's power to render false the proposition that all Nostradamus's predictions were correct. But this would not be the case according to the definition proposed in the preceding paragraph [account I], since it is possible in the broadly logical sense that Nasser have had the Sphinx destroyed and yet all Nostradamus's predictions have been correct. That is, there are possible worlds in which the proposition that all Nostradamus's predictions were correct is true and in which Nasser had the Sphinx destroyed: worlds in which Nostradamus did not predict that the Sphinx would endure till the end of the world and made no other

[2] Account I is the proposal which Van Inwagen accepted in his "Reply to Narveson", *Philosophical Studies* 32 (1977), p. 93.

predictions that would have been falsified by Nasser's destruction of the Sphinx. (pp. 67–68)[3]

In order to rule out such counter-examples, Van Inwagen suggests that we "build the past into" our definition, suggesting that we define 'S can render P false' as follows:

> It is within S's power to arrange or modify the concrete objects that constitute his environment in some way such that it is not possible in the broadly logical sense that he arrange or modify these objects in that way and the past have been exactly as it in fact was and P be true. (p. 68)

Let us call this definition "account II". Van Inwagen does not claim that this is the *only* way of ruling out the counter-examples; rather, he says that it seems to be the "best way" to do so. It should be noted that this account of 'S can render P false' has the consequence of making premise (5) trivially true – (5) follows directly from account II of 'S can render P false', and Van Inwagen exploits this fact in his presentation of his argument.

## II

### THE DENIAL OF PREMISE (6)

Whereas premise (5) is trivially true, on account II, premise (6) is controversial. Consider what Van Inwagen says about (6): "This premise would seem to be an obvious consequence of what we said about our powers with respect to the laws of nature . . . " (p. 72). His claim about the relationship between our powers and the laws of nature can be understood on the basis of the following sort of example:

> Suppose a bureaucrat of the future orders an engineer to build a spaceship capable of travelling faster than light. The engineer tells the bureaucrat that it's a law of nature that nothing travels faster than light. The bureaucrat concedes this difficulty, but counsels perseverance: 'I'm sure', he says, 'that if you work hard and are very clever, you'll find some way to go faster than light, even though it's a law of nature that nothing does'. Clearly his demand is simply incoherent. (p. 62)

Van Inwagen's point is that if performing a certain act would require that a law of nature be violated, then no human agent can perform the act. But his defence of the controversial premise (6) is a bit misleading, and, I believe, unsatisfying. It is misleading because one might deny (6) for reasons *entirely*

---

[3] For a similar criticism of a parallel suggestion made by Joshua Hoffman, see: John Martin Fischer, "Freedom and Foreknowledge", *Philosophical Review* 92 (1983), p. 72.

*apart* from any consideration of the relationship between our powers and natural laws; that is, one might *accept* everything Van Inwagen says about the relationship between natural laws and human freedom and still deny (6).

Let us suppose that one believes that in the situation described in Van Inwagen's argument, the following "backtracking conditional" would be true: If J had raised his hand at T, then $P_o$ wouldn't have obtained at $T_o$. (I shall consider the position which *denies* this backtracker below.) The conditional here is to be interpreted *non-causally*. Now, if one also believes that J could at T have raised his hand at T, then one is committed to the following conjunction of a "can-claim" and a backtracking conditional: "J could at T have raised his hand at T, and if he had done so, the past would have been different from what it actually was (insofar as $P_o$ wouldn't have obtained at $T_o$)". It follows that one believes that J could at T have rendered L false (on account II), because one believes that J could have so arranged things (raised his hand) that it was impossible that he so arrange things and the past have been as it actually was (i.e., $P_o$ obtained at $T_o$) and L be true. But since one believes that if J had raised his hand at T, then $P_o$ wouldn't have obtained at $T_o$, one *doesn't* believe that if J had raised his hand at $T_o$, L wouldn't have obtained.

So one can deny (6) in virtue of a belief in the coherence of the conjunction of the can-claim and the backtracker, and thus one can deny (6) even while accepting Van Inwagen's claim that no one can so act that a law of nature which does obtain wouldn't obtain. This claim has it that if doing X requires the violation of a natural law, then one *can't* do X. But one can *agree* with this claim and still hold that an agent might be able to render a proposition about a natural law L false. This is because (as I have just shown) one might believe that an agent can render L false *without* being able to perform an act which is such that, were he to perform it, L wouldn't obtain.

Now it might be thought that Van Inwagen has already offered reason to think that the conjunction of a can-claim and a backtracker is incoherent insofar as he has defended premise (5). But this is a mistake, since all that he has established (trivially, I might add) is that one cannot (on account II) render a proposition about the past false. But it clearly *doesn't follow* that one cannot perform some act which is such that, if one were to perform it, the past would have been different from what it actually was. As far as I can see, then, Van Inwagen's defence of (6) is inadequate: it doesn't address itself at all to a possible way of denying (6).

But is it reasonable to think that a conjunction of a can-claim and the relevant backtracking conditional is coherent? It is important to see that this view does *not* commit one to the claim that one can initiate a backward-flowing chain of causation; the relevant 'if' has to be non-causal, and the claim is that there is no reason to suppose that the truth of a "backtracking" conditional rules out the truth of the pertinent claim about freedom. So, it is important to distinguish the following two principles which express different conceptions of the "fixity" of the past:

(FP1)  If $e_1$ occurred at $t_1$, then no agent can at any time later than $t_1$ initiate a causal sequence issuing in $e_1$'s *not* occurring at $t_1$.

(FP2)  If $e_1$ occurred at $t_1$, then no agent can at any time later than $t_1$ perform an action such that if he were to perform it, $e_1$ would not have occurred at $t_1$.

Whereas it is quite clear that (FP1) is valid, it is *not* so evident that (FP2) (with the 'if' interpreted non-causally) is also valid. One might mistakenly think that (FP2) is valid by failing to distinguish it from (FP1).[4] And the truth of premise (6) requires not only the truth of (FP1), but also (as I have argued above) that of (FP2).

Van Inwagen might insist that he would reject even (FP2) and that this rejection is *not* based on any sort of confusion. He might employ the following kind of evidence to support his position:

Consider, for example, the propositions
    The Spanish Armada was defeated in 1588
and
    Peter Van Inwagen never visits Alaska.
For all I know, the conjunction of these two propositions is true. At any rate, let us assume it is true. Given that it is true, it seems quite clear that I can render it false if and only if I can visit Alaska. (pp. 72–73)

But this sort of evidence is, I think, inconclusive. It might well be true that no one can now perform an act which is such that, were he to perform it, the Spanish Armada *wouldn't* have been defeated in 1588. But it *doesn't* follow that no agent can ever perform an act which is such that, were he to perform it, the past would have been different (in *some* respect) from what it actually was. The compatibilist wants to say that it is possible that a certain sort of *conjunction* obtain – a conjunction of a can-claim (a claim specifying that an agent can perform some act X) and a relevant backtracking conditional (a claim saying that if the agent were to do X, the past would have been different in some respect from what it actually was). Now it seems to be true

[4] For this point, see: Richard Foley, "Compatibilism and Control Over the Past", *Analysis* 39 (1979), pp. 70–4; John Martin Fischer, "Incompatibilism", *Philosophical Studies* 43 (1983), pp. 130–1.

that we intuitively would never assent to the conjunction 'Agent A can do X and if he were to do X, then the Spanish Armada wouldn't have been defeated in 1588'. But this might not be because we never would assent to *any* conjunction of a can-claim and a backtracker. Rather, it might be because there is no available act of which we could truly say that if an agent were now to perform it, the Spanish Armada wouldn't have been defeated in 1588. That is, the plausibility of denying Van Inwagen's conjunction might come from scepticism about the truth of this particular conditional, rather than a *general* view that one can never have a true conjunction of a can-claim and a relevant backtracking conditional. So the example does *not* establish that (FP2) is true and thus does not support premise (6).

As I pointed out above, Van Inwagen doesn't claim that employing account II is the *only* way to avoid the counter-examples to account I. And there is a relatively simple alternative which seems to me to avoid the problems with account I. Consider account III of 'S can render P false':

> It is within S's power to arrange or modify the concrete objects that constitute his environment in some way such that if he were so to arrange them, P would be false.

This differs from I by replacing entailment by the weaker subjunctive conditional. Remember that account I had the unhappy consequence that, in the situation described above, Nasser couldn't render false the proposition that all Nostradamus's predictions are correct. But account III avoids this result. If Nasser had destroyed the Sphinx, then Nostradamus would still have predicted that the Sphinx wouldn't be destroyed. Thus, Nasser would have acted in such a way that Nostradamus's prediction would be false, and hence, on account III, Nasser would have rendered false the proposition 'All of Nostradamus's predictions are true'.[5]

It is important to notice that on account III, premise (5) becomes questionable (for the reasons adduced above). That is, no argument has been given that one can't so act that some fact about the past would have been different, where this does not require backwards causation. At least it is clear that Van Inwagen would need another argument for (5), since his argument *rests on* account II. (p. 73) In order to avoid a certain sort of counter-example to account I, Van Inwagen modified I in such a way that premise (5) became

---

[5] It might be objected that on account III, one can render false any proposition which is in fact false. So I can render it false that Walter Mondale is President in 1984. This does indicate (perhaps) that there is a divergence between the pre-analytic notion of being able to render a proposition false (if there is such a notion pre-analytically) and account III. Of course, the argument needn't use a phrase which corresponds exactly to any intuitive pre-analytic idea. And Van Inwagen points out that on his own account II, one can render false any false proposition about the past. So account III appears to fare no worse than Van Inwagen's II in capturing the intuitive idea.

trivially true; but I have claimed that one *needn't* so modify account I, in order to avoid the counter-examples, and if one adopts account III, premise (5) becomes vulnerable. So there is no account on which both (5) and (6) are uncontroversially true.

## III

## THE FIXITY OF THE LAWS

In section II, I argued that Van Inwagen's defence of premise (6) is insufficient insofar as one can accept all that he says about freedom and laws and still deny (6). In this section, I shall argue that his examples do *not* establish his claim about the relationship between freedom and laws, but only a weaker claim. Thus, there seems to be another way which is open to a compatibilist to reject premise (6).[6] Let us distinguish between two different conceptions of the fixity of the natural laws:

(FL1)   No agent can ever perform an act which itself would be or would cause a law-breaking event, and

(FL2)   No agent can ever so act that a law-breaking event would (at some point) have occurred.

And whereas it is quite clear that (FL1) is valid, it is not so evident that (FL2) is. Consider again Van Inwagen's example of the engineer and the bureaucrat: the problem is that it does not support the stronger (FL2) over the weaker (FL1). It is intuitively apparent that I cannot fly faster than the speed of light – to do so would be to perform an act which would itself be a law-breaking event. (I suppose that even the attribution of such a power to Superman was an exaggeration for effect!) And no engineer can build a spaceship which travels faster than light. To do so would be to perform an act which would cause law-breaking events. We can easily think of many examples where the fact that a possible action would itself be or cause a law-breaking event impels us to think that a person *can't* perform the action.

But suppose that I fail to raise my hand at time T and determinism obtains. Then it might be true that if I had raised my hand at T, some law which actually obtained *wouldn't have* obtained (perhaps just prior to T). Now, if this were the case, then raising my hand wouldn't itself be or cause a law-breaking event – I do not envisage that I would raise my hand at a speed which is faster than light! All that's true is that if I had raised my hand at T,

[6] Here I am indebted to David Lewis, "Are We Free to Break the Laws?", *Theoria* 47 (1981), pp. 113–21.

some law which actually obtained wouldn't have obtained. And it's not so obvious that this fact rules it out that I can raise my hand at T.

The point is that there are two different ways in which it might be true that a person can so act that a natural law would be false. And whereas it is evident that no agent can so act that a law would be false in the first way – by performing an act which would be or cause a law-breaking event – it is not so clear that no agent can so act that a law would be false in the second way – by performing an act which itself would not be (and wouldn't cause) a law-breaking event. At least it is useful to note that the examples typically adduced (and adduced by Van Inwagen) do not themselves establish the claim that the laws are "fixed", interpreted in the second way. It is *this* interpretation which is required by premise (6) and thus incompatibilism.

Having distinguished two ways of so acting that a natural law would be false, it is useful to distinguish *three* different ways in which one might think that an agent can render a law L false (on Van Inwagen's account II). In the first way, one believes that an agent can act in such a way that the past would have been different from what it actually was and L would have still obtained. (This denies FP2.) In the second way, one believes that an agent can perform an act (which itself wouldn't be or cause a law-breaking event) such that, if he were to perform it, L wouldn't have obtained. (This denies FL2.) And finally, in the third way, one believes that an agent can perform an act which itself would be or cause a law-breaking event. (This denies FL1.) Distinguishing these three ways of rendering L false can illuminate a related argument presented by Van Inwagen:

> Let us use 'T' to designate the moment of time that occurred one half hour ago. Let 'P' designate the proposition that I did not visit Arcturus at T. Let '$P_o$' designate the proposition that expresses the state of the world one minute before my birth. (Note that $P_o$ entails the proposition that at that moment Arcturus and I were separated by a distance of about $3.6 \times 10^{17}$ metres.) Let 'L' designate the proposition that nothing travels faster than $3 \times 10^8$ metres per second. We may now argue:
>
> (1) The conjunction of $P_o$ and L entails P.
> (2) It is not possible that I have visited Arcturus at T and P be true.
> (3) If (2) is true, then if I could have visited Arcturus at T, I could have rendered P false.
> (4) If I could have rendered P false, and if the conjunction of $P_o$ and L entails P, then I could have rendered the conjunction of $P_o$ and L false.
> (5) If I could have rendered the conjunction of $P_o$ and L false, then I could have rendered L false.

(6)  I could not have rendered L false.

So      (7)  I could not have visited Arcturus at T.

> This seems to be a perfectly cogent and unexceptionable argument
> for the conclusion that I could not have visited Arcturus at T.
> Anyone who thinks he can demonstrate that one of the premises of
> the First Formal Argument is false, must either show that his
> argument does not also 'demonstrate' the falsity of the correspond-
> ing premise of the 'Arcturus' argument, or else he must accept this
> conclusion and explain why the apparent truth of the premise of the
> 'Arcturus' argument is only apparent. Perhaps someone will be able
> to do one of these things, but this project does not look very
> promising to me. (pp. 76–77)

Having made the distinction above, we can undertake the "unpromising
project" as follows. In the "Arcturus" argument, the only way I can render L
false is to travel faster than $3 \times 10^8$ metres per second. That is, the only way I
can render L false is in the *third* way – by performing an act which *itself*
would be a law-breaking event. Thus, one can *agree* with Van Inwagen that
the "Arcturus" argument is sound *without* committing oneself to the sound-
ness of the First Formal Argument, insofar as the latter merely requires that
S be able to render L false in one of the first two ways, which have *not* been
shown to be incoherent by Van Inwagen! Thus, one can say that one of the
premises of the First Formal Argument is false without having to say that the
corresponding premise of the "Arcturus" argument is false: this premise is
(6).

## IV

## CONCLUSION

Finally, I wish to consider the kind of response to the arguments I have
made above which might be given. Remember, I have not attempted to prove
compatibilism; rather, I have been focusing on what I take to be *gaps* in Van
Inwagen's argument for incompatibilism. He might respond as follows.[7]
"You are simply pointing out that *if* compatibilism is true, then one of the
premises of my argument must be false. But this is obvious, since the
argument is valid! And it is clearly unfair to *assume* the truth of compatibilism, insofar as this is, after all, the question at issue. That is, you are not
entitled to assert the can-claims, given the hypothesis of determinism.
Finally, I am much more confident of the truth of all of my premises

---

[7]  See pp. 74–5, and "Reply to Narveson", *Philosophical Studies* 32 (1977), pp. 94–6.

(interpreted so as to make the argument valid) than I am of compatibilism, which is, at best, a highly controversial philosophical thesis."

I believe that this response seriously distorts the dialectical situation. My position does *not* rest on the assumption that compatibilism is true or that it is intuitively more plausible than all of the premises. Rather, the situation is as follows. Van Inwagen has presented an argument which purports to *establish* incompatibilism. Premise (6) is highly controversial and all of the examples which he adduces are compatible with its being the case that only *weaker* premises than (6) are true; so Van Inwagen does not *yet* have a convincing argument for incompatibilism. If a group of examples supports a principle P2 as firmly as P1, but only P1 renders a given argument valid, then simply in virtue of adducing the examples, one hasn't *yet* decisively supported the argument. Finally, I am not *asserting* the pertinent can-claims. All I am pointing out is that if compatibilism is true, then one must accept the coherence of the conjunction of a can-claim with a certain sort of statement. Of course, I have not *shown* that this sort of conjunction is coherent; it is Van Inwagen's job to show that this sort of conjunction is incoherent, insofar as he purports to establish incompatibilism.

It might be objected that it is unreasonable to demand that a philosopher provide examples which absolutely *require* one to accept his position. It seems that it is *necessarily* the case that if a philosopher argues for a certain general principle by giving examples, a weaker principle can be found that might be the strongest principle the examples support.[8] I believe that it is nevertheless important to see exactly where the gaps are in the incompatibilist's argument and thus to see that it is *not* an argument proceeding from premises that no sane person could doubt, by reasoning no sane person could question, to the conclusion that determinism rules out freedom. Also, it is useful to see that the plausibility of the incompatibilist's argument rests on the claims that if one accepts (FP1) one ought also to accept (FP2) and that if one accepts (FL1) one ought also to accept (FL2). The challenge for the incompatibilist consists in explaining why we ought to proceed from the weaker to the stronger principles; without such an explanation, there remains a gap in the argument for incompatibilism.[9]

*Yale University*

[8] I am indebted here to personal correspondence with Peter Van Inwagen.

[9] I have developed similar criticisms of Van Inwagen's "modal argument" for incompatibilism in: Fischer, "Incompatibilism", *Philosophical Studies* 43 (1983), and "Freedom and Miracles", forthcoming, *Noûs*. For a recent criticism of Van Inwagen's arguments, see: Terence Horgan, "Compatibilism and the Consequence Argument", *Philosophical Studies* 47 (1985), pp. 339–56.

# CRITICAL STUDIES

## THE WITHERING AWAY OF THE COGNITIVE STATE

### By Flint Schier

Stephen Stich, *From Folk Psychology to Cognitive Science*. London: MIT Press, 1983.     pp. xii+266. Price £18.25 (pb £8.95)

Stich's central claim in this complex, difficult but highly rewarding book is that cognitive science must dispense with propositional attitudes because:

(1) The taxonomy of propositional attitudes is content-sensitive and must therefore take into account both the agent's other propositional attitudes and the way the agent himself is installed in a world of fellow language-users and other external objects.

(2) The taxonomy of mental states proper to a science of mind will extrude all information regarding the way the mind is embedded in the world.

If both of these claims can be substantiated, then we will be forced to conclude, as Stich thinks we should, that we cannot conjure up cognitive science from the murky deeps of our everyday folksy propositional attitude psychology.

I

Let me begin with Stich's claim that propositional attitude (hereafter 'PA') psychology is irreducibly ecological. It is evident that an ordinary, folk-psychological explanation of an action cites the agent's beliefs and pro-attitudes, along with a host of other background character dispositions. And, clearly one can't ever explain an action without saying or intimating *what* beliefs and desires the agent was acting upon. For example, you can't explain Sergio's drinking a can of paint simply by saying "He has beliefs and desires". You have to say *what* beliefs and desires actually moved him to this eccentric behaviour, and this requires you to specify their propositional content. So it would be a sort of explanation of Sergio's activity to say "He did it because he just wanted to", for that suggests, in the context, that he *just* wanted to drink a can of paint (in Davidsonian terms, Sergio had an unmotivated primary reason for doing so). Of course, the canonical way (according to Davidson 1968[1]) of specifying the agent's beliefs and pro-attitudes is to assert a sentence of the form 'A *m*'s that' (where 'A' specifies a person, 'm' specifies a mental mode like belief or hope, and 'that' is a demonstrative which indicates the proposition expressed by the next sentence uttered), and then to follow that assertion with an utterance of some sentence *s*. The assertion will be true just if the content properly ascribed to *s* in the belief-ascriber's language is the content of one of A's mental states of mode *m*.

It should now be apparent why propositional content should be the feature in terms of which we classify (for example) beliefs, for it is only when we have specified this content in some way that we can understand the causal or explanatory significance of the belief in question. From the point of view of folk psychology, when we specify the mode and propositional content of a mental state (e.g. desire, and 'that I have a sloop') we are citing *the* explanatorily relevant features of that state. The practice of content ascription is therefore basic to folk psychology. We can no more understand what someone has done without understanding the contents of their beliefs and desires than we can understand what they have said without understanding the content of their utterance. The project of explaining action, like that of understanding speech, is irreducibly interpretative. Understanding someone's behaviour is a matter of our knowing both the mode and the content of their relevant mental states, plus a theory of how those states causally interact to produce behaviour in given stimulus conditions.

Now it is one of Stich's most interesting contentions that the propositional content of our mental states can be shown to be causally inert. This conclusion by itself would be surprising, since if the story we have just told is true, we suppose that the content of the state is one of the things we must know in order to understand how it interacts with other states to produce behaviour.

Stich's argument for the inertness of propositional content (Chap. 4, Sec. 2) appears to turn on Hilary Putnam's famous claim that "meaning ain't in the head" (Putnam 1975 a; see also Burge 1982). Putnam articulated this claim by envisaging a planet he called Twin Earth which is a mirror image of Earth down to the very last detail but one. On Twin Earth, the stuff, "twater", which looks, tastes and acts like water is not made of $H_2O$ but of XYZ. According to Putnam this stuff isn't water. Since everyone on Earth has a Twin Earth *Doppelgänger*, Earthling Sergio will have a duplicate, let's call him Sergio$_{te}$, who has exact analogues of Sergio's prejudices against Frenchmen, his penchant for Proust and his phobia of spiders, etc. Each of Sergio's beliefs, desires and so on will be perfectly mirrored in Sergio$_{te}$.

[1] For all references in this form, see Bibliography on p.172

However, there will be small differences. For example, when Sergio$_{te}$ is in a belief state that he sincerely expresses by saying "This is drinkable water" he is not in the same belief state that Earthling Sergio would sincerely express by uttering the same sentence (or the same syntactical and phonological entity). For Sergio$_{te}$ would of course be talking about twater, whereas Earthling Sergio would be talking about water. In general, we suppose that what people could possibly be talking about is a function of the stuff that they have made contact with, or which people they have known have had contact with. It would be inexplicable – a miracle – if Sergio on Twin Earth were thinking about water – given that he has never come in contact with the stuff and that he doesn't know anyone who has, nor anyone who knows anyone who has, etc.

Putnam has drawn the conclusion that meaning isn't in the head, while Burge has concluded that mental states don't supervene upon brain states. These conclusions are unnecessary for Stich's argument. We may agree that *what* people mean by '*s*', or what they believe, depends on factors outwith their crania, but this has no tendency to show that their meaning *p* by '*s*' or their believing *p* *are* states outwith their bodies. The state, for example, which is someone's meaning *p* by '*s*' may simply be a state of that person that can be described in ways which bring in factors outwith the mind-brain, rather as describing a hole in the ground as a crater or well alludes to a certain causal history (see Davidson 1963).

The problem that Stich focuses on is novel and doesn't depend on these confusions. The point is this: getting the exact propositional content of a state right doesn't seem to make any predictive difference. For example, if Sergio$_{te}$ and Sergio were suddenly to switch places, the predictions we had built up on the basis of Sergio's psychology would work perfectly well for Sergio$_{te}$, even though his beliefs about drinkable water would be quite different in content from Sergio's. So the conclusion seems to be that not all differences in propositional content necessarily make an explanatory difference.

Perhaps we can make the point clearer by recurring to the example of a well. To describe a hole in the ground as a well is to redescribe it in terms of its causal *origins*: it is a well only if it was dug by someone with the purpose of finding water. But its causal *powers* are in no way affected by how it was brought about. If a hole physically just like this one had suddenly appeared as a result of a subsidence, it would still have the same causal powers as the well-hole. If someone falls in the well and breaks a leg, the fact that the hole is a well is explanatorily irrelevant, whereas its being a hole of a certain size and shape will be relevant (perhaps a man could not have fallen into a smaller well). Thus when we say 'Bloggs broke his leg because he fell into a large hole', we might (well!) have said 'Bloggs broke his leg because he fell

into a well', but the redescription of the cause would not add any explanatorily relevant information.

Now the situation with beliefs and content ascription is rather similar. We
ascribe content to a belief and thereby describe it in terms which may well be
irrelevant to its causal powers. Sergio$_{te}$ and Sergio have different beliefs,
because their propositional content is different, but this makes no difference
to the causal powers of those beliefs. And we ascribe different contents to
the belief-states they each express by saying 'Water is drinkable' because
these states have different origins. We seem to have no way of alluding to the
causally relevant features of propositional attitudes without also bringing in
causally irrelevant factors. On this point there is obviously an important
difference between the redescription of the hole as a well and the description
of a propositional attitude in terms of its content. We have ways of talking
about and describing the well which do not allude to its well-like origins but
we have no way of reidentifying a particular belief without ascribing content
to it, and we have no way of using beliefs and desires to explain action
without ascribing content to them.

The conclusion Stich wants to draw from all this is that beliefs, desires
and the like should not figure in the cognitive science of the future. I take it
that his reason is the plausible principle that a kosher scientific term must
track only causally relevant features of the world. Therefore, in so far as
propositional content ascription appears to track causally irrelevant features
of mental states, we should reject PA-psychology as a possible basis for a
cognitive science. Stich takes it that this constraint on scientific terms
imposes a "narrowness" constraint on psychology, i.e. that a properly *scientific* psychology must be purged of any terms that can apply to a mental state
M only in virtue of M's having some relation to the world outwith the cranial
envelope.

In fact, I find each part of this argument unpersuasive. I don't think Stich
has shown that propositional content ascription does track causally irrelevant
features, nor do I think that the narrowness constraint is at all plausible. I'll
discuss the latter when I assess Stich's overall picture of psychological
explanation, so let me focus first on the former claim.

Stich's argument forgets that PA-ascription may be tracking causally
relevant features of the *whole* intracranial psychology of the agent. The point
can be made clearly if we revert once more to holes and wells. If you
characterize $x$ as a well rather than as just a hole in the ground, that may not
tell you anything about $x$'s causal powers as distinct from those of some $y$ that
is a hole just like $x$, except that $y$ was caused by subsidence. However, it
doesn't follow from this that your describing $x$ as a well contains no extra
predictively useful information, for it may tell you something interesting
about the area in which $x$ is situated – namely that, given that this is a well,

there may be people around and there may, for this reason, be more holes like $x$ in the area.

In similar fashion, the fact that Sergio's belief is about *water* does encode some general information about his mental states and capacities, namely that they are responsive to the world around him. If, miraculously, his belief had been about twater, this would tell you something about *Sergio's* causal powers, so surely the fact that his belief is about *water* likewise tells us something about his causal powers. It is true that our deductions about his sensitivity to the world around him are based on knowledge of Sergio's world. Indeed our assumptions about his sensitivity and our ascriptions of reference are inextricable. We ascribe the reference we do because of the assumptions we make about Sergio's causal powers and his world, and so these ascriptions allow others to infer facts about his causal powers and his world.

A similar point applies to bodily movements. It might be thought that describing someone's bodily movement as an action alludes to causally irrelevant features of that movement, since a kinetically equivalent bodily movement that was not caused (in the appropriately sensitive way) by the agent's primary reasons would have had the same causal powers even though it was not an action. Yet, of course, it would be mad to suggest that our ascription of purposiveness to a movement is causally irrelevant: action ascription suggests a general fact about the body making the movement, namely that it is an intelligent, goal-seeking system. So it is just a *non sequitur* to conclude that because a description D of $e$ tracks some features of $e$ that are not relevant to $e$'s causal powers, it follows that D tracks some features of the world which are causally irrelevant or predictively useless *überhaupt*.

A further analogy will help us locate precisely where Stich has gone wrong. It is evident that the theory of evolution by natural selection (and gene-drift, etc.) is a powerful and explanatory scientific theory. Yet it also seems that if one had a precise biochemical description of all the organisms within a population and a precise description of the future of their environment, it would be possible to predict their behaviour without reference to the theory of natural selection. So when we describe an organism as having been naturally selected it would appear that we're ascribing a property that makes no causal difference. After all, if we had a molecular replica of this organism that hadn't evolved by natural selection, that replica would behave in the same way. So it would appear the only descriptions of organisms that contain only causally relevant information are purely biochemical ones that do not allude to how they have come to be. Yet, of course, if the theory of evolution is a scientific theory, we expect it to tell us something about the future and the causal powers of the world. And of course it does. Just as knowing that a hole in the ground is a subsidence and not a well may, in the context of other information, lead you to form useful general expectations about the area in which you find the subsidence, so knowing that an organism O has evolved by natural selection sets up general expectations about O and other organisms. In particular, of course, the theory that O has evolved through natural selection helps to eliminate other possible explanations of O (e.g. in terms of the design of an intelligent demiurge) and the elimination of these hypotheses will also inform your expectations about O and the world. In general terms, you will expect the organisms you meet to show signs of having evolved via the rough and ready process of natural selection rather than of having been plonked down by an intelligent designer.

I think Stich's mistake, then, is to think that a truly scientific psychology must model itself on a purely mechanistic or kinematic model of explanation. On this picture, psychology would be basically a kinematics of mental states. The proper terms of such a science would have to extrude descriptions of the particular states of the system that allude to things other than the causal powers of the particular states to which they apply. Descriptions of particular states which allude globally to the causal power of the whole system would not be kosher. I'll argue later against the very possibility of this sort of psychology, answering to Stich's narrowness constraint. For the moment, it suffices to note that this conception has a parallel in biology that would entail that the theory of evolution is not genuinely explanatory.

This is the point to scotch one construction that is sometimes put on the sort of story that Stich tells. Some philosophers (e.g. Burge 1982, p. 118) have urged that the purpose of our belief-desire scheme for understanding persons is not really the causal-explanatory one that it has been cracked up to be by such philosophers as Davidson (1963). Perhaps the fact that assignments of propositional content track etiological factors that are irrelevant to the causal efficacy of beliefs indicates that what is going on when we understand a person's activities in terms of his beliefs and desires is not really causal explanation at all. Rather, folk psychology might be aiming at some non-causal understanding or *Verstehen* of human action (this suggestion surfaces frequently in Putnam 1978). This line is unwarranted. If I am right, propositional content ascription is certainly something we now do in order to effect perfectly reasonable causal explanations of action. Of course, the propositions themselves are not causally efficacious; it is rather that in assigning them as content to particular mental states we thereby succeed in tracking the features of those states which are efficacious. It is of course true that the propositional mode of characterizing beliefs and desires does supervene upon some causally impotent features of the belief state, but it would be a mistake to make a fetish of these features and suppose that they indicate that the essence of folk psychology is some kind of non-causal *Verstehen*. The features we track with our content ascriptions are not causally impotent *überhaupt*, it is just that the causal powers intimated by content ascription are partly holistic and partly atomistic. So, contrary to the resilient *Verstehen* school of metapsychology, belief-desire explanations are indeed attempts at causal explanation. To be sure, there is room for the programme of trying to characterize our belief states in terms of their functional-inferential roles rather than their propositional contents (see McGinn 1982), but the point of such an exercise is not to undermine PA psychology, but rather to decompose the different features which it comprehensively tracks. A mental state described in narrow terms would stand to the PA it realizes rather as a bodily movement described in purely kinematic terms stands to the action it realizes. On the view I'm urging, there is no rupture or incommensurability between folk psychological and functionalist theories of mind.

## II

Stich has a second argument intended to show that a causal role charac-terization of belief must be radically at odds with our ordinary, folk-psychological taxonomy. This argument turns on the holistic nature of our belief ascription. When we ascribe a belief to someone, we are intimating or presupposing various facts about his overall psychology. For example, if I ascribe the belief that all men are mortal to you then I expect that you'll agree that Socrates is mortal provided that you accept that Socrates is a man. Of course, this assumption in turn depends on my making certain assumptions about your rational powers of inference. If I decide that your powers of inference are intact, but discover you refusing what seem to me perfectly obvious entailments of what I think you believe, then I will have to adjust my view of what you believe.

Stich believes that this holistic feature of content ascription raises a certain problem. For example, maybe you and I both believe that all men are mortal, but I've heard of Socrates and you haven't. Or better: suppose you believe that 'Socrates' denotes a famous diamond. Now, given that I believe that Socrates is a man, then if I am rational and if I really do accept that all men are mortal, it would be surprising were I to deny 'Socrates is mortal'. However, we will not be startled when you say 'Socrates is forever', since you believe that Socrates is a diamond and that diamonds are forever. Stich points out that from the fact that we thus diverge in the beliefs generated by our belief in man's mortality we cannot infer that we express different beliefs when we assert 'All men are mortal'. There is a functional difference between our belief states, yet they seem to be belief states of the same type. Stich doesn't think that this divergence between functional role and pro-positional psychology presents an insuperable problem. After all, even if you're ignorant about Socrates, we can certainly endorse the following counterfactual: were you to learn that 'Socrates' denotes a man, you would acquire the disposition to accept 'Socrates is mortal'. As long as this counterfactual is true, we have nothing against ascribing to you a belief in man's mortality.

However, Stich thinks that this way of patching things up between functional role psychology and PA psychology only raises another problem. He introduces a character from his past, a certain Mrs. T. who suffered from a rather nasty form of progressive senility that gradually erased many of her memories. Although, for example, she would continue to assert (or utter) 'McKinley was assassinated', she was apparently unable to answer correctly such questions as 'Is McKinley dead?'. Stich proposes that it would not be quite right to say that she believed what we believe when we sincerely assert that McKinley was assassinated. Given that in general we have no reason to suppose that Mrs. T. is particularly foolish or irrational, we have no reason to suppose that she really *does* believe that McKinley was assassinated but is inconsistently refusing to draw the obvious conclusion. In this case, what we know about her condition suggests that it is much more likely that she has simply lost her grip on the meaning of 'assassinated'. Of course, we can't immediately infer that she doesn't believe that McKinley was assassinated. Strictly, all we can be sure of is that she isn't *expressing* this belief when she says 'McKinley was assassinated'. But let us grant Stich's claim that Mrs. T. doesn't really believe it. He thinks that this intuition will create problems for the way we have tried to patch up functional role psychology with PA-psychology. He points out that the following counterfactual may be true of the unfortunate lady: if we informed her that assassinated people die, she would accept that McKinley is dead. Now what is the difference between her case and that of the man, let's call him Jimmy, who simply doesn't know that Socrates is a man? We allowed that Jimmy can still believe that all men are mortal even though he doesn't draw the conclusion that Socrates is mortal, but we allowed this only because we thought the following counterfactual would be true of him: if Jimmy were informed of Socrates' manhood, he would accept Socrates' mortality. But then, there seems to be no important *functional* difference between Mrs. T. and Jimmy. Yet the former's ignorance causes us to feel that she can't really believe that McKinley was assassinated, while the latter's ignorance has no tendency to make us think he doesn't really believe that men are mortal.

It is obvious where the asymmetry lies, but not at all obvious how to capture it in causal or functional terms. The difference, of course, is that Mrs. T. lacks a conceptual connection whereas Jimmy merely lacks an item of information. But how are we to capture this blinding insight in terms of a purely causal or dispositional account of the states of these two people?

There is a crucial disanalogy between the way Mrs. T's ignorance affects her verbal dispositions and the way Jimmy's ignorance affects his. We can only see the difference by decomposing the expressions of the mental states in question and focusing on the predicates that feature in them. First, note that Mrs. T's use of the predicate 'was assassinated' is in general not constrained in the way our use of it is. For us, there is a general inferential connection: if someone has been assassinated, then they're dead. Consequently, we shall generally deny '$x$ was assassinated' of anyone of whom we predicate '$x$ is alive' and a host of other terms. But it is otherwise with Mrs. T. It is a global fact about her inferential psychology that states which she would express using sentences featuring the predicate 'was assassinated' differ in the inferences they generate in her from the states we would express by using the same predicate.

By contrast, the inferential disruption in the case of Jimmy is minimal with respect to other sentences which include the terms that feature in 'All men are mortal'. There are, of course, differences between our dispositions with respect to the term 'Socrates', since Jimmy is bound to use this name in rather eccentric ways. However, with respect to the terms appearing in 'All men are mortal', Jimmy will differ from us at most in respect of sentences in which 'Socrates' figures.

Of course, we would usually mark the difference between Mrs. T's case and Jimmy's by saying that she lacks a conceptual connection which he recognises. This way of putting things is misleading. We are free to say that he lacks such a connection if he doesn't assent to the sentence 'Socrates is a person'. However, the point is that he doesn't lack the conceptual connections relevant for determining whether he understands the sentence 'All men are mortal' as we do. The crucial thing is that a piece of information may be conceptual with respect to one set of terms but empirical with respect to another.

It should also be noted that I have not suggested that we make the distinction between Mrs. T's case and Jimmy's turn on which of them would have to revise more of their beliefs. It may be, in fact, that Jimmy would have to make many adjustments to his conceptual scheme upon discovering that 'Socrates' denotes a man. Perhaps he has built up an entire mythology around the diamond he takes this term to denote. None of this affects the asymmetry between Mts. T. and Jimmy. The point is that if Mrs. T. did come to accept the usual inference from 'A was assassinated' to 'A is dead', this would involve a change in her dispositions with respect to all the cases where she might have been uttering sentences involving the predicate 'was assassinated'.

The upshot of my discussion of Stich's Mrs. T. is that he has by no means established that such cases indicate that PA-psychology makes distinctions which cannot be matched by a causal role or dispositional account of mental states. In a nutshell, my claim is that PA-psychology's refusal to ascribe the usual content to Mrs. T's utterance reflects the global difference between her dispositions and ours with respect to the predicate 'was assassinated'.

Stich has tried to show that from the view point of narrow causal-role psychology PA-psychology is completely off beam, since it tracks causally impotent features of mental states and the holism of content ascription can't be reflected in the underlying causal dispositions of the agent. I've argued that both these lines of attack fail completely. However, I do not disagree with Stich's conclusion: nothing seems more obvious to me than that PA psychology can't be the basis of a genuinely explanatory theory of cognition. But the reason this seems obvious to me and not to Stich is just that I take a wider view of what psychology must do. For Stich, the purpose of psychology is *simply* to come up with a theory that will explain (that is predict) behaviour. Now, since propositional attitudes certainly seem to be in this line of business, it would seem that they might conceivably form the basis for a cognitive psychology. However, if you take a larger view of what psychology should do, as Quine does when he speaks of naturalizing epistemology, and see it as asking more ambitious questions, then PA psychology is no candidate for the foundation of such an enterprise. I'll say more about this in Section VI.

## III

In the process of arguing that content-based psychology cannot dovetail neatly into functional-role psychology, Stich touches several times on the notion of mental representation. For example, he devotes some space to considering the view of philosophers like Harman (1973), Fodor (1978) and Field (1978), who hold that the best explanation of belief, on the folk theory, is to suppose that beliefs are sentences inscribed in the head. Stich handles these views far too gingerly for my taste. He does pose the notorious problem that such "sententialism" provides no account of the content of our utterances until some account is given of how these internal sentences themselves get content, and I think he's right to claim that no sententialist can avoid embracing some functionalist theory of content for his brain-inscribed sentences. However, he is strangely reluctant to dismiss the sententialist theory altogether and, as we shall see when touching upon his own "Syntactic Theory of Mind", he himself embraces a conception of mental states that has some bad points in common with sententialism.

Stich thinks that he can make us receptive to the sententialist message by pointing out that we already accept that a thing may have sentences inscribed in it without displaying the visible or audible signs of sententiality. He says that books recorded on cassette tapes are "unproblematic" instances of sentences inscribed in an unrecognizable medium (p. 37). If you accept this story, you might as well buy the whole sententialist approach. To be sure, when I hear the tape played, I hear sentences. But does it follow that sentences are inscribed in the tape? You might as well say: because I hear a parrot recite 'Polly wanna cracker' a sentence must be inscribed in the parrot's brain. And if you think that Polly's "utterance" betokens a sentence on her brain, that must be because you are already tempted by the view that our dispositions to utterance must be grounded in sentences inscribed in the brain. But no one who seriously questioned the sententialist thesis would allow that any such thing is obvious.

In any case, having remarked that sententialism cannot, by itself, provide an explanation of the content of our beliefs or utterances, Stich does not issue the obvious challenge to explain what explanatory function the brain writing hypothesis *does* serve. If the content of a belief state needs to be explained functionally, then it is not clear that we illuminate anything about beliefs by ascribing sententiality to them, unless something about their functional interconnections can only or best be explained on the assumption that they are sentence-like in structure. But given that the brain writing theory provides no account of content, the most it can provide is an account of structure. The structure of the state of believing that snow is white must have the very structure of a sentence (perhaps of 'Snow is white'). In other words, the belief state has a syntax. Here we are in the realm of sheer fantasy. At the moment we have no reason to treat a belief as anything other than an extremely complex disposition of the believer. It may be true that dispositional states must be grounded in something that can be described in a way that isn't constitutionally iffy, but it would be gratuitous to suppose that the disposition which constitutes my believing that snow is white, which includes *inter alia* my disposition to assent to 'Snow is white' in certain circumstances, can be grounded in a little sentence inscribed in the brain. The disposition may well be grounded in structural facts about the brain, but nothing at all obliges us to suppose that these structural facts can best be characterized as a code or set of internal representations.

To suppose that our symbolic behaviour (including silent verbal thought and manifest talk) must, or even can, be explained by positing an internal set of symbols would be like adopting Leibniz's notorious homuncular theory of *emboîtement* (encasement) according to which the shape of the outer man is explained by supposing it to be an enlargement of an invisible little man that was present all along in the father's sperm. It is a mystery to me how anyone could think it possible to explain some phenomenon – e.g. speech, or the structure of a body – by positing an invisible duplicate of that very phenomenon in some other medium (the brain, sperm). What is so objectionable about sentenialism is not really the idea of internal representation *per se* – for this idea is innocuous properly understood. We represent the world as much when we think as when we talk, and presumably the brain is where we do that. What is objectionable is the idea that *beliefs* are representations, for this idea explains nothing.

IV

Stich has a further complaint against PA-psychology. He thinks content ascription is inherently vague, and that there may be some cases where it positively breaks down altogether, so that we may be convinced someone is in some mental state M, but unable to characterize it in terms of M's content. Moreover, we may believe that M obeys certain generalizations, but then these can't be based in PA-psychology, for the generalizations of such psychology will only range over states with an ascribable content. I'll consider Stich's argument in two stages. I'll look first at his account of content-ascription and then at his claim that folk psychology is doomed to overlook certain potential applications of true and important psychological generalizations.

According to Stich, when we say of someone that they believe P, we're saying roughly that they are in a state that is similar to the one which *would* play a central role in a typical causal account of our own assertion of 'P', were we to assert 'P'. At first blush this account has some odd features. For example, it makes it a condition upon the correctness of a belief-ascription that there should be a typical causal account for my own actual or possible utterances of 'P'. I don't see why I couldn't use 'P' to ascribe the belief that P to S, even though all *my* utterances of 'P' involved widely varying causal chains. More importantly, however, it seems to me that I could ascribe a belief that P to S by saying 'S believes P' even though I'm eccentric and would myself assert 'P' in all sorts of strange circumstances, perhaps with a view to misleading people.

I can imagine some modifications that might promise to save Stich's account. For example, instead of supposing that when I ascribe a belief that P to S I'm comparing S's state to my own, it might be suggested that what I do is compare S to typical members of the community whom I'm addressing. My belief-ascription will be correct provided that typical members of that community would assert 'P' only if they were in circumstances or conditions similar to those which S is in. But this analysis also breaks down, since of course the members of A may all be hypocrites and liars with respect to matters pertaining to P, while S might be a perfectly sincere person. If the ascriber is known to be a reliable belief ascriber, he could certainly inform members of A of S's belief by uttering 'S believes P' even though members of A would be in a state quite unlike S were they ever to utter 'P'.

Of course, it is true that if I tell members of A that S believes P, I'm telling them that S is in a state *similar* to the one that they would be in were they to believe that P. But this is hardly news. Indeed, it is not clear to me what Stich meant to accomplish with his analysis of content ascription. He certainly doesn't take himself to be providing an analysis of what it is for someone to *believe* something, rather he is essaying an account of the features of a belief state that makes it a state of believing P. However, he is trying to give an account that doesn't pretend to provide an answer to the question "In virtue of what does someone mean P when they utter 'P'?". He is taking the notion of the meaning of something by an utterance for granted and trying to give an account of the content of belief in terms of the notion of the meaning of an utterance plus a certain complicated counter-to-fact causal story. As I've said, I don't see how his analysis can work. Of course, one could wheel in the notion of *sincere* assent. If I say 'S believes P', then I'm saying that S is in a state similar to the one I'd be in were I to assent sincerely to P! True enough, but clearly this is no good for Stich's purposes, since assent to 'P' (where 'P' means P) is sincere just if the assenter believes P. But then the analysis of sincere assent requires us to ascribe content directly to a belief, just what Stich wants to avoid.

Indeed, it should have been evident from the start that Stich's analysis is circular and uninformative. For, if he is taking the state of someone's meaning that P by 'P' for granted, he is taking the notion of the content of PAs for granted, for (as Davidson has pointed out) S's meaning P by 'P' is itself a PA. S's meaning P by 'P' is precisely a (mental?) state of S that we characterize by assigning it a propositional content, just as we characterize S's beliefs by assigning them such contents.

Stich touches upon a very congenial point when he notes that the warrant for a content-ascription does not have to take the form of undefeated evidence for an *identity* between the belief-content and the content of the content-ascribing sentence. I may say that 'S believes that P' even though I know that S's belief state is only very similar to the state I'd be in were I to assent sincerely to 'P'. Such an idea would be attractive to anyone proposing that mental states should be classified in terms of the causal-inferential roles they perform, since such a theory must obviously recognise a spectrum of beliefs ranging from those that are very similar in their inferential roles to those that are very different. It is vain to expect there to be a precise rule for specifying the degree of causal–inferential similarity that any two states on this spectrum must possess in order to count as having the same cognitive content. Since PA ascription is sensitive (*inter alia*) to cognitive role, the vagueness in the notion of cognitive content will be reflected in ascriptions of PAs.

In Chapter 7, Stich argues that the vagueness and interest-relativity of the "same-belief" relation suggests strongly that it would be healthier for cognitive science to forget about characterizing mental states in terms of their content and to concentrate instead on depicting their narrow causal role. He dubs the contrary view, that the generalizations of cognitive science will be defined over states with content and that these generalizations will hold *in virtue* of the contents of the states in question, the Strong Representational Theory of Mind (SRT for short). According to Stich, the trouble with this position is that our capacity for cognitive explanation sometimes outstrips our capacity for content-ascription.

Stich notes (p. 130 ff) that some psychologists have conjectured that people have a general tendency to believe something even after their original ground for believing it has been undercut. For example (pp. 133–4) experimental subjects who have been informed that their performances on certain tests indicate hidden homosexual desires will continue to believe that they own such tendencies even after the experimenter has assured them that this is not after all what the tests indicated. The generalization such cases inspire might be stated in terms that clearly require one to know the content of a belief before applying the generalization to it: 'If S believes that $p$ only because S believes that $q$, and S ceases to believe $q$, S will continue to believe that $p$'. (I assume that S will invent some new reason to legitimate his continued belief in $p$). Here the variables clearly range over a domain of propositional contents and hence the generalization is applicable only to PAs.

But Stich thinks we have good reason not to restrict such generalizations to propositionally characterizable mental states, for sometimes we will feel that the generalization might apply even though we can say nothing about the content of the mental state(s) in question. Thus, Stich invites us to consider someone with quite eccentric views about sex, perhaps with views like those expressed by the transexual in Gregory McDonald's *Fletch and the Widow Bradley* who informs the hero that a person's sexuality is a spiritual, not a biological, fact. Such a person might feel that they are gay because they are attracted to females and, although biologically male, they feel spiritually female. Now Stich suggests that their conception of sexuality is so eccentric as to make it impossible to know whether to ascribe to them the belief that they are homosexual. Consequently, if one of these eccentrics were subjected to the belief-perseverance experiment described above, it would not be possible to apply to him the generalization as it stands, since it is couched in terms of PAs and we simply can't say what content should be ascribed to the eccentric's beliefs. Stich also reminds us of the fact that we have difficulty in saying what Mrs. T. believes, given that we've agreed that she doesn't believe that McKinley was assassinated. Moreover, similar problems bedevil the ascription of content when someone conflates distinct people. For example, someone may hear various stories about someone named 'John', to the effect that 'John is tall', 'John is blond' and 'John is a wiz at maths'. But it may be that unbeknownst to him, all of the speakers were referring to different Johns. Here, Stich suggests that we may be completely unable to assign a reference to the mental state that this man expresses by saying 'John is tall, blond and a mathematical wizard'.

In each of these cases Stich is guilty of a *non sequitur*, since in all of them he moves from noting that we would have difficulty in ascribing content to someone's belief by using a particular sentence – 'McKinley was assassinated', 'He is a homosexual' or 'John is tall, blond and mathematical' – to the conclusion, wholly unsupported, that there is no sentence that could be used to ascribe content to the mental state at issue. But this is transparently untrue. If someone acknowledges a desire to go to bed with someone they believe to be spiritually of the same sex, we may connive in their usage by ascribing to them the belief "that they are gay". To be sure, we'd want to cancel the usual implications of this in the context, but it doesn't follow that we have failed completely to characterize what they believe. Likewise, although we can't say that Mrs. T. believed that McKinley was assassinated, we may elicit enough from her to ascribe to her some vague belief to the effect that something unpleasant happened to McKinley. But vague content is better than nothing. Finally, the man who has got his referential knickers in a twist over 'John', can certainly be said to have some propositionally characterizable belief, even if we can't say that this belief is about John (or indeed about anyone). We can at least say that our man believes that there is exactly one man called 'John' about whom all his informants were talking and who is tall, blond and in command of mage-like mathematical powers. Of course, it may be *difficult* to ascribe content, and we may feel that some ascriptions are closer to the literal truth than others, but it is hard to imagine a case where we'd be convinced that we know something about some mental state M of S but have no idea at all of what content to ascribe to M.

Of course, these cases of interpretative difficulty do show something important about PA-psychology: it is not an exact science, and most of the explanatory work is done at the interpretative level, at the level of achieving a realistic portrayal of what someone believes. The generalizations of folk psychology are feeble to the extent that their application in a particular case will always require prior interpretative work of some intricacy. The contrast with physics is stark. Steven Weinberg can tell us what the first three minutes of the universe were like on the basis of a little information (about fossil radiation) and a lot of theory. In this respect, psychology once again proves its affinity to the biological sciences, since here too any evolutionary explanation will require a fund of particular historical data (see Hull 1984): and this affinity once again intimates that biology may be a more appropriate model by which to judge the explanatory claims of folk psychology.

## V

In a chapter entitled "The Syntactic Theory of Mind" Stich tries to divine the shape of (non-content based) cognitive psychologies to come. According to Stich this hallucinated science will depict the mind as a system of causally interacting, but semantically uninterpreted, syntactic tokens. He does not of course attempt to fill in the picture himself; that task is left to empirical cognitive science. Instead, he tries to show that there are no good reasons for supposing there to be explanatory or predictively useful generalizations that would elude a syntactic theory of mind just because it is not content sensitive. The discussion is bold and ingenious but it leaves many lingering doubts.

First, we should remind ourselves of Stich's declared intention that a syntactic theory of mind (STM) be a narrow one. In characterizing the mind, STM's not only jettison all information regarding the purported contents of the subject's mental states, they proceed as though in ignorance of the subject's particular causal embedding in the world, although general causal laws may of course be exploited. This world-denying principle requires that we should make no use of information concerning the subject's transducer and effector states that involves redescribing them in terms of their causal connections to the world at large. For example, a predicate like 'is seeing an apple' would not be regarded as a properly projectible predicate of cognitive science, because it could only apply to a transducer state in virtue of that state's relation to some causative agent. It should also be noted that Stich also requires narrow psychological theory to turn a blind eye to *intentional* objects. Thus such opaque predicates as 'is having an experience as of seeing an apple' and 'is trying to peel an apple' are extruded along with the transparently world-referring ones just mentioned. I take it that Stich wants to extrude such terms because they involve the ascription of content and he takes himself to have shown that content-ascription is sensitive to causally irrelevant factors – in any case it is certainly sensitive to factors outwith the cranial envelope. In this respect he has seen the consequences of the narrowness constraint far more clearly than other writers. It is one of the merits of this book that throughout he thinks matters through to their final consequences.

The gist of Stich's defence of the STM is just his claim that the STM can explain anything the representational theory can explain, whereas there are some things the STM can explain which the representational theory can't. I shall not concern myself with the second half of this claim: it turns on the success of Stich's argument that there are occasions when we can't ascribe content to the states over which a cognitive process is operating. I've said I don't think Stich's argument for this claim works. Nor will I directly attack the first half of his claim. Instead, I want to depict briefly the sort of thing he has in mind by a 'STM' and then ask whether such a thing is properly called a "theory of mind".

Let us sample the sort of explanation of behaviour a STM might throw up. Suppose Mary runs out of the front door of her condominium. Let us suppose that everyone, including Mary, agrees that if any folk-theoretical account of her behaviour on this occasion is warranted, the following is: Mary believed the building to be on fire, and that only by running out of the building could she save her life. She wanted to save her life. So she ran out of the building. In this account, we have made use of the following very crude folk-theoretical generalization: 'If S desires $p$ and believes that $q$ is necessary for $p$ and that A will achieve $q$, then if S is able to A and has no countervailing beliefs or desires, S will do A'.

Any application of this generalization would require ascribing contents to her beliefs and desires, so the narrow cognitive theory of Mary must find some way of replicating this generalization in terms that require only a syntactic characterization of her mental states. Stich proposes that the syntactic theory might begin by simply taking over certain features of PA-psychology. It might postulate that there are B states (corresponding to beliefs) and D states (corresponding to desires). Mary's B and D states would simply be mapped onto formulae having a certain syntax. Thus we might map Mary's belief that her building was on fire onto some formula like P(C) (where 'P' is a syntactic token replacing 'is on fire' and 'C' is a syntactic token replacing 'the building'). Of course, we can ascribe syntactic structure in a much more fine-grained way than this. Moreover, a cognitive role psychology might try to track the particular connections of particular *parts* of (say) Mary's B states with particular transducer conditions. Now for any B state of Mary's, an STM would characterize this in terms of its syntax and causal role within her narrow psychology (in other words, her psychology syntactically characterized). If we were to carry out such an exercise for all of Mary's states, we could then start to apply and test various cognitive generalizations. For example, part of the content-sensitive generalization that was used in the folk-theoretical account of her flight behaviour might be replaced by something like this:

> For all subjects S and all well-formed formulae A and B: If S is in a B state that we can map $A \supset B$, and S is in a D state that we can map onto A, then S will be in a D state that we can map onto B.

Of course, this generalization is ridiculous, but it gives one the general flavour of the project. The main point is, initially, to show how one can replicate folk-theoretical generalizations in a purely syntactic form.

I have several doubts about Stich's proposal for a STM. First, I do not know of any means for forming plausible hypotheses about the syntax of a mental state that wouldn't require the ascription of content. Stich's proposal will work only if we are warranted in ascribing syntax to mental states independently of ascribing content to them. He hasn't shown that this can be done. Of course, one can describe the syntax of an observable sentence without describing its semantics, but this has no tendency to show that one could ever be warranted in ascribing a certain syntactical structure to an unobservable mental state without having formed some idea of its content. Stich might reply that it wouldn't matter if the ascription of syntax were parasitic on the ascription of content, so long as we understand that only the ascription of syntax is relevant for the purposes of scientific explanation. However, he can't use this argument if he is going to insist that there are cases where M is a mental state with syntax but without any conceivable content.

But the next question is: what is the difference between saying that Mary's mental states have a syntax and simply saying that their structure is relevant to understanding their causal interactions with each other and with Mary's transducers and effectors? I cannot see that Stich has adequately motivated the proposal that Mary's states possess syntactical, as distinct from merely structural, features. Generally speaking, one motive for assigning syntax is to prepare the way for an ascription of content, where the content ascribed to the whole is a function of the content ascribed to the parts and where syntactical rules help to say what that function is. Saying what formulae are well-formed gives one a class of formulae that are potentially the bearers of truth-conditions and of cognitive roles. But given that Stich does not think that cognitive science will *see* the content of mental states, it is unclear to me that there is any more motive, within cognitive science, to speak of the syntax of mental states than there is to speak of the syntax of the assemblage of cars that make up a freight-train. Indeed I have no idea what Stich thinks will be the use or point of a criterion for the well formedness of mental state formulae. (Note that cognitive science can't rely on what speakers say about the well- or ill-formedness of their utterances, since cognitive science is supposed to turn a blind eye to the contents of utterances).

But until some motive has been provided for thinking that it is especially appropriate to think of mental states as having a syntax, not just causally significant structure, it should be clear that we could treat a lot of non-mental systems as having a structure analogous to the image of mind enshrined in the STM. Of course, one may object that non-mental entities can't have B and D states, but Stich has not explained what these are yet – indeed, I doubt that any narrow psychology can explain what makes a mental state a *mental* state. As he is holding up an uninterpreted calculus to nature, we have to ask what ground there is for supposing that only mental processes can be mirrored in it. For all Stich has shown, the working of the gut or liver would be as successfully modeled by his uninterpreted calculus as the workings of the mind.

Perhaps what makes for the mentality of a system is that its states interact in terms of *computational* processes. But this is a notoriously difficult idea to spell out: the conditions for ascribing the following of a rule to a system are not easy to spell out and if the system is not allowed to have any representational powers I think the problem of distinguishing rule-following from simple regularity becomes insuperable. It requires a system at least to register its mistakes and successes (even if it doesn't require the system to have an explicit formulation of the rule). The system, in other words, needs to be able to track and evaluate its own performances. Now since Stich denies that cognitive science will treat the mind as a representing thing, I do not see how it can treat the mind as a system of *rule-governed* manipulations of syntactic tokens, since one then has to suppose that the mind is evaluating them by asking itself questions like 'Is that (syntactic) derivation valid?' and 'Is that formula well-formed?'.

There is a strong suspicion that by extruding all the intentional, extracranial features of mental states, the STM is left with no account of what makes them *mental* states. Stich might reply: so much the worse for the distinction between the mind and other sorts of systems. He would want to ask whether the *explanatory* power of syntactic theories is in any way reduced by their applying to systems other than minds. But I don't think he should really be happy with this sort of reply. After all, he set out to tell us what cognitive science is going to be like and it seems his futuristic depiction turns out to be rather bland: cognitive science will tell us how parts of a system causally interact, where these parts may themselves have parts that have distinct causal roles.

## VI

But perhaps the truth will turn out to be boring, perhaps the logic of Stich's position should move us to accept that the elimination of mind from the realm of nature is on the cards. Is the elimination of mind unavoidable?

I now want to try diagnosing where Stich has gone wrong and briefly cast doubt on the idea of a world-denying psychology. We can begin by looking at a rather revealing section of his chapter on the STM in which he tries to supply an argument for adopting a narrow, brain-in-a-void psychology. The general principle he seeks to vindicate is something he calls the "Autonomy of Psychology" (Fodor has concocted different arguments for the same idea under the head of "methodological solipsism". See Fodor 1980).

The argument works as follows. The purpose of psychological theory is to explain, that is predict, behaviour. Factors which are irrelevant to predicting behaviour are irrelevant to explaining it. But evidently, facts about the particular conditions that inform the development of someone's mind must be irrelevant for the purposes of predicting his behaviour, because two people with identical brain-in-a-vat psychologies will behave identically in the same circumstances, even if their psychologies have different developmental histories. Stich illustrates his point with something called a "replacement argument". If an evil demon atomizes Sergio one day and replaces him with a duplicate (perhaps Sergio$_{te}$) who is indistinguishable from Sergio in his intracranial psychology, the duplicate will behave just like Sergio. The predictions that were true of Sergio will be true of the duplicate. And if explanation *is* prediction, explanations true of Sergio must be true of the duplicate and explanations false of the duplicate must be false of Sergio. But facts about Sergio's developmental history turn out to be in principle irrelevant to predicting his behaviour, because his duplicate's behaviour could be predicted, and therefore explained, on the basis of a knowledge of Sergio's intracranial psychology alone.

If this is supposed to be a non-question begging argument for a narrow, content-insensitive psychology, it surely fails, since the states which in fact causally explain Sergio's behaviour will be quite unlike those that explain his duplicate's behaviour. The adherent of PA-psychology will point out, for example, that Sergio will have many beliefs and desires that his duplicate (e.g. Sergio$_{te}$) can't have, simply because the contents of those beliefs and desires will not be transmitted to the duplicate. Consequently, any adherent of PA-psychology should spurn the conflation of 'explanatory theory' and 'predictively useful calculation device'.

The nub of my disagreement with Stich is over his characterization of the aim of psychological theory as "explaining behaviour". On the face of it, this vision of the goal of psychology seems astonishingly unambitious. Surely a science of mind, or a theory of mind, if such a thing is possible, should attempt to answer such questions as: How have intelligence and rationality come to be? What is memory? What function is served by dreams? Are there stages or moral, cognitive and affective development? I take it that this more ambitious view of psychology is the one endorsed by Quine when he proposes the naturalization of epistemology, but it is clear that there is no way to do this sort of psychology without taking a diachronic-developmental and evolutionary view of minds, human and non-human. However, on Stich's conception of psychology, none of these extra-cranial facts plays a role. He wants psychology simply to explain the mechanics of the mind without inquiring into its origin. Why does he accept this restriction of psychology's scope? I suppose he believes that the more ambitious theory of mind will obviously not be pure psychology, but an amalgam of sociobiology, developmental psychology, evolutionary theory, neurobiology, cultural anthropology and so forth. But then what does he mean by "pure" psychology, and why suppose that it is inscribed in the book of nature that such an enterprise should be possible or interesting? I can only suppose that Stich's idea of pure psychology consists of the kinematics of PAs minus the content and facts about origin. But surely this is the wrong picture. It makes two mistakes: it supposes that the basic theoretical entities of a theory of mind are going to be the things we now describe in propositional terms, and it assumes psychology is going to be or should be a purely mechanical theory like (say) chemistry. Both views are false: if psychology is asking how intelligence and representation are possible, PA-psychology and the entities it refers to are what need to be explained by psychological theory, so they can't possibly be themselves basic parts of the explanation. Moreover, the evolution of mind should be regarded as part of the developmental history of particular forms of life. In so far as psychology is anything as unambitious as Stich's "autonomous psychology", it is not clear to me that we are likely to improve upon the basic conceptual scheme of PA-psychology. In so far as psychology asks more ambitious questions, neither Stich's syntactic theory of mind nor PA-psychology are going to provide the right sort of answers.*

University of Glasgow

*. Talks based on this critical study were given at the Universities of the Witwatersrand, Cape Town and Glasgow and I am grateful to colleagues present on these occasions for very useful criticisms and advice.

## BIBLIOGRAPHY

Burge, T. 1982: "Other Bodies", in Woodfield 1982.
Davidson, D. 1963: "Actions, Reasons and Causes", in Davidson 1980.
Davidson, D. 1968: "On Saying That", in Davidson 1984.
Davidson, D. 1980: *Essays on Actions and Events* (Oxford).
Davidson, D. 1984: *Inquiries into Truth and Interpretation* (Oxford).
Field, H. 1978: "Mental Representation", *Erkenntnis* 13
Fodor, J. 1978: "Propositional Attitudes", *The Monist*, 61
Fodor, J. 1980: "Methodological Solipsism Considered as a Research Strategy in Cognitive Psychology" *Behavioural and Brain Sciences* 3.
Harman, G. 1973: *Thought* (Princeton).
Hookway, C. 1984: *Minds, Machines and Evolution* (Cambridge).

Hull, D. 1984: "Historical Entities and Historical Narratives", in Hookway 1984.
McGinn, C. 1982: "The Structure of Content", in Woodfield 1982.
Putnam, H. 1975 (a): "The Meaning of 'Meaning'", in Putnam 1975 (b).
Putnam, H. 1975 (b): *Mind, Language and Reality* (Cambridge).
Putnam, H. 1978: *Meaning and the Moral Sciences* (London).
Woodfield, A. 1982: *Thought and Object* (Oxford).

# SENSE AND CONTENT

## By John Campbell

CHRISTOPHER PEACOCKE, *Sense and Content: Experience, Thought and Their Relations.* Oxford: Clarendon Press, 1983. Pp. ix + 221. Price £17.50 (pb. £6.95).

## I

Work on the way in which thought represents often relies upon study of the way in which language represents. The inquiry concerns the general form of a theory of meaning for a language, and the constraints to which such a theory is answerable.

The motivation for this approach is provided by the idea that grasp of a public language is constitutive of one's grasp of the idea of objective truth, of things being so whether or not they seem to be so. As Davidson puts it, "Our sense of objectivity is the consequence of [a] sort of triangulation, one that requires two creatures. Each interacts with an object, but what gives each the concept of how things objectively are is the base line formed between the creatures by language."[1]

In *Sense and Content*, Professor Peacocke provides an alternative approach to content. He aims to provide an account of thought which does not depend upon an account of language. His discussion focuses, as it is natural for such an account to do, on what he calls the Basic Case: the case, that is, of an organism capable of elementary spatial thought about its perceived environment.

It is natural for such a thought-theoretic approach to focus on the Basic Case, because the thought-theorist will take grasp of the concept of objective truth to be given not by grasp of a public language, but by the conception of oneself as in a spatial world. One will think of oneself as tracing a route through a world in which whether things are so is independent of whether they seem to be so.

There are two main strands in Peacocke's positive account of thought, both organised around the Basic Case. One is in a broad sense reductive. The book opens with a distinction between "representational" and "sensa-

---

[1] "Rational Animals", *Dialectica* 36 (1982), 317–27.

tional" features of perception. To ascribe "sensational" features to someone's perceptual experience does not directly involve ascribing concepts to him; whereas the exercise of concepts is involved in his experience's having representational features. Let me try to put this account in context.

We might contrast Peacocke's approach with Austin's. The discussion in *Sense and Sensibilia* of the character of perceptual experience leaves little question as to the complexity of ordinary English usage here. It also, however, makes it apparent that fruitful systematic approaches to phenomenology are unlikely to be found by focusing directly on ordinary uses of verbs of perception. We need some independent grip on what the phenomena are to which ordinary usage is responding. Peacocke's approach in effect finds such an independent grip in information-processing accounts of perception.

Thus consider colour vision. The capacity for colour perception is a capacity to keep track of surface reflectance characteristics of objects through a variety of conditions of illumination. A central task for an information-processing account is to explain how features of surface reflectance are separated from features of the illuminant. The nature of colour experience "from the inside" is affected by the spectral characteristics of the light reaching the subject – that is, it is affected by the way things are at that stage in the information-processing at which surface reflectance characteristics have not been separated from features of the illuminant. It is *also* affected by the way in which the separation is carried out, by which specific shade one perceives the object to be. This complexity in the phenomenology is reflected in the instability of the use of 'looks' in ordinary English. Does the door look the same colour all over? Yes, because there is certainly no question of there being, for example, a splash of red amongst the green; it is presented as having the same surface reflectance characteristics all over. No, because it is dappled by shadow, so that some parts look darker than others. We are provided with an independent grip on the complex phenomena to which the ordinary English use is responding here, if we bear in mind the possibility of an information-processing approach to vision.

In experiencing the door as being thus dappled by shadow, or as being that particular shade, the subject is not plausibly taken to be exercising concepts he possesses. To say so would be to suppose him capable of a range of propositional states – beliefs, hopes, desires – which are targeted very finely onto particular colour shadings, or particular undifferentiated colour-appearances. But such fine-grained conceptual capacities are not plausibly a precondition of ordinary colour experience. Peacocke develops this type of point for a wide range of cases, indicating a host of features of experience, such as size in the visual field, which cannot plausibly be taken to involve the subject's exercise of concepts. These are what he calls "sensational" features of perception.

To characterise these unconceptualised aspects of colour experience, Peacocke introduces primed versions of ordinary colour predicates. These are explained as true of a region of the visual field just in case it has the sensational property which is produced by an object satisfying the unprimed predicate, in normal conditions. So for example understanding 'red'' is "knowing that it is the sensational property of the visual field in which a red thing is presented in normal circumstances" (p. 21).

This apparatus cannot deal comprehensively with the phenomenology of colour vision. It provides no way of characterising that dimension of colour experience which is prior to separation of properties of surface reflectance from properties of the illuminant – experience of a white wall dappled by shadow will be white' throughout the relevant region. And at the level at which the separation has been effected, it provides only a rather coarse description. For the colour words of our language do not cut as finely as would be needed for Peacocke's method of introducing primed predicates to characterise the fine differences there can be between colour experiences. For example, perceptions of perceptibly different shades of snow will all be characterised as white'. And perhaps this problem for Peacocke's approach is irremediable; perhaps we could not introduce colour concepts – concepts of recognisable colours – which differentiate objects as finely as our experiences are differentiated.

Yet Peacocke's approach may nevertheless be adequate for the main purposes to which he puts it. Centrally, he aims to provide a reductionist account of grasp of such concepts as 'red', in terms of the evidential sensitivities of the subject's judgements to red' experiences.[2]

Peacocke also uses his notion of a sensational feature of perception in providing a direct analysis of the Basic Case; of what it is to be capable of elementary spatial thought. I shall expound this account in §II below.

I said that there were two main strands in Peacocke's positive account of thought. The second is an extensive treatment of demonstratives, which are said to be ways of thinking integral to the capacity for elementary spatial thought. He aims to characterise the contribution of demonstratives to fixing what counts as "canonical" evidence for thoughts in which they figure. Evidence is said to be "canonical" if it is constitutive of grasp of the thought that one recognises that evidence, when confronted with it, as *prima facie* evidence for the truth of that thought. Peacocke does not defend his evidential approach to sense, nor does he provide any further development of the notion of canonical evidence. Rather, he gives accounts of the senses, thus conceived, of a range of demonstratives, including perceptual demonstratives. To do so he introduces his notion of the "constitutive role" of a

[2] For discussion of this account, see Michael Smith, "Peacocke on Red and Red'", *Synthese*, forthcoming.

demonstrative, which characterises its sense. We shall return to this notion below, in §III.

There are two general theoretical purposes to which he puts this idea of "constitutive role". One is provision of a criterion of demonstrative type, an account of what it is for a way of thinking to be demonstrative. I shall comment on this account in §IV. The other is a reconstruction of Russell's Principle of Acquaintance, which I shall consider in §V.

Finally, there are two chapters which I shall not discuss further. In Chapter 4, Peacocke conjectures that no-one could have the conception of a spatial world in which he is located, unless he had spatial observational concepts. And he provides a positive account of what it is for a concept to be observational. Chapter 8 discusses the notion of a "language of thought". This chapter is remarkable for its portrayal of the dispute between realism and instrumentalism in the philosophy of mind as a dispute over whether and in what way thought requires syntactic vehicles.

II

I said that it is natural for a thought-theoretic approach to focus, as Peacocke's does, on the Basic Case. For the thought-theorist will take the notion of objective truth to be provided by the conception of oneself as in a spatial world. That is, he ought to take the capacity for spatiotemporal thinking to play the role in his account of content which the proponent of a communication-theoretic account of content assigns to grasp of a public language.

A thought-theorist's direct analysis of the Basic Case ought to exhibit the features of the Basic Case which make it so central. Peacocke's analysis, however, does not.

He introduces the concept of "perspectival sensitivity"; that is, the capacity to "recentre intentional webs". Possession of an "intentional web" consists in possession of an experience with a particular set of sensational properties, and a set of dispositions to move in such a way as to come into contact with the objects presented in the experience, should one intend to do so. The capacity to "recentre" such an intentional web is the capacity to have one's dispositions to movement suitably updated as one's perceptual presentations change.

The capacity for elementary spatial thought is explained as possession of "perspectival sensitivity"; that is, this capacity to recentre intentional webs. We must ask whether this analysis really does exhibit the features of the Basic Case which make it so basic for the theorist of thought. Does it show how elementary spatial thinking makes available the conception of objective truth?

It seems apparent that it does not. Our conception of objective truth goes beyond mere intersubjective agreement; it relates to that which *explains* our perceptions. And Peacocke's account does nothing to show the structure of this conception.

Indeed, there is a sense in which his analysis is solipsistic. For it assigns a quite unparalleled place to the subject himself; it assigns an unparalleled role to his own dispositions to movement. It does not describe the materials which would make it intelligible to the subject that his viewpoint is simply one among many possible viewpoints. Far from showing what makes the notion of objective truth intelligible, the account does not even show what makes the idea of intersubjective agreement available.

Even so, it might be that Peacocke's analysis articulates a fundamental feature of our spatial thinking, a feature which is not derivative upon those aspects of spatial thinking which *do* make available the notion of objective truth. I shall return to this way of motivating his analysis in §VI.


### III

I want now to point to a line of thought in *Sense and Content* which runs counter to emphasis on the Basic Case; and which, I think, explains Peacocke's failure to remark the significance of the solipsism in the perspectival sensitivity analysis.

In providing for the conception of objective truth, spatial thinking provides for the conception of *oneself* as one percipient among a possible plurality of percipients. Yet Peacocke maintains that the meaning of 'I' is given by "the person with *these* conscious states", where the embedded demonstrative is a peculiarly intimate way of thinking of one's present conscious states, made available by the fact that one is *in* them.

The intuition behind this account is in outright opposition to the idea that spatiotemporal thinking is required to provide for one's core conception of *oneself*. It suggests that one could engage in thought of oneself and one's conscious states without using one's capacity for spatial thought. It thus entirely undermines Peacocke's contention that the capacity for thought in general depends upon the capacity for spatial thought (p. 57).

Let us consider Peacocke's account of the first person in more leisurely detail. The formula 'the person with these conscious states' seems to be conceptually more sophisticated than the first-person way of thinking it is designed to analyse. The notion of "constitutive role" is introduced to meet this difficulty. The suggestion is that the first-person way of thinking can be characterised by 'the person with these conscious states' in the sense that the formula gives an *indirect* characterisation of the contribution of the demonstrative to the canonical evidence for thoughts containing it; that is, that it gives its "constitutive role".

To see how the account works, consider a sophisticated thinker who grasps the thought, 'the person with these conscious states is $F$'. There are many states which he can recognise as evidence for that thought. Among them will be some whose availability to him does not draw upon his advantages in conceptual sophistication over a thinker who has only what is necessary to grasp 'I'-thoughts. For example, simply being in pain will provide our sophisticated thinker with evidence for 'the person with these conscious states (including this pain) is in pain'. But it does not require conceptual sophistication to be in pain.

When an unsophisticated thinker, who has only what is necessary to grasp 'I'-thoughts, is in such a state, we can say that he has "evidence*" for the thought 'the person with these conscious states is $F$'. He cannot grasp the thought, but he has evidence* for it. (Ordinarily, to say that someone has evidence for a thought would suggest that he grasped that thought; hence the need for notation.) So, for example, an unsophisticated thinker, simply by being in pain, will have evidence* for 'the person with these conscious states is in pain', though he cannot grasp that thought.

The doctrine that the constitutive role of 'I' is given by 'the person with these conscious states' may now be explained as follows. Anything which is evidence* for 'the person with these conscious states is $F$', is canonical evidence for 'I am $F$'. Thus, for example, simply being in pain is canonical evidence for 'I am in pain'. On the present account, its status as such is secured by the fact that being in pain is evidence* for 'the person with these conscious states is in pain'.

That is how Peacocke plans to retain the thesis that 'the person with these conscious states' gives the sense of 'I', while acknowledging that the former is conceptually more sophisticated than the latter.

I think Peacocke's picture is that we have a *core* way of identifying ourselves, which can in this way be specified by reference to current conscious states, and that the capacity to find one's present and past location on the basis of perception and memory is extraneous to this core conception.

He does allow that the capacity to locate oneself through perception and memory is intrinsic to the ordinary, full-blown, first-person concept. His view is that it is constitutive of grasp of the concept that one be able to locate oneself; but that it is also part of grasp of the concept that there are circumstances in which one will not take perception and memory to reveal one's location. Thus one's apparent memories may be merely q-memories in Shoemaker's sense. They may be caused in an appropriate way by the events they concern, but those events need not have happened to the person who has the q-memories; they may have been transplanted from the original observer. In such a case one will not take memory to advise one of one's own past location. Peacocke thus stresses that the capacity to locate oneself depends upon background beliefs or presuppositions. And he says that the constitutive role account of 'I' as 'the person with these conscious states' is "intended to capture what is essential to the first-person m.p. [mode of presentation], in the sense that it does not take any background beliefs or presuppositions for granted" (p. 148). It captures only our *core* way of identifying ourselves.

What motivates this account is an asymmetry between self-ascriptions of conscious states and self-ascriptions of location. Consider a self-ascription of pain, made on the basis of felt pain. Here there is no possibility of one's making the judgement because *someone* is in pain, but not the person one took to be in pain, namely oneself. The explanation is, Peacocke in effect suggests, that the core way of identifying oneself is in a way characterisable by reference to current conscious states, such as pains. In contrast, consider a memory-based self-ascription of past location, such as 'I was on an ocean liner'. It may be that one makes this judgement because *someone* was on an ocean liner, but not the person one took it to be, namely oneself. What is responsible for one's apparent memory may ultimately be brain surgery, together with some *other* person's having perceived that location. The apparent memory may be a transplant. What make this possibility intelligible to us, Peacocke in effect maintains, is that one has another, more fundamental way of thinking of oneself than as the person located thus-and-so by memory and perception. For one may think of oneself in the core way specified by the constitutive role, 'the person with these conscious states'.

I think it is clear what one would want to oppose to this picture of Peacocke's. One would want to press a view on which the most fundamental way of thinking of ourselves we have is by reference to location. On this view, one depends upon the availability of this core conception when thinking of oneself in a way which can be characterised by reference to one's current conscious states. Here I want only to remark upon how such a view might deal with what is for it perhaps the most difficult point in Peacocke's argument here: the impossibility of getting wrong the owner of a self-ascribed experience. What explanation could we give of this, if our most fundamental way of thinking of ourselves is by reference to location?

The alternative explanation, I suggest, would be an account of what assigns a particular experience its owner. What assigns an experience its owner, on this account, is the possibility of self-ascription of it by him. This view can explain the fact that there is no possibility of this type: that one makes a self-ascription of pain on the basis of felt pain; that one forms the judgement because *someone* is in pain; but that that person is not oneself. The explanation why this is impossible is that what makes the pain one's own just is the possibility of self-ascribing it, so there is no possibility of a self-ascription getting wrong the owner of the experience.

In any case, we have now seen Peacocke's analysis of the first-person way of thinking, and seen that it does not take the capacity for first-person thought to depend upon the capacity for spatial thinking. The analysis is thus in conflict with his contention that the capacity for any thought at all is dependent upon one's capacity to engage in spatial thinking. In contrast, an account of the first person which took its core to be the capacity for self-location could do something to explain why spatial thinking might be so fundamental.

A full defence of the thesis that one's core conception of oneself is by reference to one's location would have in the first instance to press the solipsistic character of Peacocke's account of the first person. That account leaves it unintelligible to the subject how there could be *other* selves. There is nothing in the direct evidential sensitivity Peacocke characterises to make such a conception intelligible. (In contrast, conceiving of oneself in terms of one's location does make it intelligible how there could be other selves.)

The thought-theorist ought not to stop here, however. He ought to go further, and explain *why* the solipsistic conception of oneself and one's states is not a genuine option. Here he must, I think, depend upon an account of the way in which the conception of truth for self-ascriptions of conscious states is ultimately made available by the capacity for spatiotemporal thinking.

Finally, the aspects we have stressed of his analysis of the first person may serve to explain Peacocke's failure, in his "perspectival sensitivity" analysis, to exhibit the features of the Basic Case which make it so basic; to show how it makes available the concept of objective truth.

## IV

As I remarked, however, it might be held that the "perspectival sensitivity" analysis characterises a feature of our spatial thinking which is fundamental, which is not derivative upon those aspects of spatial thought which *do* make available the idea of objective truth. I shall discuss this view in §VI, after considering Peacocke's reconstruction of Russell's Principle of Acquaintance. To understand that reconstruction, we must look at his account of what it is for a type of mode of presentation to be demonstrative.

This account of demonstrative type appeals to Peacocke's notion of "constitutive role". As we have seen, the intuition behind this idea is that we can model the evidential sensitivities of an unsophisticated thinker upon the evidential sensitivities of a sophisticated thinker who is thinking reflectively about his own conscious states.

It is, Peacocke says, a necessary condition for a type of mode of presentation to be demonstrative that its constitutive role at any given time concern the then current psychological states of the thinker. So for example, in the constitutive role of 'I', 'the person with these conscious states', the embedded demonstrative refers to the subject's present states. Similarly, the constitutive role of a perceptual demonstrative such as 'that bowl' is 'the bowl responsible, in the way required for perception, for the experience as of a bowl in *that* region of my visual field'. Here again, constitutive role relates to current psychological states.

Yet we may question whether this condition on constitutive role really is essential to the criterion for demonstrative type. As it stands, the condition is necessary only; to find a sufficient condition we must supplement our account. As we shall see, the supplementation Peacocke provides seems to yield a sufficient condition in itself.

The condition given so far is necessary only. For the aim is to find a fundamental class of *simple* demonstratives; and mixed descriptive-demonstratives may have constitutive roles which concern the thinker's current psychological states. To use Peacocke's example, 'my paternal grandfather' has the constitutive role, 'the paternal grandfather of the person with these conscious states' (p. 153). One might think that the problem is that we do not yet have any control over just how the thinker's current psychological states may enter into the constitutive role of a demonstrative. But this is not Peacocke's reaction; and I think that to react thus would be to misconceive the problem.

We might draw a parallel between Peacocke's condition and the view that demonstrative expressions are, in Reichenbach's phrase, token reflexive – that each token of a demonstrative term refers by referring to itself. To say this is not to put any bound on how reference to the token is exploited. The expression 'my paternal grandfather', glossed as 'the paternal grandfather of the person who produced this token', is just as much token-reflexive as 'this', glossed as 'the object causally responsible for the production of this token'. It would be wrong-headed to suppose that one might go on to provide a criterion, in terms of how reference to the token is exploited, for distinguishing simple demonstratives such as 'this' from mixed descriptive-demonstratives. On a token-reflexive analysis, the *only* fundamental demonstratives are those which refer to themselves, such as 'this token'. All others turn out, under analysis, to be mixed descriptive-demonstratives.

The point of the parallel is to suggest that in terms of the "constitutive role" approach, there is only one type of demonstrative which we shall be justified in singling out as especially fundamental. That is the class of demonstratives immediately referring to the subject's own current conscious states, such as 'these conscious states'.

Yet the general character of Peacocke's account means that we need not confine ourselves to appeal to constitutive role. For constitutive role provides only an indirect characterisation of the contribution of a demonstrative to the canonical evidence for thoughts containing it. It may be, therefore, that we can find an account of the fundamental class of simple demonstratives at the level of a direct characterisation of sense.

That is the strategy Peacocke employs. He introduces the notion of a mode of presentation being "constitutively identificationally basic". The intuitive idea here is that grasp of some singular modes of thought directly involves the capacity to make knowledgeable judgements using them which are, in Peacocke's phrase, "identificationally basic". A judgement '$a$ is $F$' is "identificationally basic" if it does not rest upon a pair of judgements of the form '$a$ is identical to $b$' and '$b$ is $F$'. So for example, grasp of the first person may be held to require the capacity to make knowledgeable self-ascriptions of conscious states, or of location, which do not depend upon one's having made judgements of the form 'I am identical to $b$' and '$b$ is in pain' or '$b$ is located thus and so'. Similarly, grasp of a perceptual demonstrative may be held to require a capacity to make knowledgeable, identificationally basic judgements such as 'that bowl is blue'. Peacocke calls such ways of thinking, "constitutively identificationally basic". I shall in general speak simply of a mode of presentation's being "basic".

Peacocke now proposes a two-part definition of demonstrative type. For a type to be demonstrative, he says, its constitutive role at any given time must concern the thinker's then current psychological states; and furthermore, it must be "basic". This second condition is not met by mixed descriptive-demonstratives; as Peacocke says, "'my paternal grandfather' is not a genuine demonstrative: it is not a requirement for employing this m.p. that one be able to make empirical, non-derivative judgements to the effect that one's paternal grandfather is thus-and-so." (p. 157).

Yet Peacocke's second condition by itself already seems sufficient to delineate the fundamental class of simple demonstratives. It does so, more-over, in a way which makes immediately intelligible the significance of the classification. It defines a class of singular modes of thought by reference to their distinctive cognitive role.

Peacocke himself remarks that it is difficult to see how there could be a "basic" way of thinking which was not demonstrative (p. 164). The imme-diate implication of this parenthetical remark is, however, that the constitu-tive role condition falls away as redundant.

Indeed, if we take the demand for "basic" character to be directly definitive of the notion of a demonstrative, we can see why the constitutive role condition should have seemed plausible. For one might suppose that knowledgeable, identificationally basic judgements must be made on the basis of one's current psychological states. One might then suppose that one can give an indirect characterisation of the evidential sensitivities of someone using a demonstrative, by reference to the evidential sensitivities of someone thinking explicitly of those psychological states. One might, that is, suppose that the evidence to which the unsophisticated subject must be sensitive will be a straightforward subset of the evidence to which the sophisticated subject is sensitive; the "evidence*", in Peacocke's term.

Yet simply by trusting one's perceptions, one arrives only at judgements with the very same contents as those perceptions. It is, therefore, only through reflection and inference that a perception with the content, 'that bowl is $F$', can serve as evidence for the judgement 'the bowl responsible, in the way required for perception, for the experience as of a bowl in that region of my visual field, is $F$'. Consequently, the bare perception alone is not "evidence*" for the sophisticated judgement; hence Peacocke's account does not in fact secure the status of the bare perception alone as part of the canonical evidence for the judgement, 'that bowl is $F$'. For anyone wanting to make serious use of the notion of canonical evidence, that conclusion is surely not tolerable. The evidential sensitivities of the sophisticated and unsophisticated subjects are not in fact related in the straightforward way Peacocke requires.

The intuition behind the constitutive role account thus seems questionable. And as we have seen, the concept of constitutive role does not seem fitted for the theoretical use to which it is put in providing a criterion of demonstrative type; we do best to dispense with it in favour of the notion of "basic" character.

V

I turn now to Peacocke's use of the idea of constitutive role in reconstructing Russell's Principle of Acquaintance. The Principle is that "every proposition which we can understand must be composed wholly of constituents with which we are acquainted" (*The Problems of Philosophy*, p.32). It is, *inter alia*, a principle about singular reference in general; it holds that genuine singular reference to an object requires acquaintance with it.

Peacocke offers his notion of a thought's being "indexed" by a thing as a reconstruction of Russell's notion of an object's being a constituent of a thought. The "indexing" of a thought by an object thus apparently consists just in the thought's being one which makes singular reference to that thing.

Peacocke also offers a reconstruction of Russell's notion of acquaintance. A subject is said to be "acquainted" with an object just if he is thinking of that thing under a mode of presentation of a type whose constitutive role concerns the thinker's current psychological states (p. 182).

This account of singular reference seems however to be unduly restrictive. On Peacocke's own terms, we have to allow for other types of singular reference than demonstrative reference. There are, for example, the singular ways of thinking of objects which are made available by one's capacities to recognise those objects. Yet his account seems to rule out such forms of singular reference, for these "recognition-based" ways of thinking cannot be represented as "acquainting" the thinker with the thing, in Peacocke's sense. Peacocke sees the problem, and maintains that his account does acknowledge such a form of acquaintance: "There will be some complex relation such that the thinker's judgements that $c$ is $\phi$, where $c$ is such a [recognition-based] m.p., are sensitive to evidence that the thing that bears the complex relation to the kind of experience which produces recognition is $\phi$." (p. 181). Peacocke supposes that this shows the constitutive role of a recognition-based idea to be such that it *can* "acquaint" a thinker with a thing. Yet this simply misses the point that a subject may be thinking in a recognition-based way even though "the kind of experience which produces recognition" is not one of his *current* conscious states. Peacocke's account does not succeed in finding its proper place for recognition-based singular reference.

There is thus a way in which Peacocke's account is too restrictive. There is also a way in which it is not restrictive enough. As we saw, a mixed descriptive-demonstrative such as 'my paternal grandfather' has a constitutive role which concerns the thinker's current psychological states. So on Peacocke's account, we can be "acquainted" with objects under mixed descriptive-demonstrative modes of presentation. The notion of "acquaintance" has however now become of no use in explaining what genuine singular reference consists in.

There is however another role which Peacocke finds for his notion of "acquaintance", namely, to illuminate the role of singular ways of thinking in what we might call "relational" psychological explanations. A "relational" explanation is one which relates a subject's propositional states to characteristics of the things in his environment. For example, if my Twin Earth *Doppelganger* and I simultaneously open doors, one may want to know why he has acted upon one object whereas I have acted upon another. What is required is a pair of relational action-explanations. They would appeal to our separate propositional states to explain the resultant door-openings. Or again, if my *Doppelganger* and I both know that our doors are open, there may be a pair of relational explanations to be given. One will explain how he knows that his door is open; the other will explain how I know that my door is open. Here our propositional states are explained by the properties of the things around us.

According to Peacocke, "indexing" indicates which thoughts are capable of figuring in which relational explanations. Thus for example, to say that my thought about an apple is indexed by that apple is to say that that thought is capable of figuring in relational explanations relating my states to those of that apple. The indexing of thoughts by objects is, however, to be effected only in cases where this would not be "redundant". What Peacocke means is that it would for example be redundant to index purely descriptive modes of presentation. For relational explanations will invoke purely descriptive thoughts only mediately, through their relations to states which are not purely descriptive, such as demonstrative states; and it is these latter states which will *immediately* affect and be affected by the characteristics of the objects in the thinker's environment.

Peacocke appeals to his concept of "acquaintance" to explain what it is that makes the indexing of certain thoughts non-redundant; what enables them to play this "immediate" role in relational explanation. Yet this appeal seems misguided. A mixed descriptive-demonstrative such as 'my paternal grandfather' has a constitutive role which concerns the thinker's current psychological states. One can thus on Peacocke's account be "acquainted" with an object under such a mode of presentation. And in the redundancy of indexing them, mixed descriptive-demonstratives would seem to be on all fours with pure definite descriptions. If I act upon an object, my thinking of it as 'my paternal grandfather' will enter into explanation of the action only *via* my grasp of an identity of the form, 'my paternal grandfather is *that* man'. Again, it is surely only *via* my grasp of such an identity that the object can directly affect my cognitive states concerning it. Whatever it is that makes indexing non-redundant, it thus cannot be "acquaintance" in Peacocke's sense. We need a fresh start.

I think that the first move in providing a better approach to singular reference must be to abandon altogether the notion of constitutive role. There is, so far as I can see, no way of putting it to serious theoretical use.

The second move is to give due centrality to elementary spatiotemporal thinking in characterising what singular reference is. We have, centrally, to understand the role in our most elementary spatial thinking of recognition-based and demonstrative ideas. Peacocke says little about recognition-based ideas, and I shall not consider them further here. Yet we can look to his comments on demonstratives.

A first step must be to inquire into the relation between the two roles which Peacocke gives to "indexing": as definitive of genuine singular reference, and as concerning potential role in relational explanation. I think the answer, which is certainly Russellian in spirit, must be that in the first instance, we have to characterise singular reference in part by giving an account of the role of demonstratives in our most elementary thinking.

What I am suggesting is that a distinctively thought-theoretic characterisation of singular reference will proceed by giving an analysis of what Peacocke calls the Basic Case. The correct analysis of the Basic Case should be the theorist of thought's first concern.

## VI

Earlier I raised the question whether Peacocke's "perspectival sensitivity" analysis articulates a fundamental feature of our spatial thinking, one not derivative upon other aspects of it.

It certainly does seem plausible that the capacity for spatial action is somehow internal to our grasp of spatial concepts. This intuition would be caught by the idea that the capacity to have intentional webs, to have one's intentional actions appropriately controlled by one's spatial perceptual input, is internal to spatial thinking. (Even here, there is a question whether this capacity is not best viewed as derivative upon other features of our cognitive lives. Perhaps it might be held to depend upon a combination of very simple pre-conceptual relations between sensation and movement, and the episte-mic role which this simple perceptual system has for a creature possessed of spatial concepts. But I shall not pursue this line of inquiry here.)

Yet the focus of the "perspectival sensitivity" account is anyway not on the capacity to have intentional webs. Perspectival sensitivity consists in the capacity to *recentre* intentional webs. Appeal to this idea of "recentring" goes far beyond the intuition that the capacity for spatial action is internal to grasp of spatial concepts.

What then is the idea of "recentring" *for*? Peacocke maintains that the capacity to recentre intentional webs constitutes possession of a mental map of one's environment. And, relatedly, he thinks that it is what provides for the capacity for self-location; the capacity to tell where one is (p. 76).

Yet it is hard to believe that his account achieves that. All it provides for is the brute capacity for changing spatial action in response to changing perceptual input, on the basis of one's spatial intentions. How *could* that be what provides for the idea of oneself as in an objective spatial world?

We can throw the point into relief by contrasting a cognitively oriented account of grasp of spatial concepts. On this view, one's grasp of spatial concepts is constituted in the first instance as an element in one's grasp of a simple theory of perception. This theory involves some sense of the objective order one is perceiving, and a grasp of the general enabling conditions of perception. So for example, one's having a perception as of *a*'s being *F* may be explained jointly by the fact that *a* is E, and by the fact that one is correctly located with respect to *a*, appropriately oriented, and there is nothing in the way, so that one can see *a*'s *F-ness*. The suggestion is that grasp of such facts is part of the most elementary use of spatial concepts.

The subject thus takes it that the course of his own experiences is to be explained by the general enabling conditions of perception together with the particular natures and locations of the things in his environment. The further condition which completes the explanation, specifying the subject's own route through that environment, is one which may be intelligibly filled out in any of a variety of ways. That, I have suggested, is how the conception of a possible plurality of subjective routes, of which one's own is merely one, becomes available.

It is against the background of the possibility of some such account as this, I think, that we have to view the failure of Peacocke's "perspectival sensitivity" analysis to give a credible account of the capacity for self-location. The fundamental problem, I suspect, is that while Peacocke does see the centrality of the Basic Case for a thought-theoretic approach to content, he does not have a secure grip on *why* it is so crucial.

The centrality of the Basic Case, I have suggested, is owed to the fact that the thought-theorist must take spatiotemporal thinking to be what provides originally for our grasp of the conception of objective truth; of things being so whether or not they seem to be so. There is no very evident way in which the idea of the recentring of intentional webs might be taken to provide for that concept. The thought-theorist does better to focus on the suggestion that grasp of a simple theory of perception is what provides originally for the concept of objective truth.

The unvarying intensity of the discussion in *Sense and Content* occasionally makes for difficulties of comprehension. There is a lack of sense of *scale*; issues of rather different orders of importance and profundity are all treated with equal, maximum, seriousness. This however is compensated by the exceptional clarity of the book's compact treatment of fundamental questions; the thought and its expression are invariably sharp, clear and penetrating.

The book discusses its chosen topics at the very highest level; the treatment is quite unusually intense and sophisticated. The discussion of representational and sensational features of perception is unquestionably successful. The analyses of secondary-quality and spatial concepts are new, intuitive, and of major interest. There is a flood of insightful observation on demonstrative thought.

This is a major work. It matters for the sophistication and the wealth of detail with which it challenges the tradition that the study of thought must depend upon the study of language.[3]

*Christ Church, Oxford*

[3] For criticism of earlier drafts, I am much indebted to Michael Dummett, Naomi Eilan, Robert Gay, Gavin Lawrence and Penelope Mackie.

# INDEX